Advance Praise for
Forged in Chaos

"I've known Tyler for the better part of my adult life but after reading his book, I realized that I never truly knew him until now. His ability to identify and address issues with life experiences are unlike those of anyone I have encountered. His ability to coach and set people up for success has been invaluable to me and my life. I'm excited for you to read his book and improve yours as well."

—Justin Melnick, SEAL Team Actor

"Being a warrior is a choice—one that reshapes how you see the world. The path is demanding, the rewards hard-earned, and once you take the first step, you never look back. This book tells that story—from one who has walked it, understands its highs and lows, and offers a path to fight the war within."

—Patrick Van Horne, US Marine and co-author of *Left of Bang*

"A powerful contribution to the cannon of military literature of our time; Tyler depicts the realities of the warrior archetype and illuminates the virtues that lead us through perpetual transformation and strife. His work is humble, raw, and real."

—Josh Mantz, bestselling author of *Beauty of a Darker Soul*

"*Forged in Chaos* shows how war never leaves those who fight it. Tyler Grey's story is a raw look at combat and the "invisible" war many continue to fight. Grey illustrates both his struggles and salvation. It's a motivating, gritty, and illuminating read for our warrior class and everyone who wants to lead."

—Morgan Lerette, author of *Guns, Girls, and Greed: I Was a Blackwater Mercenary in Iraq*

"*Forged in Chaos* is an electrifying, unfiltered journey into the heart of combat, written by one of our nation's most elite warriors. Raw, fast-paced, and relentless, this book doesn't just tell a story—it immerses you in the chaos, the intensity, and the unbreakable will forged in battle. More than just an exhilarating read, it's a book that will leave a lasting impact, shaping perspectives and inspiring action. A must-read for anyone who values courage, grit, and the warrior spirit."

—Darrell Utt, Green Beret, author of *Grit to Glory*

"One of the most exceptional memoirs of our generation. A fast-paced, gripping, and deeply profound story that must be read by every warrior, leader, coach, and executive that wants their team to know what winning looks like when you've been through the dark side of war."

—Major Scott A. Huesing USMC (Ret), Award-winning and bestselling author of *Echo in Ramadi*

"To complete the circle, a warrior must become an artist and a teacher. A former T1 Operator turned actor has now produced a story that I believe cements his status as an artist, for good. Tyler could have filled these pages with war stories that would have echoed throughout time. He instead chose to present his testimonials of the inevitable consequences that come with war. He became a teacher, so that others may find their way through as well. He is as close to closing the circle as one can be. That's the definition of a hero to me."

—Pete DePrez, Retired SWAT Officer

"Reading this book felt like Tyler was writing about my life. Though the details and events may differ, the principles and mindset struck a deeply familiar chord. If you see yourself as a warrior—whether through military service, law enforcement, first response, or as a defender at heart—this book is for you. Join Tyler on his powerful journey of recovery and discover the first steps of your own."

—Kris Quinby, Military and Law Enforcement Veteran

"A highly intense story, full of raw honesty, rich in insight and imagery. Tyler Grey not only fought in Afghanistan and Iraq as a Delta Force Commando, he also strategically chose to become a self-described 'Patient Zero,' battling the effects of deep-level trauma for himself and the good of his fellow warriors. Read this book and be awed. Be inspired. Be challenged. Be grateful. You won't be disappointed."

—Marcus Brotherton, *New York Times* bestselling author

"*Forged in Chaos* is an absolute must-read that shatters every expectation you might have about military memoirs. Tyler Grey's raw, unflinching account of his journey as a Delta Force operator takes you beyond the battlefield into the war that rages within. Grey doesn't just tell war stories; he masterfully weaves together the complex threads of his life, from his childhood in Bakersfield to firefights in Fallujah, revealing how the warrior ethos shapes every aspect of existence. What makes this book extraordinary is its brutal honesty. Grey isn't interested in glorifying his service or painting himself as a hero. Instead, he offers something far more valuable: authentic truth about warriors' psychological battles. Grey and Lauren Ungeldi have created something rare, a memoir that functions as both personal confession and universal insight into the warrior mindset. Whether you're a veteran, know someone who serves, or seek to understand the profound human experience of those who fight our wars, this book will transform your perspective. This isn't just another military memoir, a roadmap for understanding the complex psychology of modern warriors, and the battles they continue to fight long after returning home."

—Dr. Jason Piccolo, US Army Infantry Captain and retired Special Agent

FORGED IN CHAOS

A WARRIOR'S ORIGIN STORY

TYLER GREY
AND LAUREN UNGELDI

KNOX PRESS

A KNOX PRESS BOOK
An Imprint of Permuted Press
ISBN: 979-8-89565-262-6
ISBN (eBook): 979-8-89565-263-3

Forged in Chaos:
A Warrior's Origin Story
© 2025 by Tyler Grey and Lauren Ungeldi
All Rights Reserved

Cover design by Ben Sledge/Solid Copy Media

This book, as well as any other Knox Press publications, may be purchased in bulk quantities at a special discounted rate. Contact orders@posthillpress.com for more information.

All people, locations, events, and situations are portrayed to the best of the author's memory. While all of the events described are true, many names and identifying details have been changed to protect the privacy of the people involved.

No part of this book may be reproduced, stored in a retrieval system, or transmitted by any means without the written permission of the author and publisher.

Permuted Press
New York • Nashville
permutedpress.com

Published in the United States of America
1 2 3 4 5 6 7 8 9 10

I dedicate this book to Cristiane Santos, whose unconditional love and support changed me forever and allowed me to share this story. You are my soulmate and have given me the love I have searched for my entire life. You are the best thing that's ever happened to me, and I couldn't have done it without you.

TABLE OF CONTENTS

Introduction 11

Chapter 1: Raw Meat 17
Chapter 2: Traffic Jam in Fallujah 24
Chapter 3: A Goddamned Superhero 36
Chapter 4: Knuckle Dragger 52
Chapter 5: Aftermath 62
Chapter 6: Tube of Misery 71
Chapter 7: Praying for Turds 76
Chapter 8: My Scrotum in Sadr City 86
Chapter 9: Just the Beginning 97
Chapter 10: You Should Be a Therapist 106
Chapter 11: Augusta 111
Chapter 12: Beautiful Chaos 116
Chapter 13: Tableful of Strippers 121
Chapter 14: Gargoyle 126
Chapter 15: That's Not How It Feels 135
Chapter 16: Into the Fire 145
Chapter 17: Collateral Damage 152
Chapter 18: Square One 157
Chapter 19: Don't Miss a Day 162
Chapter 20: No Heroes Here 174
Chapter 21: Room 406 185
Chapter 22: The List 198
Chapter 23: Hollywood Isn't Dead 203

Chapter 24: Suicide Squad 210
Chapter 25: New Orleans by Friday 221
Chapter 26: Crash 232
Chapter 27: Purgatory 239
Chapter 28: Warriors Heart 249
Chapter 29: Anatomy of a Warrior 259
Chapter 30: The Fractured Warrior 273
Chapter 31: The War Within 286
Chapter 32: War Plan 317
Chapter 33: Seven Minutes 334
Chapter 34: It's Not the End 343
Chapter 35: Everything Will Be Okay 346

Acknowledgments 349

INTRODUCTION

LET'S START BY GETTING ONE thing very clear: I am not a hero. I am not a badass. I am not a role model to emulate or a champion to salute. What I am is a warrior. Most people think being a warrior means being a fighter or soldier, needed only in times of danger or war. Others equate it with violence or aggression.

To me, being a warrior extends far beyond any uniform. A warrior embodies a strong sense of duty, an innate connection to a higher purpose, and a clear mission. A warrior remains calm amid chaos, possesses natural mental fortitude, and acts bravely in the face of resistance. A warrior is someone who stands up for what they believe and holds fast in their convictions. A warrior is willing to sacrifice themselves for the greater good, even risking their life to protect others. This is who I am by nature—my raw essence, my DNA. I couldn't change if I tried.

The pages that follow, however, are not filled with heroic tales or accounts of courageous deeds. Instead, they contain confessions, raw truths, and uncomfortably real stories that reveal a side of warriors often hidden in the shadows. They say you should never meet your heroes, and there's a reason for that. You're about to see a portrait of a warrior that may forever change how you view those you may look up to. You will see me as a superhero and a villain, a warrior and a destroyer—a courageous giant full of purpose and power, and a broken man struggling to piece himself back together. I'm warning you now so you know exactly what you're getting into.

The stories in this book are not just a collection of curated moments from my life that I felt compelled to memorialize. They are, in fact, *clues*. Each one is a piece of a puzzle that will come together to reveal a larger picture in the end. So, no matter how unusual, comical, unsettling, peculiar, or tragic you find a particular story, read it carefully.

Every single one has a purpose. And if, in the pages ahead, you think I sound like an asshole or a jerk, conflicted or confused, hypocritical or arrogant, it's because I was exactly that—*at that time*.

You see, most books are a collection of memories polished by time and experience, painted with the smooth and flattering brush of hindsight. Mine is not. I want you to experience the events as they happened and immerse yourself in my inner dialogue as it unfolds. Through this unfiltered lens, you'll uncover both shards of truth and fragments of deception. As you witness my inner dialogue, note it carefully because the truth can sometimes masquerade as a lie, and lies can cloak themselves as truth. And the lies we tell ourselves can be far more insidious than those we tell others. And maybe as you listen to my inner dialogue, you'll hear your own voice.

I need you to gather all of it—the lies and the truths—because both are crucial for unraveling the mystery. Luckily for you—or perhaps unluckily, depending on your perspective—my inner dialogue is laced with a twisted sense of humor and an affinity for sarcasm. And if any of the jokes in here offend you, just remember that this is INNER dialogue, so technically, I *didn't* say it out loud.

So now, if you're anything like me, you're probably asking, "Okay, so what's the mystery?" Good question. That will become clear as you read. But let me offer you at least a hint before we dive in or this whole introduction is just a bunch of dramatic bullshit.

Many of you know that I fought in Afghanistan and Iraq, serving as a special operations forces (SOF) operator and spending nearly four years as a 2nd Ranger Battalion sniper. What most of you don't know is that I also waged a battle on another front—a secret war against a nameless enemy. The collateral damage from this secret War Within was profound, affecting every aspect of my life—physical, emotional, mental, spiritual, and sexual. For years, I felt like I was grappling with symptoms of an undiagnosed illness, exhausted from a battle against an unnamed enemy in my own mind. I felt like I was trying to piece together the fragments of a fractured identity, and nothing seemed to fit. I even legally changed my identity. Day after day, no matter how bruised and battered I felt, I kept fighting and refused to quit. When people asked how I was doing, I kept saying I was *fine, just fine*, because I had been trained to contribute to the team and never take from it—a master of the art of silent suffering. But I couldn't ignore the fact that there was a disease spreading, mutating, and ravaging every part of my life, consuming me from the inside out.

Everyone kept naming the enemy PTSD (post-traumatic stress disorder), diagnosing my struggle with those four little letters. They told me I felt the way I did because I was living in some post-traumatic purgatory that was wreaking havoc on my brain. But that label never quite fit me. Maybe it wasn't *incorrect*, but it was certainly *incomplete*. And I couldn't help but wonder: If PTSD diagnoses and treatments were effective, why have we lost nearly four times as many veterans to suicide as we have in combat? Why are mental health struggles and suicide rates among veterans, law enforcement officers, first responders, and other service members escalating? Why was "fine" often the last word spoken by too many of our beloved warriors, days or even hours before they took their own lives?

Awareness is higher than ever, a broader range of recovery and treatment options is more available than at any time in history, and yet the problem is getting worse.

I just couldn't shake the feeling that there was more to this mystery than we'd uncovered. And I developed a strong suspicion that PTSD wasn't the only culprit involved. While it was undeniably a symptom, I wasn't convinced that it was the disease.

Like a detective in an old whodunit, I started following clues, convinced that the faceless enemy I'd battled was more than a disorder caused by a single event. I chased clues, followed patterns, and asked questions. As I began to unravel the mystery, it fundamentally transformed my life. I experienced peace for the first time, and honestly, I didn't know what to do with myself after being at war for so long. Initially, my discoveries were personal and private. A part of me wanted to ride off into the sunset and enjoy that newfound peace and unconditional love all by myself. But then, two things happened.

First, I had an *oh shit* moment. It started when I opened my big mouth and began talking about the breakthroughs I'd had and the discoveries that led to them. During that time, I went on *The Shawn Ryan Show* podcast and shared my story: unscripted, raw, and honest. That's when the dam broke and a tidal wave of calls, texts, emails, and DMs came at me by the hundreds:

"I felt like you were describing me."

"I went through the same thing."

"How did you know?"

"I thought I was the only one."

"When I heard you speak about how you felt growing up, it was like it came from inside my own head."

Warriors from all backgrounds and locations across the country kept reaching out, week after week, month after month, year after year. Suddenly, I realized that what I had discovered wasn't a fluke. I'd been so afflicted with a case of terminal uniqueness that I believed I was alone in my struggles. I thought I was the only one. But I was wrong. Hundreds and thousands of warriors were fighting similar wars within themselves. I might have been a prototype, but the mold was the same.

As I looked at the faces behind the messages, I understood the gravity of the situation. These weren't just messages; they were distress signals from a darkening battlefield. Every one of these warriors was grappling with the same inner struggles I had faced, fighting to gain the upper hand. I couldn't just sit back and withhold my discoveries and strategies that could change the course of this war to save our warriors.

That's when the *oh shit* moment happened. I knew exactly what I needed to do. I needed to be patient zero. I needed to lie down on the examination table, turn on a big bright light, open up, and allow my life and experiences to be dissected and used as a template to study the disease. That's why, in the pages ahead, you will see my secrets—all the gross little pockets of infection, weird ingrown abscesses, fractured bits, and misshapen parts. And while that's uncomfortable, it's also necessary because it's the only way to find a cure.

The second thing that happened after my *oh shit* moment was that I started having really strange encounters with a handful of brilliant doctors, counselors, and medical researchers. They listened to me rattle on about my discoveries and then looked at me with that glow of academic knowledge that seemed to say, "You're onto something." And that's when things got *really* interesting. It turns out that my discoveries weren't just inspirational anecdotes; they were scientifically proven medical breakthroughs that had taken place in research labs but had yet to be fully utilized to turn the tide in the war to save our warriors. That's when my mindset shifted.

Now, I'm in full battle mode. We're not at war as a nation, yet our warriors are dying daily. This means the enemy is coming from within. I won't stand by while it continues to claim more lives than any foreign adversary has in years. I won't stay silent while the lives of good families and relationships become collateral damage in this unseen war.

To the Warrior Class—not just the active military, veterans, first responders, firefighters, law enforcement officers, and medical warriors, but anyone who chooses to fight rather than surrender—I hope my story inspires you. If you are on the front lines of a War Within, don't give up. Don't accept defeat. Victory is possible. But first, we've got to understand the true nature of the war we're fighting and unite to win it. Recovery isn't the end game here; it's just the beginning. We need you to recover and heal so you can fulfill your purpose and complete your mission. Your family, community, country, and world need you more than ever right now. My hope is that the insights I share here will turn the tide before it's too late. I hope it will help you gain the upper hand before you harm those you love and suffer the pain of losing them. Most of all, I hope the space between your ears becomes a safe and peaceful place, and you experience truly living without a war raging inside. I have finally experienced it, and I promise you, it is everything I had hoped it would be. Inner peace is the greatest feeling I have ever had.

And to all those who love a warrior—a spouse, partner, friend, son, daughter, parent, or other family member—I hope my story will articulate all the things your warrior feels but hasn't said. I hope my story will foster greater understanding, connection, and compassion between you and the warrior you cherish. And in case no one has said it in a while: *Thank you.* Your love changes everything.

And so, with that, I offer you my life stories for forensic analysis. Read the pages ahead carefully. Gather evidence. Pay attention to fragments of truth and even closer attention to lies. Every story, every relationship, every heartbreak, every encounter with addiction, and every friction point you're about to read is a clue—a piece of a bigger puzzle.

Let's solve it together.

CHAPTER 1
RAW MEAT

Somewhere in Baghdad, January 2005

I'M PRETTY SURE WE RAIDED the wrong house.

I'm standing in a bedroom bathed in the unmistakable hue of NOD (night optical device) green. In front of me is a man shouting in broken English, a woman screaming bloody murder, and two wailing children—all dressed in pajamas. One kid is staring at me, frozen and whimpering, while the other's face is buried in his mother's thigh. The mother weeps and then starts screaming again. I pull two fruit-flavored suckers from my pocket and offer them to the children. I always keep suckers and a handful of pencils in my pocket for nights like these. It's not going to change the fact that the kids just woke up to an assault team bursting into their bedroom at 1:30 a.m. looking like transformers with short-barrel rifles. But it does let them know that I have no intention of involving them in a game they never signed up for. The children accept the suckers, and the mother's screams turn into a low whimper for a minute. The rest of the team moves on and searches the house to identify our target while I stand guard over the family. The target should be here. All of the intel points to this exact location. But I don't think we're in the right place.

After enough time in the field, you develop a gut feeling, a premonition, an elusive sixth sense that gives you the ability to smell the intent to kill, and there isn't so much as a whiff of it in this house. It took time for me to learn that a person carrying a gun isn't always an enemy poised to take your life, and likewise, a person without a gun isn't necessarily a friend who means you no harm. It's not about a gun or a particular behavior that's the tip-off. It's the pure evil that emerges from behind the eyes, the monster inside the human suit—glowing with wicked intent that just can't stay hidden.

When I was eight years old, my grandpa told me about the worst fight of his life in his entire career as a police officer while working the night shift in downtown Bakersfield, a fight with a woman who weighed less than a hundred pounds soaking wet. "She was like a rabid Tasmanian devil, that one. It didn't matter that she weighed less than a handful of salt. Took every bit of strength I had to stay alive. It was the worst fight of my life." My grandpa was a stout man who could hold his own, and I remember looking at him up and down as he told the story, wondering how a slight woman like that could have given him a run for his money. And then he said something I'll never forget: "It wasn't the size that mattered; it was the fact that she was intent on doing me harm. It was like a superpower. Couldn't escape the bitch."

I didn't really understand the story until I was much older. Not just the fact that the woman in Grandpa's story was a hooker—that part became clear later on—but all that intent-to-harm business. I learned that in a remote field in Afghanistan when a farmer pointed a gun directly at me and I almost killed him on the spot. I'm still not sure where the old fellow came from; he was the first person we'd encountered outside the wire, in the middle of nowhere, on our way to an off-site location. In less than a second, four infrared lasers were on his body, four of the world's best-trained snipers just a flick of a finger away from taking him out. I was the team leader, and they were waiting for me to make the first move. I looked at the farmer, and then at the barking dogs who knew we were there. The farmer stared into the darkness; he couldn't see us, but he damn well felt us. We all stood there for a while in a silent standoff. And then I understood. That man had no intention of harming us. He'd heard his dog barking and had come to see what the fuss was about. I wanted to kill him, if I'm being honest. When you've trained for that moment for the last four years, it's hard to suppress the urge. And at that moment, I knew that if I pulled the trigger, no sirens would follow my shot, and there would be no crime scene investigation or clean-up crew to mop up his spattered brain. One conversation with my officer in charge and the whole thing would be over. The choice was entirely mine to make.

I switched off the laser that day instead of pulling the trigger. The other three dots vanished in a second as the team followed suit. That old farmer was lucky that I happened to give a damn about his intentions. He lived to see the morning even though he'd drawn his weapon on a highly trained assault team, giving us every right within the rules of engagement to end him on the spot. *Not everyone who carries a gun is an enemy poised to take your life, and not everyone without a gun is a friend who means you no harm.* I learned to spot the difference in that muddy field. I learned it again when they taught us to find the terrorist hiding in a group of hostages by just looking in the eyes. The eyes never lie. The monster just can't stay hidden, that gleam of pure, evil intent. I've seen it peer out from behind the eyes of humans more times than I can count. Truth be told, I've felt a monster inside my own chest before, clawing up from somewhere deep inside me, full of unadulterated destructive intent. I always hide it. Shove it down and make it disappear. Tell myself I'm a warrior, a superhero—not a villainous destroyer. But some days I'm not sure. Some days I wonder if there's a terrible person hiding beneath this heroic character I've created. And it's an unsettling thought.

For fifteen minutes, I stand guard in the bedroom with the family, waiting for the rest of the team to finish the search. The kids are holding suckers now, and the screaming has quieted down, though it's not gone altogether. I'm staring at the faces in front of me that are painted with a lot of things: fear, shock, anger—it's all there. But the monster isn't. We've got the wrong house. I just know it.

How do I know? Easy. The mother and two kids are still going apeshit crazy. That's always the telltale sign. A guilty man's family is silent, blank-faced, and compliant. Not because they aren't scared but because they aren't confused. They aren't surprised that Dad's line of work got everyone into trouble; they're just upset that tonight's the night. An innocent man's family raises hell because they have no idea what the fuck is going on. This family can't seem to catch their breath between all the crying and screaming. My radio crackles with a call for two teams, including mine, to gather outside while the third waits with the family inside. I make my way out and join the rest of the group.

"They said this isn't the house," our team leader says. *No shit.*

My night started just after sundown, like it always does, with a brief on tonight's target. We're after a man with strong ties to none other than Abu Musab al-Zarqawi, the infamous terrorist leader singlehandedly responsible for countless bombings, beheadings, and brutal attacks on American forces and innocent civilians. These days, Zarqawi is a name we speak daily.

Our target tonight could have solid intel on Zarqawi's location. What's more, he's responsible for organizing his fair share of terrorist activity. If we can get him alive, we'll work on extracting intel about Zarqawi's whereabouts. If we have to kill him on-site, we'll still have done the world a favor. If we're lucky, Zarqawi himself might even be there. The target's house is located in a neighborhood in Sadr City, where I find myself now. Sadr City is the armpit of Baghdad—filled with violence, poverty, and dirt roads. A freezing February rain shower hit yesterday, turning all that dirt straight to mud. A SEAL team is attached to our troop for this entire deployment. We're not short on manpower to get the job done; we just have bad intel.

"We need to be in that house," our team leader says in a low voice, pointing to a dark structure about a hundred yards away. It's clear that the intel nerds have been hard at work to get us to the right location. We begin to walk. Thick mud clings to my boots from the washed-out dirt roads. A dog barks in the far distance. The air is cold, but I don't feel it. Our feet barely make a sound. Within two minutes, we approach the house. Without a word, the SEAL team breaks off and heads to the front entrance. They'll clear from the front; we'll clear from the back. The SEAL team disappears from sight. Thirty seconds later, the earsplitting sound of gunfire pierces the air. It is relentless. Like the grand finale of the Fourth of July parade an inch from your face. Like nothing I've ever heard before. "I'M HIT!" "I'M HIT!" "I'M HIT!" With the sound of those two words over the radio, my legs begin to pump until I reach the wall that surrounds the house. There's no time to set a charge to get through the entrance. I reach up, and my hands connect with the concrete. I pull. I jump. I'm over the wall and running the moment there is solid earth beneath me, in step with my buddy Russ.

"I'M HIT, I'M HIT!" It's a different voice on the radio this time, but the sound of suppressed pain is the same. The gunfire has yet to cease. They knew we were coming, and they are ready for a fight. "I'M HIT!" It's a third voice this time. Three SEALs wounded in less than thirty seconds. *Fuck. Fuck. Fuck.* I'm at the back door now and breach it quickly. Sink, counters, cabinets: kitchen. We move into another room on the left. Laundry, cleaning supplies, boxes: storage room. The gunfire still hasn't relented, and I have no idea what the SEAL team is up against or if we even have the SEAL team anymore. I move through another doorway, make an immediate right, and walk directly into the barrel of an AK-47. As the nose of the gun hits my chest, everything becomes slow-motion. I look at the man holding the weapon. I can see him perfectly; I'm nothing more than a dark shadow to him. My first instinct is to kill him. But a movement catches my eye. A silhouette, a purple nightgown in the moonlight. There's a woman right behind him. *Not a player.*

I do not kill him. The woman's body is not sprayed with the blood of the man she slept with, and there is no bullet that flies through his chest and then enters hers. Instead, I grab the barrel of his gun, twist, and *WHACK*. His head is bashed in, and blood pours out. The time that elapses between the moment his gun touches my chest and he falls to the ground is less than a second. It feels like minutes. I pull him up and drag him from the bedroom to the kitchen. Blood courses down his neck. More team members have made it into the house, and someone grabs him. Seconds later, my shoulder unites with my buddy at the start of a long hallway, and we fall in step, guns up. One step, two steps, three steps. We're three yards in before all hell breaks loose. A great concussive force envelops my skull, and it pounds and pounds and pounds until I feel like I will explode. It's as if my head has been strapped to a loudspeaker on full blast at a rave and the sound will crack open my skull, tear apart my eardrums, and spray my brain across the wall. Someone is unloading one, if not two, full mags of AK gunfire through the wall at close range, and I feel my body reacting to the sheer power of it, but my mind is steady. No panic. No fog. Every part of my brain is turned on. *Clarity. I am made for this.* Then the walls begin to break. I see them tearing, shredding, vibrating, falling. I'm sprayed by a torrent of fragmented rocks as the mud walls come apart. *So this is what it feels like right before you die.*

"I'M HIT! I'M HIT!" my buddy shouts, and we take refuge in the kitchen. He's cradling his left arm and shoulder. He's been shot at least twice, and I know it's probably hurting like a motherfucker, but he's taking it like a champ.

Mikey appears at my right, ready to go, but it's clear that we can't move forward down the hall. I'm weighing our options. We need to throw a grenade if we want to make it through the doorway at the end of the hallway—it's the only thing that will pack enough punch. But the doorway is positioned off to the right, which puts us at a severe disadvantage. We're going to have to make it down the hall in one piece and then throw the grenade at a curve to ensure that it blows through the doorway and doesn't hit the wall and bounce back on us. And the trouble is, if they have the same bright idea to throw one in our direction, they only have to open the door, serve up a hooked throw, and it's a straight shot down the hallway to where we are.

"You prep a grenade, I'll lay down fire to get us down the hallway, then you throw it." I'm not sure if I yell the words or just mouth them and use hand signals; it's hard to tell with all the noise. Communication in the heat of combat becomes nonverbal somehow. Either way, we understand each other. He reaches for the grenade. Then my entire world explodes.

I'm lifted, flying, suspended. The Hulk has picked me up in his big green fingers and is lifting me. I don't know which way is up or down because he doesn't just have me, he has the entire house in his hands and he's shaking it like a cocktail shaker, and now I'm the ice inside, breaking, shattering, falling apart. My head hits the roof, then the roof becomes the floor, and then I'm not sure which is which as everything collapses. I'm tumbling through open space, weightless. When the impact comes, so does the darkness. My NODs are blown off my face. My bones are toothpicks. I feel my body slamming into the ground with brute force, but I don't feel pain. I just feel insignificant. I feel small. So very *small*.

After the impact, I lift my head from the hard surface of the floor, and I see a light glowing softly in front of me. The light catches dust, dirt, and smoke and swirls them into a single vortex at the end of the hall. The vortex glows like embers of a fire, like a portal opening to another place, and then it slowly begins to close, but I am not moving. A strange feeling washes over me. I have forgotten something, something very important. *No, that's not it.* It's not that I've forgotten something, but there is something I need to know. Something my body is trying to tell me, and it's very important. But I don't know what it is—only that it's there again, a faint signal buried in the back of my darkened mind. It's not pain. It's not a sensation. It's not even a fully formed thought. Just a dull alarm, like a muffled voice beneath the ringing in my skull.

A deep, instinctual awareness that something is missing. There's something I should be feeling—but I'm not.

It claws its way up now, ripping through the fog. And when the message finally breaks through, it's no longer a whisper.

It's a full-blown scream.

I need to look down.

I need to find something.

I need to find my arm.

Because I'm pretty sure it's not attached anymore.

CHAPTER 2
TRAFFIC JAM IN FALLUJAH

One year earlier...
Fallujah, Iraq, 2004

I SLAM MY BOOT ON the gas pedal of an Alfa Romeo, and the car lurches forward, picking up speed. The tension in the area is palpable—not just inside our vehicle but throughout the entire operational theater. Fallujah has become a symbol, and retaking the city is a crucial step in breaking the insurgency's grip. Politically, the stakes couldn't be higher. Failure is not an option, but the cost of success is mounting by the hour. Washington is under immense pressure, the world is watching closely, and every civilian death fuels anti-American sentiment.

Today's objective is to drive from Fallujah to Baghdad and link up with the rest of my troop and the Task Force 160th helicopters waiting there. Once we arrive, my team will get our target package details. But as luck would have it, the authorities have granted a rare clearance for the evacuation of civilians from Fallujah today. This is their last chance to leave before the Marine invasion begins. The roads leading out of the city are choked with heavy-duty five-ton trucks loaded with military-age males, most of whom are on supply runs to prepare for the impending conflict. Like us, a fair share of them are headed straight for Baghdad.

My priority list for the day is simple. First, blend in. If any of the fighters catch so much as a whiff of an American-flavored fart in the air, they will have no problem opening fire on us. We can't afford even the slightest tip-off that highly trained SOF operators are sandwiched between hundreds of Fallujah fighters headed down the highway.

Second, don't become a human smoothie. I know full well that if we hit an IED (improvised explosive device) on the way, there's nothing I can do about it. But I also know that the key to decreasing the chances of one's brain becoming asphalt art after hitting an IED is speed. If you barrel down the desert roads fast enough, you might stand a chance at outrunning the click-to-bang and missing the blast radius. So I keep my foot pressed down on the gas pedal, maintaining a speed of nearly 120 mph.

But while blending in with the armed Fallujah fighters and not getting blown up are high on my priority list, there's one more that is a solid contender at the top: Don't get killed by a Marine convoy. War has a funny way of showing you what your priorities are. You think you know what they are, you talk a big game. But you don't actually know until the stakes are high enough and you act on pure unadulterated instinct. That's when you find out precisely *what* ranks *where*. Whether you agree with that particular order is meaningless. It is what it is.

Our biggest threat on any given day is getting taken down by an American convoy. If we're doing our job right, even our fellow American soldiers will have no idea who we are and what we're up to. The cost of training and armament that has been invested in each of the men sitting inside the vehicle comes in at several million dollars a pop. It would be a damn shame to waste the American taxpayers' hard-earned dollars by becoming roadkill just because of a little friendly fire. Besides that, it's just a bad story. Death isn't the part that scares us; it's the idea that the curtains might close before we have a chance to be who we want to be, who we've trained to be. Maybe not heroes exactly, but at least something close. Getting hit by a friendly isn't the script any of us have rehearsed.

When I see a line of brake lights flashing ahead, a wave of unease washes over me. Suddenly, all traffic comes to a complete standstill. Trucks packed with Fallujah fighters are gridlocked as far as we can see. One minute ticks by. Then two. Then ten. Then thirty. On a typical day, the drive from Fallujah to Baghdad takes just over an hour. And while nothing in Fallujah in 2004 can be considered ordinary, this is unprecedented.

Movement in the rearview mirror catches my eye. A handful of gruff, bearded men get out of their vehicles, making their way down the line to get a better view of what's happening up ahead. That's when my heart rate starts to pick up speed. I am not afraid of a good fight. Let me run into a building or go head-to-head with the enemy, and let's see how the odds play out. If I come out on top, I live to fight another day. If it's my time to go, at least I'll go out with a damn good story. So far, my odds have been pretty good. But this is different. We are boxed in on every possible side. I glance in the rearview mirror and watch an armed figure moving closer to our vehicle. At first, I feel claustrophobic. Then something else: sheer terror. I've heard other people describe fear before—the paralysis, the sweating palms, the racing heart. I've never had that feeling.

Now, I can't shake it. It's like a monster clawing from the inside out, coiling its fingers around my throat until I feel like I can't breathe. I look in the mirror again. Two heavily armed fighters are getting closer. *Please don't stop.*

I move my submachine gun just under the window and keep my eyes focused straight ahead. *Please don't stop.* One of the men is almost parallel with our vehicle now. If he knocks on the window and asks a question, I'll be dead in about five seconds. The thought isn't a hypothetical indulgence for a fearful mind. It is just pure fact—a matter of statistics and logistics. We are completely closed in. Zero tactical advantage. Outnumbered and overwhelmed. I clamp down on the handle of the gun. No one in the vehicle speaks. We don't need to tell each other what we know to be true.

The fighter edges into my peripheral vision, but I keep my gaze straight ahead. When he passes our vehicle without stopping, I feel no relief. Another fighter follows, then another, each passing with a suffocating intensity that makes it hard to breathe. After what feels like an hour, sweat pours down my temples, pooling under my armpits and soaking the back of my neck.

At last, the vehicles begin to inch forward again. The veins on the side of my head throb as if they might burst. The fighters return to their trucks, and we slowly move forward, searching for any clue about what had caused the delay. As luck would have it, the whole ordeal turns out to be the result of an impromptu Marine checkpoint. And now we are back to the first order of priority: *Don't get killed by a Marine convoy.*

◂▸

Days later, I'm standing in a small Texas airport, watching a beautiful girl in the bus station waiting line. I've got two weeks of leave, and I've been waiting for this moment for four months. I can account for about two showers between conducting a live mission in Fallujah and standing here in Podunkville, Texas, staring at Miss American Beauty. It's the third time I've locked onto her sea-green eyes, and this time, I let my gaze sweep down her spine and back up again. She smiles and turns her head slightly, and that approving glance means everything. Thirty seconds later, her eyes are back on mine, this time more inviting.

We're strangers, but we shared the same flight from Raleigh, North Carolina, to Dallas. A mighty Texas thunderstorm forced us to land here in Podunkville, and now we're waiting for a bus to carry us the remaining four hours to Dallas. Everyone is exhausted and angry.

I, on the other hand, have spent every waking hour of the past four months with a team of men without so much as a smile from a pretty woman. Now, I'm locked onto an adorable brunette, with a long open road ahead. Backpack slung over my shoulder; I close the distance between us. Her cheeks are slightly flushed with excitement, and she tilts her head to look into my eyes when I pause near her. The boarding is about to begin, and I know exactly what I want to do.

"Hey, do you know where the cool kids sit?" I whisper.

"I guess I don't," she giggles.

"Come with me, and I'll show you," I say, holding out my hand.

She breaks into a smile and puts her tiny, beautiful hand into mine. God, I'd forgotten. How soft. How feminine. How delicate. Only then do I notice the thick calluses on my trigger finger as I slowly glide it just a centimeter across her silky skin before leading her onto the bus.

She follows me to a bench at the very back where three seats are open. She takes the window seat, and I sit beside her. A round, sleepy-looking man whose face I barely notice settles in next to me. After everyone boards, the bus pulls away from the airport, and by 2:00 a.m. the fatigue from the delayed landing has set in. Within minutes, the man beside me is fast asleep, and soon the entire bus follows suit.

"So what brings you to Texas?" My lips almost touch her ear when I ask the question.

"I'm here for a Beach Body conference," she whispers.

She leans close to me as she speaks, and I can feel her breath on my face. Lightning tears through the sky for a moment and illuminates her silhouette in the darkness. I didn't realize how much I'd missed this feeling. This drug. This high. Being close to all those beautiful lines and curves. Woman. What a beautiful creature. When our lips meet, everything else fades. I'm only aware of the sound of rain pelting the bus and the taste of her lips. It's intoxicating. We don't stop until the bus does, four hours later. When we arrive at Dallas Fort Worth International Airport at 6:00 a.m., she sends me off with a kiss on the cheek and her phone number. I save it and walk outside where a car is waiting.

"It's so good to see you!" says the woman in the front seat as she pulls me into a tight hug and kisses my cheek. She's the reason for my visit to Dallas.

Flying from Baghdad International Airport to Fort Bragg, North Carolina, takes about 15 hours and 35 minutes. Add in one quick stop in Germany, and you're looking at roughly 24 hours of total travel time. This leaves you just enough time to catch a crick in your neck, watch a few movies, eat crappy airline food, and maybe get some free gin if you're charming enough to flirt with the flight attendants. When my phone finally reconnects to good ol' American cell service, I check my messages and decide to refresh my connection with a handful of girls I'd kept in touch with via email while deployed. One of them had invited me to visit her in Dallas, so that's where I went—the beautiful girl on the bus was a delightful, unexpected surprise. Then again, life seems to surprise you a little more often when you're twenty-eight years old, never miss a day at the gym, and you're a Special Mission Unit (SMU) commando.

Besides a few days of fun, I've made no promises to Miss Dallas. We've only seen each other a handful of times, with our connection largely built on virtual flirting. But within an hour of being together, it becomes clear that she has written a full script for our weekend. She has a full itinerary planned, and it's clear that I've been cast as the White Knight in her play. Unfortunately, that isn't a character I'm cut out for, at least not right now. I'm more suited for the role of stranger you kiss on the back of the bus than the guy you take to a prescheduled couple's massage. I feel stifled and irritable. It's all too much—too many expectations, too many planned events.

By our second day together, she's visibly disappointed and ready for me to leave. I clearly haven't given her the reaction she hoped for. When she heads to the gym, tearful and frustrated, leaving me alone in her empty apartment, I realize it's time to move on. I grab my phone and call my buddy Kyle.

"Get on the bus at midnight tonight and come see me in Olathe, Kansas," he says when I tell him how things are going. "We're having a party here."

That's all the invitation I need. I've already disappointed Miss Dallas enough. I politely say my goodbyes and head for the bus station. But first, I make a phone call to the green-eyed beauty I met on the bus. This whole Dallas trip was a bust, and I need a win. As luck would have it, she's still in town for the Beach Body convention and staying in a gorgeous upscale hotel just a stone's throw away from the bus station. She invites me up to her room. My bus is scheduled to leave at midnight, and it's just after 9:00 p.m. Plenty of time. For two hours, I stay with her at her hotel and finish what we started on the bus. When I leave the hotel, the confidence I lost from being rejected by Miss Dallas has been restored and then some.

Then I spot movement out of the corner of my eye. A group of more than ten stunning women crosses the street, all impeccably dressed in professional clothes that accentuate every curve. I have no doubt they're in town for the Beach Body convention. It seems like my lucky day. My gaze locks onto one woman in particular—a walking prototype of my dreams. Even from a hundred yards away, I can see she stands out. She glances at me for a split second before quickening her pace. The rest of the group moves on, throwing smiles over their shoulders as I approach the well-built beauty with the glossy blonde hair.

"Hi, my name is Tyler, I—"

"No, no, no you don't," says another blonde as she steps between me and the green-eyed woman I can't take my eyes off of. "You can't talk to her until you go through me first and then everyone else."

"Alright, what do I need to do?"

"For starters, do you know where the closest McDonald's is? We're starving." She raises one perfectly shaped eyebrow, challenging me.

"Of course I do." I smile confidently. "I'll walk you there."

The truth is I've never been to this area of Dallas in my life, and I have no idea where the nearest McDonald's is. But I'm absolutely sure of one thing: If you walk in a straight line long enough in any downtown city in America, you will run across a McDonald's. I check my watch. I have forty minutes until it's time to board the bus.

"So, what other questions do you have for me…uh, I didn't catch your name?" I ask the tall blonde—clearly the gatekeeper of the group.

"Cassie," she says without a smile.

"Nice to meet you, Cassie; I'm Tyler Grey. Now, what do I have to do to talk to your friend?"

We walk for more than fifteen minutes, and Cassie and her friends launch a full-scale interrogation into my life. Little do they know I'm specially trained in counter-interrogation techniques. *Give me everything you got, girls.*

They want to know everything. I quickly find out that they are not only Beach Body sales reps but also Cadillac directors in town to present awards to their team at the convention. They are confident and used to being in charge. My clock is ticking, and the stakes are high. But this is my sweet spot—performing under pressure and thinking quickly on my feet. There are always guys who are more handsome or muscular than me, but I can outtalk just about anyone. The girls lay on questions like a crew-served machine gun, and I go full Neo in *The Matrix*. I have just over twenty minutes left to get to the bus station, and as luck would have it, a McDonald's comes into view, just as I'd predicted.

"Okay, last question." Cassie looks at the McDonald's and back at me. It seems I passed the first test, and now I'm facing the final boss.

"Let's say my friend here wins the Beach Body Director of the Year Award and you take the stage as her boyfriend and have to give a two-minute speech for the entire audience. What will you say?"

Cassie smiles, her chin in the air, victorious. It's the final challenge, and she is sure I will fumble on the home stretch. I toss one look at the beautiful blonde who still hasn't spoken a word and then stare at Cassie.

"Ladies and gentlemen, I'm profoundly grateful to see each of you here this evening. It is with immense pride that I stand before you to introduce someone who epitomizes both professional excellence and personal grace. Not only is she an inspirational leader, but she also holds the esteemed title of being the woman in my life—my beloved, gorgeous girlfriend."

I stand on the sidewalk and deliver a speech for exactly two full minutes, and when I finish, all ten girls clap.

"Time to vote!" Cassie shouts. "Everyone in favor of Mr. Tyler Grey talking to our dear friend, raise your hand."

Ten hands shoot into the sky.

"Hi, I'm Tyler Grey. What's your name?" I take a step closer to the one woman in the group who has captivated me since I saw her from a hundred yards away.

"Hi, Tyler, I'm Vanessa." Her voice is as sweet as her face.

"Can I have your number, Vanessa?" I ask.

"You live in North Carolina, as I understand. I live in South Beach, Florida. What are you going to do, hop a plane and come all the way to South Beach to take me on a date?"

She laughs, waiting for me to see the ridiculousness of it all.

"That's exactly what I'm going to do." I look at her straight in the eyes, and we hold each other's gaze. Her eyes ask questions, and mine answer them all.

"I never do this." She shakes her head as she gives me her number, more of an admission than a compliment.

"I'll see you soon, Vanessa." I smile at her, thank the ladies, and sprint to the bus station. I arrive with just five minutes to spare. Five days later, I call her and we talk until the sun rises.

Three weeks after that, I arrive in South Beach, Florida, just as promised, to take her on a date. I'm nervous when I see her standing in the mall parking lot where she told me to meet her. Damn, she's just as pretty as I remember and still way out of my league. Now the pressure is on. After flying across the country to see her, it would be a shame to waste the night awkwardly sitting in a stuffy restaurant. I need to think on my feet and pull off something unexpected.

"How about a hike?" I ask after we say hello.

"Love it," she smiles.

The natural walking trails surrounding the South Beach area are bright with fresh rain, and we fall into easy conversation as we walk. We laugh, we chase conversational rabbits, we form strategies to solve all the world's problems and our own.

"Okay, so here's a question: If you could travel anywhere, where would you want to go?" She tosses a look in my direction.

"Hawaii," I answer without hesitation. "I don't know, I always had some feeling I would meet my future wife in Hawaii."

It's admittedly a strange and stupid thing to even think about, let alone admit out loud, but something about her sweet smile and green eyes makes me feel like telling her everything. "Well, you never know; you could be wrong. That's not where we met." She dares me with her eyes, and I'm surprised at how my entire body reacts to her words.

Holy shit. Do I really have a chance?

When we reach the end of the trail, she turns around to face me. Everything in me wants to wrap my arms around her, taste her lips, and pull her close. But Vanessa is a real woman, not a girl you kiss on the back of a bus. She's a businesswoman, she has a master's degree in psychology, and she's more confident than any woman I've ever met. I see my reflection in her eyes—a version of myself I've never seen before—and I don't want to look away. When she turns to look at the setting sun, I inch closer until her back is against my chest. Just the proximity is enough.

"You hungry?" I whisper after we stand in silence for a while, gauging the time we have left to walk back to the trailhead before it gets dark.

"Definitely."

"Tell me, where is the best fine dining restaurant in all of South Beach, Florida? Because I want to take you there."

She grins.

"Well, I do know this one place...I've never been there, but everyone says it's the best."

"Then we better get changed." I wink at her and lead the way back down the trail.

Two hours later, we're sitting across from each other at a small corner table covered with a white tablecloth. I traded my T-shirt for a white button-down—wearing a shirt with a collar to a fine dining restaurant just seemed like the thing to do. Vanessa's dress is a brilliant blue. I scan the other tables and realize with pride that the prettiest girl in the room is sitting at mine. When the menu comes, I take it and thank the waiter graciously in my most sophisticated low voice. I scan the menu for several minutes but don't understand a single word I'm reading.

What the am I looking at here? Is this written in Latin? The dish names are confusing and tough to pronounce, and the descriptions are just as baffling. "Served with truffle oil compound butter," one reads, but I still can't figure out what the main dish is, let alone the side. And truffle oil compound butter—what is *that*? Valentine's Day chocolates mixed into some special butter? I'm scanning the menu, hoping to find a familiar word to save me—chicken, steak, or potatoes. But I'm out of luck. I haven't found a single word that sounds like food except that damn truffle oil butter.

Vanessa gently sets down her menu and throws an encouraging smile at our waiter, who has been standing in the corner watching us like a studious old English butler. He begins to walk in our direction, and now the pressure is on. Vanessa clearly knows what she wants, and I still have no idea what I've been reading for the past five minutes. *New strategy: Pick the most pronounceable menu item so you don't look like a total fucking idiot.*

The waiter is hovering just above me now. "Have you made your selections for the night?" he asks smoothly.

I nod at Vanessa to order first in a show of gentlemanly deference, but the truth is I need all the time I can get.

"No, you go ahead," she smiles sweetly.

Fuck.

"I'll have the..." I start, struggling to pronounce the next word, fully aware that I'm about to butcher it.

"I'll have the...this." I point to the one thing with the side of the other thing with the truffle butter. How bad can butter and chocolate be?

"Excellent choice," the waiter approves, and I sit a little taller. "And for the lady?"

"I'll have the same," Vanessa smiles.

When the waiter disappears, Vanessa leans close.

"Honestly, I couldn't understand a word on that menu. I was waiting for you to order first," she giggles.

"Well, shit. That's bad news for both of us because I just panic-ordered and pointed to something random."

We laugh like two school kids until the waiter returns with our drinks. Our conversation never stops, except to finish our big plates of small food. Turns out the truffles they've got around here are mushrooms, not chocolate treats.

"I don't want this night to end," she says when we finish dessert.

"It doesn't have to." I still can't take my eyes off of her. "Let's go for a walk."

On the street corner in Dallas, this was all a game and I just wanted to earn the highest score. But as I reach for her hand, everything changes.

I feel my world shifting, narrowing. Suddenly, there is only one. There is only her. She grabs a bottle of wine from the local 7-Eleven—the first I've ever tasted—and we take it to the beach. Under the light of the moon, we savor the wine and each other, letting the night slip away until the sun begins to rise. Time is passing quickly and slowly all at the same time. I try to hold onto it, but it falls through my fingers like water. There is still one thing that I need to say. When I say her name, she looks at me so sweetly and innocently that I almost close my mouth without continuing.

"Vanessa, I'm going to have to take a trip soon. I'll be away for a few months." She tilts her head, processing. "I think I need to tell you about my job."

CHAPTER 3
A GODDAMNED SUPERHERO

MY NAME IS TYLER GREY, and I'm a superhero. My job is to extract hostages, breach fortified doorways using surgical explosives, and neutralize villains with a flick of my finger. More specifically, I'm an SOF operator. I also spent nearly four years as a 2nd Ranger Battalion sniper.

I joined the Army in 1998 because I fell for the propaganda. Not the flag-waving, finger-pointing Uncle Sam type shit—there's an audience for that kind of stuff, but I was never one of them. That's not to say I don't love America, because I do. But my America was *Die Hard* and *Robocop*; it was *Rambo* and *The Magnificent Seven*, *Dirty Harry*, and *Raiders of the Lost Ark*. America, to me, was its movies, those onscreen stories of brave loners and outcast heroes fighting for justice, freedom, and vengeance. That's the propaganda I fell for: the action movies, spy flicks, sci-fi extravaganzas, and crime capers.

From the time I was a boy, it seemed that on any given weekend, at any theater, you could watch Schwarzenegger battling a brooding and violent Stallone, or an impossibly cool Harrison Ford. What's more, cable television was airing almost every action movie ever made—from classic, patriotic World War II movies like *The Longest Day* and *Sands of Iwo Jima*, to thought-provoking Vietnam War films like *Platoon* and *The Deer Hunter*, sometimes even reaching back to the Civil War with *Glory* and the Old West with *The Good, the Bad, and the Ugly*. My childhood television presented a hundred different versions of American history and what it meant to be an American man. They were goddamned superheroes. And I would become one too.

But, like most superheroes, I never really wanted to be one as a boy. I had other dreams. My first dream was to become just like my father.

I was no exception to that primal instinct in most boys to model their character after their father. *I'm going to be just like him when I grow up*, I thought, and I gave it my best shot. Until I ran into one major obstacle.

At six years old, I wasn't allowed to do the one thing my father did best: *drink*. Nobody lets you drain half a bottle of vodka on weeknights or finish off two six-packs of beer on a Saturday when you don't even have a single hair sprouting on your balls. It's not like I wanted to drink the stuff anyway—the smell of it reminded me of my father's sour breath and how it would fill the room every time he erupted in a fit of anger. The red-hot lava of my father's rage always smelled like alcohol. *I'm going to be just like him when I grow up*, I thought as I got a little older. *Only I won't drink the weird-smelling drinks*.

Every week, I would beg my dad to take me hunting. I loved being outside and was dying for a chance to shoot a real gun like the ones I'd seen in the movies.

"Hold your horses there, son," my dad would tell me when I reached the fifteenth plea. "This weekend I've got things to do. Maybe, but we'll just have to see."

On Saturday morning, I'd wake up early, scarf down my bowl of cereal extra quickly, and wait for him to wake up. The cartoons on television barely held my attention as the hours dragged on. Finally, his bedroom door would open, and he'd shuffle into the kitchen. I'd wait, hoping to hear him call my name. But he never did. I'd hold out hope until morning turned into evening, watching a cluster of empty beer cans pile up on the floor beside him.

I'm going to be just like him when I grow up, I thought. *Only I'll take my son hunting every weekend*.

One night, when I was seven, that volcano of anger and rage erupted again. This time, that red-hot lava didn't just fill the room with the smell of alcohol—it incinerated everything in its path, including my dream of being just like my father. I only remember the pattern of the couch fabric, the blue light of the television, and the sound of my mother screaming as my father's hand connected with the side of her face. When I heard it, I looked up at my father's face in horror. But it wasn't him staring back at me. It was someone or some*thing* else, the eyes of a destroyer—bright with anger and capable of anything. My body froze, but my mind started racing. *I'm going to be just like him when I grow up. I'm going to be just like him when I grow up. Oh NO, NO, NO...I DO NOT WANT TO BE JUST LIKE HIM WHEN I GROW UP!*

Everything in me wanted to stand up and stop him. I wanted to hug my mom and erase that awful look on her face, the one filled with confusion and disbelief as she stared at my father like he was a stranger, like she didn't even recognize him anymore. I promised myself then and there to find a new role model—one who didn't drink or erupt in red-hot rage and make his woman cry. The next morning, I began my search. I wanted to be a real-life Han Solo—smart, strong, and quick on my feet. But becoming Han Solo didn't seem like an easy thing to accomplish, and besides, I was more like lonely ol' Luke Skywalker. So I considered the path of a cowboy, then a fireman, and then a cop. Yet none of these roles seemed to quite hit the mark.

I opened one of the worn picture books my mom had picked up from a second-hand store to find an illustration of a man peering back at me through the eye slit of a shiny steel helmet. I flipped to the next page. And then the next. And the next. By the time I had finished the book, I'd made my decision. I would take up the helmet of righteousness, gird myself in the armor of truth, and set forth to pursue a most honorable profession—a vocation held in high esteem by bright-eyed young children and elderly British actors.

I would become a *knight*.

In my seven-year-old eyes, a knight represented everything that a boy ought to aspire to become. Knights were brave and noble warriors. Knights were bold and free adventurers. Knights stood up in the face of danger and protected the weak. More importantly, no true knight would ever drink himself into a rage and scream insults at his child. Nor would he surrender to a great cloud of depression and lie for weeks on a couch, moving only to take a swig of vodka. Most importantly, no knight would ever hit his lady.

For all these reasons, my new role model seemed far preferable to my former. These were naïve assumptions, of course, made years before I read about the atrocities committed by Christian knights at the siege of Jerusalem during the First Crusade or at the sack of Constantinople during the Fourth. As a bright-eyed American child, and even as a Dungeons and Dragons-obsessed adolescent, I readily accepted and reveled in the popular, Arthurian version of the European knight: a mighty warrior, clad in steel, riding atop his noble steed, a lance in his hand and virtue in his heart. I did not see them as feudal henchmen, keeping the vast majority of the medieval populace enslaved to hereditary lords through intimidation and violence. No, to me, they stood for justice, freedom, fairness, and most of all, for the protection of the weak against the strong. I wanted to be a warrior of righteousness. But that wasn't easy, not in the late 1980s and early '90s, and certainly not growing up in Bakersfield, California.

One and a half hours north and inland from Los Angeles, Bakersfield is a small, dusty shitpit of a city, growing like an ingrown hair on the slapped ass of California's Central Valley. It's not a pleasant place, not even in hindsight.

As a child, I always imagined that the town had been built by pioneers who had lost hope on their journey to the Pacific and decided to quit the trail. If they'd only had the chops to stick it out for a couple more weeks, they would have ended up in Malibu or Santa Monica. Instead, they threw up their hands, cursed the western ocean as a lie, and settled down in the desert wasteland to build a city of broken dreams, a monument in commemoration of giving up. Luckily for those imaginary pioneers, oil was discovered around the town a generation or so later, and it wasn't long before prospectors were trundling in to find a rig to work or a competitor to screw. Bakersfield became a roughneck mecca, full of hard-working and hard-drinking men, cantankerous whores, and a whole lot of gunfights over slight misunderstandings.

The first time I deployed to Fallujah, Iraq, I remember thinking that it reminded me of my hometown. I didn't tell anyone that—they'd have shot me down if I did with a thousand reasons why my comparison was untrue and illogical.

Still, to me, at least, there are undeniable similarities between these two unofficial sister cities. Both are desert towns, oppressively hot and dusty, and relatively isolated from the rest of civilization. There's the stink of oil about both of them, populated as they are with pumps and rigs and the tired, filthy men who work them. There's violence. Armed gangs. Religious fanatics. Tensions between groups, be they Sunnis and Shiites or rednecks and immigrants. The populations of the cities are nearly identical—or at least they were before the Marines ordered every noncombatant out of Fallujah. Both cities have a river running through their center: the Euphrates in Fallujah and the Kern in Bakersfield.

They are also both heavily dependent on freeways. Bakersfield draws life from the 5 and the 99, while its Iraqi counterpart clings like a barnacle to Highways 1 and 11.

Most of all, both cities suck ass.

As a child, the sense of imminent danger I felt on the streets of Bakersfield provided me with just a tiny taste of what I would experience years later fighting in Fallujah. Of course, there weren't any IEDs going off downtown or snipers taking potshots at me as I walked to school, and most of the adults in my neighborhood seemed to be relatively decent and hard-working folks. But their children—those muddy-handed, black-hearted, snot-nosed, crooked-toothed terrorist offspring—made the Bakersfield of my youth into a nightmarish, Fallujah-esque battleground.

On my block alone, there were ten-year-old racists who would spit slurs or throw dirt clods at anyone even a half shade of white; there were pint-sized psychopaths who would laugh like maniacs as they kicked their dogs or shot baby frogs out of garden hoses; and then there were the run-of-the-mill bullies, one or two to every household, all of whom seemed to be able to smell weakness from a hundred yards away.

"It's so lovely outside," my mother would say. "Why don't you and your younger brother go out and play?"

My mom worked full time and put herself through school—a dream she had to put on hold when she met my dad at the Pearly Cue, a pool hall nestled at the foothills of the Tehachapi Mountains, right on the edge of Bakersfield. She was a waitress, and he was a pool shark. After they got married, they bought a small house in Bakersfield, where I was born. My brother came along three years later, and Mom's college aspirations went on hold until we were old enough to eat solid food and wipe our own asses.

When school was over, Mom would sweetly encourage my brother and me to play outside while she studied. Of course, we would never just put on our shoes and leave the house. That would be madness, pure stupidity, a surefire way to get caught. Instead, I would insist on doing some reconnaissance: cracking open our vinyl blinds to peer out over the heat-hazed cement of our cul-de-sac, scanning each ramshackle ranch house and brown front lawn for our enemies.

It didn't matter what time of day it was—morning, noon, or twilight—there was always some gaggle of despots gathering together to sharpen their plastic shovels or throw dog shit at one another. My brother's and my objective was to put as much distance between ourselves and these urchins as possible without being seen. So when the time was right, while the little fuckers were distracted with the sacrificial burning of an anthill or the ritual mutilation of some poor unfortunate rodent, we'd run out our front door and flee in the opposite direction. Better to meander the sidewalks all day, was our thinking, than to spend the next eight hours being targeted by the juvenile criminal element.

To make matters worse, we were exceedingly easy targets. Not because either of us was particularly small or extraordinarily ugly—though I'll admit, I was pretty goofy-looking. No, we were easy because we were trusting and naïve. Maybe that sounds sweet, lovable, or even precious, but in the real world, whether you're a kid or an adult, being sweet and trusting makes you easy prey for the not-so-sweet and not-to-be-trusted. We couldn't help it, though. Some people are just born with a sweet disposition. Despite her troubles, my mom was one of the sweet ones, and my brother and I took after her.

My brother was plagued with a multitude of health issues, which meant that my parents had to focus on his needs more than mine. He had just about every allergy and health problem you could imagine. He screamed endlessly, refused to eat, and didn't like to be touched. Because of this, I had to learn how to take care of myself at a young age. I saw it as my duty to be as low-maintenance as possible and to do my best to keep the peace during my parents' arguments, trying to prevent things from escalating into violence. I was the unofficial peacekeeper of the family—a knight or a superhero in my own right. Despite my role, I never picked fights or stood up for myself. In fact, I think my parents forgot they had two kids most of the time. But I kept a mental ledger of all my good deeds and sacrifices, convinced that one day, my high moral standing would earn me respect from my peers and the love and attention I craved from my parents.

My very best childhood friends were named Gauge and Desoto. Only I could actually see them since they existed in my imagination. Anytime, day or night, they were always up for an adventure and always knew just when to swoop in and save the day.

When the sound of my dad's drunken shouts and my mom's tears filled the house, I'd see one of them in the corner, motioning for me to go outside. Once I was outside, Gauge and Desoto would brief me on the complex mission we were tasked with for the night. The intricacy of the problems always demanded my full attention. As much as I wanted to fix my parents' latest argument, I couldn't afford to be distracted—I needed to bring my A game until the mission was complete. So when it was clear my dad intended to drink beer for dinner and my mom was too busy helping my brother or studying to cook supper, I'd make myself a sandwich and play with Gauge and Desoto until dark. We'd pretend to rescue hostages from a high-security building, complete daring missions, defuse imaginary bombs, and face off against ruthless foes plotting world domination. We used discarded rope from the garage for scaling imaginary walls, fallen tree branches as makeshift rifles, and old, worn-out blankets as tactical vests—some real MacGyver-style shit. We'd strategize how to breach locked doorways with makeshift tools and tactics and capture notorious villains by setting up elaborate traps and ambushes. Gauge and Desoto were legends. They never backed down from a fight and kept me on my toes.

When the sun set and I could no longer see more than a few feet in front of me, I'd start heading back to the house. As I walked home, I'd wonder if anyone had noticed my absence—maybe I'd open the door to find Mom saying she'd been worried sick and Dad scolding me for being out too late. But the only sound that greeted me was the muffled hum of the television, casting a blue light into the otherwise dark living room. Dad would already be passed out on the couch, beer bottles strewn across the floor beside him. Mom would have retreated to her bedroom to avoid the inevitable conflicts with Dad. I'd check on my little brother and then tuck myself into bed for the night.

Then came the part of the day I dreaded most. Once everything was quiet and my head was on my pillow, my mind would begin to race and ruminate. But it wasn't scary monsters or bullies at school that occupied my thoughts. Instead, my mind would run through a list of catastrophic world problems, fueled by scraps of information I'd picked up from watching the news with my parents, reading the newspaper, or overhearing adult conversations. I couldn't find a way to shut off this constant barrage of fear and anxiety.

But that wasn't the only reason I dreaded the night. Every single night, without exception, I would wake up in a puddle of my own urine. I wet the bed every night until I was at least fourteen, and somehow my parents never noticed. To minimize the mess, I developed strategies to make cleanup easier. I always slept on top of the quilt, never between the sheets. Even with these routines in place, I still dreaded the night. I hated that I couldn't control my body and stop the bed-wetting.

Sleepovers at a classmate's house were even worse; they became a full-scale operation. I'd come prepared with my own sleeping bag and a change of clothes. I'd wake up at the crack of dawn to dispose of my pee-covered pants before anyone could see me. I'd crawl on my belly, tiptoe, and change in the dark to avoid discovery. And only once did I get caught.

I was in full stealth mode, just about to reach the bathroom to change, when I came face-to-face with my classmate's father, who just so happened to be a Kern County Sheriff. He took one look at my pee-soaked pants and knew exactly what I was doing. I expected him to get angry or shame me, but instead, his eyes were filled with compassion. He offered to bring me towels and help me, allowing me a shred of dignity. What's more, he never spoke a word about it to anyone. That fresh towel he gave me was one of the kindest acts of care I'd ever received as a child.

But I was still all big, dumb, genuine smiles and misty-eyed empathy in those days. I soon learned that the real world is no place for a sensitive kid. For a few blessed years, I wasn't the primary target of the neighborhood bullies. They'd let me hang around in an effort to pull me to the dark side. But I recognized their cruel and unusual activities for what they were. Despite their taunting, I'd refuse to take part. I was a knight, after all. No knight would ever de-pants his little brother or throw rocks at wandering pets just to fit in. Nor would he harrass toddlers or spit on people's door handles in an effort to please. My disagreement with their proposed activities wasn't just because every "prank" they planned was petty and mean-spirited, or even that their idea of "fun" was never actually that.

The biggest problem was that their targets were always innocent or weak—the exact types of people that a knight was sworn to protect. It wouldn't have bothered me so much if they'd just gone up against each other, bully against bully. In that case, they both would have signed up to play the game, making any damage incurred an unsurprising side effect. *May the best man win.*

But these bullies didn't pick on the other players of their evil game; they picked on the weak, the ones who never asked to be put in the middle of a fight, the ones who could not protect themselves. I hated that. You can play the game all you want inside the board, but you never, ever attack the innocents beyond that boundary.

The bullies kept inviting me to participate in their evil scheme of the day, and I kept saying no. I wasn't an enemy; I was just a non-participator. But that wasn't a position I could maintain forever. One day everything changed. I declined their offer to toilet paper an elderly neighbor's house on the grounds that it would make me too sad to watch the old man clean up the mess. That's when I discovered that there is nothing in this world more vicious than a middle school-aged child on a rampage to punish a fellow kid who goes against the grain. I remember the wolfish smiles creasing their tiny terrorist faces after I gave my refusal. I can still see their bright, evil eyes darting back and forth, shining with devilish delight. Fresh prey was among them. From that day on, they cursed me with a single word that would hang around my neck like an albatross for the rest of my life: *nerd*.

And then things got worse. One day, on my parents' front lawn, an argument erupted among the group. It wasn't just a disagreement among friends; it was three boys—each two years older and at least a head taller—blaming me for something I hadn't done. I pulled out my mental ledger, trying to prove my innocence and show them how illogical their accusations were. But they didn't care.

"Get him!" one of the boys yelled. In an instant, rough hands were all over me, pushing, pulling, and shoving. I hit the ground hard. When I tried to get back on my feet, I could barely move. One boy had my legs pinned down, another was above me, pressing his knees into my shoulders, grinding me into the dirt. The third boy straddled me. I pushed with all my might, trying to break free, but the more I struggled, the harder they laughed and held me down. Panic surged as I realized I was completely at their mercy, completely powerless. My shouts of resistance turned into desperate, high-pitched screams. The biggest boy's twisted smile widened as he reared back his head, pursed his lips, and spat right in my face. As that pool of mucous-laced saliva landed on me, I felt humiliated, alone, and powerless. When they finally released me, I jumped to my feet, ready to fight back. But they just laughed and walked away.

From then on, each "lovely day" that my brother and I left the house, we were hunted. Being a nerd was about the worst thing a kid could be in Bakersfield. This was a place where bullying was encouraged as an essential form of social Darwinism. At that time, the prevailing wisdom among Bakersfieldians was that if you were a wimp, getting your ass kicked was the best way to toughen you up; if you were homosexual, taking a few hard shots to the teeth would knock the gay right out of you; and if you were a nerd who believed himself a knight, well, being bullied every day might just force you to hang up your sword. In a final effort to end my suffering, I did what no kid ever wants to do. I tattled. I told my parents and teachers what was happening and asked for help. They were quick to run to my aid with life-changing advice.

"You gotta find a way to fix this yourself, Tyler."

"They wouldn't be picking on you if you weren't so strange, Tyler."

"Why don't you man up and fight back, Tyler?"

What a fool I was to believe that my pitiful entreaties might dent the ironclad prevailing wisdom of the Bakersfieldians. That was before I realized that the cruel world is no place for being who you are. I still clung to the notion that if I were good, kind, and quiet enough, maybe I would earn a second look from my parents, more friends, and luck with the girls.

But it didn't matter what I did; every day remained open season on "little Tyler Gay," or, as I was known to the less imaginative bullies: "that pussy nerd f*%#%t." The girls kept flocking to the assholes who treated them like trash, and I was out of luck. But I kept trying. By the time I reached high school, I was a chameleon. I'd hang out with the jocks one day, the black-trench-coat-wearing intellectuals who could have been voted Most Likely to Shoot Up the School the next, and the film nerds the following.

As the hammer of puberty fell, I morphed into something unrecognizable from the scrawny kid I once was. Aggression, height, power, and strength surged through me, reshaping the way I saw the world—and myself. Then I found my dad's stash of *Playboy* magazines, a raw, unfiltered introduction to a world I wasn't ready for but couldn't turn away from. Suddenly, the girls around me weren't the same snotty-nosed kids I'd played tag with at recess; they had turned into beautiful, otherworldly beings with captivating new shapes that I couldn't tear my eyes away from.

This revelation hit me again as I walked through our local Blockbuster, trying to pick out a Friday-night movie. Elisabeth Shue, Winona Ryder, and Mia Sara stared back at me from the video covers, and I found myself pressing the rewind button more than once to watch Princess Leia in her golden bikini. But nothing compared to Wonder Woman—strong, curvaceous, and drop-dead gorgeous. I hung her DC comic book poster on my wall and vowed to find a Wonder Woman of my own someday. Just once in my life, I wanted to experience a grand, epic love story like the great warriors in books and films.

So, when a pretty brunette named Allison caught my eye in ninth grade, I went out of my way to be nice to her. But she was far more interested in Mario, who was, quite literally, the epitome of a walking asshole. After enduring more rejections than I could count, I gave up and moved on. This time, it was Diana who humiliated me at a school dance. The cycle seemed endless: no matter how kind, genuine, polite, or sweet my gestures were, I was always met with rejection. I soon learned that love in the real world wasn't like the comic books and movies where the good guys win the girl and the bad guys are punished.

Still, I kept rising above the lying assholes who treated girls poorly. I rose above the fights that came my way, striving for a mental high ground of moral superiority—as if participating in schoolyard brawls was beneath my knightly dignity. I kept tallying up my good deeds, politeness, sacrificial acts, and righteous endurance of torture in my ledger of justice, believing that someday it would prove my worth and silence my enemies forever. But the list kept growing, the black eyes kept coming, and I remained alone, overlooked, unseen, and ground into the gravel. I tried every way I knew to fake my way into the cool crowd, but none of it worked.

So, one day I decided to pull out the big guns. I would invite all my friends to my favorite place in the world—the one place that always made me feel safe and happy: *Disneyland*.

There are a handful of happy childhood memories I hold dear: the time my soccer team won and my dad told me he was proud of my performance; the time my grandfather, a World War II veteran and respected member of the Bakersfield Police Department, took me to his basement and showed me his collection of souvenirs from thirty-five years on the force—bullets, brass knuckles, zip knives, and countless other items he'd kept from his battles against the meanest bullies on the Bakersfield playground; and the time my parents took my brother and me to Disneyland.

The best part about Disneyland at the time was its strict no-alcohol policy. For one perfect Saturday, my father was sober, my mom was smiling, my brother wasn't crying, and I felt genuinely happy. As we waited in line for rides, devoured fried food delicacies, and cheered on the roller coasters speeding down the track, I felt like we were a real family.

And if Disneyland was magical enough to bring my family together, I figured it might just be the key to making some real friends at school. Once a year, all the high schools in the area convened for Grad Night—an entire night of fun at Disneyland after it closed to the public. I invited a handful of old friends from a neighboring high school to meet at the bench on Main Street at the entrance right across from the fire station at 11:00 p.m. so we could all hang out together. When Saturday night arrived, I showed up at 10:15. By 10:55, I started looking for my friends, wondering who would show up first. By 11:30, I was questioning why they were late. By midnight, I worried they had the wrong time. By 4:00 a.m., I realized they weren't coming at all, and I suddenly had no desire to ride any of the rides. My mind kept racing with the same questions: *Why am I always invisible to my parents and detestable to my classmates? What is wrong with me?* No matter what I did, my environment never changed. I couldn't escape the pain, rejection, and neglect. I couldn't earn approval. *Am I just a bad person? Am I just not good enough? Is it me?* I couldn't silence the questions that echoed in my mind.

One day, another fight broke out, once again on the front lawn of my parents' house. They were at it again. Taunting, laughing, kicking, and slapping. I cocked my arm and clenched my fist. I wanted to defend myself but was afraid that my knuckles would connect with all the force of a light breeze, eliciting laughter from my opponent before he struck back and cracked my skull. I just wanted them to leave me alone. I just wanted to feel safe. I just wanted peace.

The biggest kid, Matt Marley, shouted an unimaginative slur and slapped my cheek. The pain of the insult, even more than the sting of his palm on my face, cracked open something inside of me. *Maybe they're right. Maybe I'm not good enough to be liked. Maybe I'm not strong enough to fight.* All this time, I had believed I was a knight. All this time, I'd tried to prove to myself that I wasn't on the dark side…no, I was *good*. My ledger was so packed with polite smiles and good deeds that there should be no question on the verdict of my identity as a knight, as a hero. But the question persisted: *Why me?* My moral high ground wasn't high enough to avoid a black eye and bruised ribs or earn me the attention of a beautiful girl. And I was beginning to think that the ledger didn't exist. I had earned nothing but rejection, pain, and torment. Maybe I was going about this all wrong.

The other kids seemed to gravitate toward the two-faced, superficial "cool kids" and bullies at their parties. The girls preferred the bad-boy assholes over the nice guy who smiled and tried to be a gentleman. And despite my best efforts, my good behavior still hadn't won me any approval from my parents. Inside my home, there was tension and chaos; outside, there was ridicule and rejection. I had no safe or happy places left to run. Soccer was over, along with my dad's approval; Disneyland had been ruined; and even my grandfather's basement was cleaned out after he passed away.

The chaos swirled around me, the ugly faces of the bullies closing in, snarling with menace. That's when I realized I wasn't going to change this environment. There was no safety to be found, no ledger of good deeds that would buy me peace. The world was dark, cruel, and painful—nowhere for a kind, sensitive guy like me. The kind, naïve, trusting little boy on a quest to do the right thing needed to go. I needed to change the rules of the game or become the best player. Maybe I'd do both.

In that split second, I knew what I had to do: create an entirely new identity. Something inside me began to shift, change, and split apart. There was the Tyler Grey I had always been, and now there was a new character emerging—the Tyler Grey I would become. This new Tyler would play the game and do it better than anyone. He wouldn't take shit from anybody. He would be confident, ruthless, and aggressive. He wouldn't need anyone's approval or feel neglected, because he could take care of himself. He would never find himself powerless amidst the chaos; instead, he would be on the offensive, the creator of the chaos. I'd kept the destroyer in the shadows long enough, and now it was time to let him take control.

As I drew back my fist, an involuntary animal screech erupted from my throat, fueled by a surge of adrenaline that spilled over uncontrollably. I hurled my fist toward Matt Marley's face, driven by years of suppressed anger and hatred. The moment of impact was explosive. Pain shot through my hand, up my arm, and into my elbow, as if my knuckles had spontaneously combusted. My heart thundered in my chest. Matt toppled backward onto the turf and scrambled away on his elbows, but I moved toward him, kicking and still screaming like a banshee. Out of the corner of my eye, I saw the front door of my parents' house swing open. My father stepped outside, took in the scene—me on top, Matt pinned beneath me—and shouted with a gleam in his eye, "KICK HIS ASS, SON!" And I obeyed.

I stood over Matt, kicking his legs, ribs, and arms with relentless fury. I shouted, punched, slapped, and kicked some more. Every retaliation I had held back, every comeback I'd never voiced, every fistful of anger I hadn't released came crashing down on poor ol' Matt Marley. My father watched silently from the front porch. Eventually, Matt stumbled to his feet and fled, turning back to his friends. As he ran, I inhaled the breath of a new identity that had taken hold of me from the inside out. My mind, once clouded with fear, was now crystal clear. The chaos raged all around me, just like it always had. But this time, I was calm. I felt no panic, no stress, no desire to run away. It was the first time I realized I had a superpower—one that would be with me for the rest of my life. I was in the game. And I was ready for more.

"Come on!" I yelled at them, my fists clenched so tight that my fingernails cut into my palms. "Come the fuck on!"

When they heard the sound, they looked at my face. Suddenly everyone froze. Because it wasn't the Tyler Grey they had always known staring back at them. It was someone or some*thing* else entirely. My eyes burned with the intensity of a destroyer—bright with dominance and capable of anything. I had taken down their buddy with one swift punch, and now none of them wanted to step in where he had failed. They were afraid of getting their asses kicked—by me. *I* was powerful, and *they* were scared.

As I slowly lowered my arms and unclenched my fists, none of them dared to move closer. I smiled then, baring my teeth at the pack, and walked away. And at that moment, I knew I wasn't a knight anymore. He'd had his shot and he'd failed. I was something much better. I was a warrior. I was a destroyer. I was a goddamned superhero.

CHAPTER 4
KNUCKLE DRAGGER

Somewhere in Baghdad, Iraq, January 2005

MY DAY STARTS AT SUNDOWN. When my alarm goes off, I rub the sleep from my eyes, take a shit, hit the gym, and eat. Within an hour, I find myself seated on a cold metal chair in a small briefing room—it's time to see what Command has planned for the night. A four-month rotation consists of approximately 120 nights, and the Army intends to make the most of every single one. Lousy weather is about the only thing that gets you a night off around here because that's the only time the helicopters can't fly. Hours, days, maybe even weeks of meticulous planning have led up to this moment when we finally learn the who, when, where, and how of tonight's mission. In front of me is a board displaying images of our target location, and tonight we're in luck: we have several photos. Sometimes we're only given one grainy snapshot, which isn't much to work with.

Our team leader begins the briefing. Tonight we're going after one of the most prolific vehicle-borne improvised explosive device (VBID) makers in the city. This fellow isn't just tinkering around with a couple of used cars in his backyard to make extra cash; he's running a full-blown operation that is responsible for the death of numerous Americans and Iraqis. As I listen to the briefing, I don't feel anything at first. There's no rage, emotion, or surge of aggression that rises up in me. This is procedural. This is my job.

"...is responsible for killing two Marines last week..." the team leader says. *Deserves full retaliation.*

"...is responsible for the deaths of women and children..." *Deserves to suffer and die.* Now feel something. It's not red-hot rage or savage aggression. Not a feeling that makes me shout some godawful cliché, "C'mon boys, let's get this fuckin' low-life bastard!" It's not like the movies. My feeling is quieter but just as lethal. As the gavel hits the wooden block in my mind, I feel a clean, sharp sense of finality. This man broke the cardinal rule. He harmed innocents who never signed up to play our game. Sure, I'm pissed that he took out American soldiers, but they were players; they signed up for this game, just like I did. We advance, they push back. We show up in their backyard, they take a shot at us. This is war, and we all knew the rules of the game when we signed up. But the women, the children—they didn't sign up. They aren't players. That's where I draw the line. They should be off-limits. You can play the game all you want inside the board, but you never, ever attack the innocents beyond that boundary. My mind is clear and calm—now it's just a matter of protocol, logistics, and execution.

The plan is to hit the VBID maker's house while he's asleep and apprehend him and anyone else of interest who happens to be there. One team will come from the back door, one from the front, and one from the rooftop. The flat-roof houses commonly found in Iraq are multilevel structures—utilizing sun-dried mud bricks for their walls, which provide insulation against the intense heat. The locals use the rooftop like another room of the house, for everything from social gatherings to water storage space to sleeping areas on warmer nights. I'm in charge of breaching the rooftop entrance so we can pay Mr. VBID Maker a surprise visit. When the briefing concludes, I study the images on the board to help me calculate the charge needed to breach it. The images were taken overhead and at a distance, but I can still see the approximate dimensions of the door. Judging by the look of it, I have a good idea of the building material. The rest is just math. Specifically, algebra.

When I pull out a pad of paper and begin calculating, I am transported back to 1993—my sophomore year of high school. I remember sitting there in that uncomfortable seat, roasting in the sweltering heat of the classroom, taking my very first exam of the year. I was stuck on the first question, asking myself why the hell a math problem had the letter x right in the middle of it. For a while, I stared at the problem in such concentration and stress that sweat dripped onto the paper until a thought came to me: *I'm never going to use this again.*

Suddenly, I felt my stress melting away. Everything would be okay, and why shouldn't it be? After all, I wasn't going to be a scientist or accountant, let alone a mathematician. So, what did it matter if I understood the math problem with letters in it? It was all nothing but a big waste of time and considerable brainpower. Now I was free. Free to spend my mental energy on more important things, like calculating the odds of whether the green-eyed girl in the corner would go out with me. My predictions about life seemed to be accurate when I joined the Army. Nobody needs algebra when you're busy running, shooting, and fighting, right? Turns out I was duped. They lured me into the job with the promise of learning and mastering the cool stuff: stalking an enemy location, counterterrorism, hostage rescue, direct action, special reconnaissance, long-range sniping, and the list goes on. Until I uncovered the truth: The United States military tricked us all into becoming nerds. Lucky for them, I already was.

This epiphany came to me in the mountains of eastern Afghanistan on the Pakistan border in 2002 as a US Army Ranger sniper team leader when I sat inside a hide site figuring out x with a calculator. I had ballistic formulas scrawled across Rite in the Rain notebook paper. And that's when the thought came to me: *How in the fuck did I get here, doing this? I am NOT a scientist, accountant, or mathematician! I'm in the Army, for Pete's sake, and an Infantryman, no less. This wasn't the job I signed up for.* For a minute, I analyzed the set of choices that led me to that exact moment in time— joining the Army, yep, I did that. Airborne, yes. Ranger Battalion, uh-huh. Sniper, check. But no, I definitely didn't volunteer for math duty. Maybe I just did too well on my ASVAB (Armed Services Vocational Aptitude Battery). Hell, I don't even remember taking the damn thing. I think I just checked A, B, C, D, then reversed my guesses D, C, B, A, because it seemed more logical to alter the sequence for the most fitting answers. Statistics, right? Can't be. So I asked myself again: *How did I get here?*

Truth is, I joined to be a knuckle dragger—slightly derogatory military slang for infantry combat troops that I'm personally quite fond of. I joined to be the razor's edge of democracy's spear, a member of "the Unit," an SOF operator, a bona fide Chuck Fucking Norris. But the more I learn about my job, the more I realize that they tricked us all into becoming mathematicians and scientists. Sniping or long-range shooting is nothing but math, physics, and geometry, all combined into a badass-sounding job package that tricked all of us unsuspecting math dropouts. I questioned my knuckle-dragger status a thousand times while I took classes on waveform antenna theory, learned to calculate slant angle, and studied wind, ballistic coefficients, or my personal favorite, the Coriolis effect. I concentrated so hard I thought blood was going to come out of my nose and ears. *Dammit, they got me.* I honestly didn't see it coming.

It's a product of the changing times and the evolution of warfare, I suppose, which necessitates the natural evolution of its participants. Truth is, everything is science. It's how we understand the world, and war is no different. And it doesn't take a genius to recognize that science has transformed the battlefield drastically over time, and the pace of that change is ever-increasing. Warfare is no longer mindless hordes of humans running at each other with sharpened metal rods, at least not usually. Modern warfare is complex and requires warriors with intelligence. Now, you not only gotta be able to get to the top of the mountain like a champ, but you have to do some math when you get there to figure out the enemy's range to take your shot. The days of the all-brawn, no-brain warriors are gone. Nowadays, you gotta be both. Modern warriors need to be thinkers. We are building smarter warriors for smarter warfare. So, my advice to the bright-eyed kids at home dreaming of joining the military? If you want to be a knuckle dragger someday, you should pay attention in algebra class.

"Looks like the Bakersfieldian bullies were right," I laugh to myself as I hunch over my pad of paper, calculating what type of charge I'll need to breach the rooftop of tonight's target location. The thing is, if you know how to make the correct calculations and have enough explosives on hand, you could breach the front door of the Great Pyramid of Giza.

Breaching is easy if you don't care about the destruction on the other side. Make a big boom, and you're through. But we're a hostage rescue unit, which means that the big boom method doesn't work for us. If we breach with an explosive that takes out the very hostages we're trying to save, we'll be out of a job. That's why we took surgical breaching so seriously and trained for it over and over until we saw *new* formulas in our dreams. We had to learn to use only the exact amount of explosives to open the entrance without demolishing anything on the other side. But determining that exact amount means considering a variety of factors, like the room's size, dimensions, net explosive weight, and how much freakin' overpressure gets unleashed. Overpressure is an extraordinarily complex calculation, based on a myriad of factors. It's a math problem that just keeps getting trickier the more factors you introduce into the question. But if you train enough, it becomes instinctual.

I study the photo and make calculations based on my estimations from what I can see and then head with the rest of the team to get geared up and ready to go. Then I set to work building chargers for the breach. I always bring at least four with me so I have a solid contingency plan for each specific door type that I might be facing. I have a solid guess as to which one I'll end up using tonight, but it never hurts to have a backup charge, a tertiary, and a backup to that backup. I haven't miscalculated a breach before, and I don't intend to start tonight. My buddy Mikey is building charges right alongside me.

It's well past midnight when we begin to transport from the Green Zone, where we are headquartered, to the location of the VBID maker. We arrive in less than an hour. The house is large, and a tall concrete wall surrounds the property, which is not unusual for the area. A ladder is placed against the wall, and two teams climb over in total silence and then head to their respective positions—one at the back door, one at the front. My team places a ladder against the wall surrounding a neighboring house directly adjacent to the target's home. It doesn't take long for us to gain access to the top of the neighbor's roof. From there, we extend a ladder to the roof of the target house so we can crawl over without being detected. Once in position at the rooftop entrance, we'll coordinate with the other teams to set the charges, and three, two, one...*boom*. We'll start clearing the house from every direction until we converge in the middle. I crouch down and wrap my hands around the ladder and begin crawling toward the target's rooftop. Suddenly, rapid gunfire cracks through the air, piercing the silent night.

POW. POW. POW. POW. POW. POW. It doesn't stop. *Fuck*.

My mind is crystal clear, my body is acting on pure instinct. I'm running now, holding the sides of the ladder for stabilization until I make it onto the target's roof. The gunfire doesn't relent. No fewer than thirty rounds have been fired by the time I reach the rooftop doorway. I glance at the doorway, grab charger number three, set it, and *BOOM*, we're inside. I can hear voices shouting from the floor below us, and the sound of gunfire echoes through the entire building. I scan the room, gun raised in a ready position, elbows flexed. The floor is empty. If we were in the movies, this is the part where we'd yell, "Clear!" In reality, we don't need to say a damn thing.

All the action is going on below us. I see a staircase and sprint to it. One...two...three...steps, and then I see bodies. The floor is covered in bodies...four, five, six bodies, maybe more. I can't count.

I step off the staircase and into the hallway. My balance suddenly falters, like the floor is sliding, like there's something wet beneath me, like Mom just mopped the floors and will be mad that I'm walking on them, like a puddle of goo underneath my boots. I'm sliding in blood from one of the bodies nearest to the stairwell. *Goddammit*. You don't realize how much blood a human holds until it starts draining out. I steady myself and take another step forward. I see my buddy up ahead in the next room. Then there's a loud grunt, and a man comes flying at him from the other direction and tackles him to the ground. The two are struggling on the floor, a tangle of arms and legs. I step over two more bodies in the hallway, clearing each room, one by one, getting close to my buddy who's just taken a fall. There are three more bodies in the kitchen and two more in the living room. Blood oozes across the concrete floors, seeping into the rugs and gathering in pools. I glance in my buddy's direction again. He's back on his feet; the assailant is pinned down. Fucking bastard didn't have a chance. When we come together in the center, all rooms have been cleared, and no one has escaped the home. No team member has been injured.

"Just before we breached the front door, these fuckers decided to grab AKs and pick a fight. Had to hit 'em first. A bunch of fucking suicide bombers all sleeping in the front room, getting ready to roll out in the morning."

That explains the gunfire. We'll stay on-site for several more hours. We always do. If we successfully bring a target in alive, we stay and question him to see if he'll give up the location of any of his nefarious buddies that might be of interest to us. More often than not, if you intimidate them into thinking that they are about to die, they'll roll on their pals. If we do get promising intel on a follow-up location, we'll load up and head straight there. If we successfully identify that target and take him down, we'll go through the same process again: scare the living shit out of him, make him roll on somebody else. Once, we got four Grade-A bad guys in one night just because they kept giving each other up. Fear is a powerful tool.

Tonight, we only have one live one, the same one who tackled my buddy, and as luck would have it, it's Mr. VBID Maker himself. And he isn't talking. That might change when we bring him in.

Various duties need to be completed before we can head back to the Green Zone for breakfast and a day's worth of sleep before we go again. We need to search each room for weapons and other items of interest. I'm on dead-guy photo duty. One snapshot of each man's face will be given to the intel nerds, who will run their facial recognition software to try to identify each person. I do a quick walk-through of the house to get the lay of the land. Dead bodies cover the floors, nearly a dozen in total. My boots are tracking bloody footprints all over the place, but there's nothing I can do about it. I can't go more than a couple of feet before hitting another puddle of blood.

In the kitchen, two men lay lifeless on the floor, blood seeping from their chests and heads. There's a third man in the corner, and the body is still moving. I walk a few steps closer to get a better look. He's a chubby fellow, not more than thirty to thirty-five years old. Blood seeps from his abdomen and chest where he's been shot multiple times. But he's still breathing. I can tell by the ragged sound that a lung has collapsed already. In this condition, I'm surprised he's still holding on. It's not always easy to gauge how long someone's got left by the look of things. I've seen guys survive a bloodbath and others go down on the spot from a bullet that didn't make much of a splash. But the sound never lies. That labored, uneven breathing always comes right before death. I move on to the next room. He'll die any second now.

It doesn't take long for us to complete the initial search. The other team members continue with a full SSE (Sensitive Site Exploitation) as I move on to dead-guy photo duty. I pull out my camera and start with the body closest to me. He's lying face up, which makes my job easier. I don't need to touch him. I hate getting their blood on me, and I've already burned more Nomex gloves than I can count. *Click*. On to the next. I head back to the kitchen to get photos of the three bodies located there before moving on to the hallway and main room. Then I hear it again. That jagged, raspy breath. How is that fucker still alive? I move closer to him until I'm standing right over him.

Watch him die. The thought comes like a command from somewhere deep inside me. And I obey. The man's eyes are open, and he's staring at me, but there is no light of recognition there. They are empty. Another strained breath comes and goes. I kneel down in front of him and lean in until I'm no more than a foot away from his face. We are eye to eye, and he's looking straight at me. Another long, agonizing breath comes and goes. I'm betting it will be his last, but he keeps holding on. For more than an entire minute, we stare at each other. He struggles to breathe, and I don't move. And then it happens. His eyes change as the life drains out of him. His chest does not rise for another breath. He is still now, eyes fixed, and I sit in silence. I'm waiting. Waiting for some feeling to come, any feeling—satisfaction, victory, power, resentment, guilt, regret, anger, sadness—anything. I don't even care what I feel; I just want to know that I'm still capable of it. I realize that I've arranged a test for myself. To see if the mechanism still works, that human-feeling valve should be firing about now. Nothing comes. Absolutely nothing.

I don't feel satisfaction, victory, or power. I don't feel sadness, anger, or guilt. I feel nothing, nothing, nothing…until I feel concerned that I feel nothing. *You're supposed to feel something; this isn't normal,* half of me thinks. *Look who's in control now; you're invincible,* the other half whispers. I stand up, snap a photo of the man's face, and then keep moving. The sun is just beginning to rise when we bring the VBID maker to the designated holding location.

"Tyler, why don't you join me for this one?" My team leader motions me to accompany him to interrogate the VBID maker. He knows that I'm working on my interrogation techniques and need the practice. The VBID maker is in a metal chair—hands and feet tied. His stare is vacant, eyes misted with indifference. For several hours, I listen and observe as our team leader thoroughly questions the man. By the time he finishes, he's systematically covered just about every question related to the operation that could provide us with actionable intel. He's good, and I'm taking notes.

"Got any questions to add?" he says when he finishes. I nod my head and stand up. I begin with a few operational questions, filling in details and ironing out discrepancies that I noted while listening. But I'm not done.

"I got one more question for you." I stare straight into the VBID maker's eyes, gaze sharp. "Look, I can understand why you want to blow up guys like me. I'm a foreign troop in your country. I get it. If you were in my country, I'd blow the fuck out of you too. I wouldn't give a damn *why* you're there. If you came to my back door saying that my president is a horrible leader and tried to gain control of my city, I wouldn't give a fuck about your reason. I'd tell you to get the fuck out of my country and I'd try and blow your brains out, just like you're doing to us. That I understand. But here's what I don't get and want to understand.

"If you were in my country, I wouldn't blow up twenty American women and children to kill fucking five of you. I wouldn't do that to kill a hundred of you. I wouldn't do that to kill a thousand of you. How can you possibly consider it okay to slaughter your own women and children just to take a shot at me?"

My eyes are digging into him, searching. The translator finishes relaying my message, and I wait to see something. A flash of guilt, an oh-shit-why-didn't-I-think-of-that, or even some look of defiance that says I just don't care. But his eyes are dead and his mouth is rattling, spitting out lines like a tape recorder. Something about infidels, something about a martyr's death, something about Allah. He repeats the lines without feeling, which could all be summed up to mean that Allah's got the situation under control, and the women and children who died will get a one-way ticket to heaven as long as they went out helping to kill the infidels. Classic. But I'm not ready to stop.

"Okay, I get that, I get that you believe that." I will not let up until I get to the bottom of this. "But what are you going to say to the father of one of the children you killed? How are you going to look him in the eyes?" Again, I'm waiting to see something, anything. Remorse, sadness, regret, empathy.

"But the father already knows that what I have said is true. He knows." I take a breath and lean closer.

"Okay. But what if the father doesn't share your beliefs? Who are you to make that decision about his own child for him?"

I'm inches from his face. He doesn't even pause to consider what I've said. The moment he understands, he blurts out a response. "Then the father would be wrong."

Now I do feel something. Rage. Deep rage. Because now I understand. This isn't an evil man. This is a stupid man. I'd respect him more if he'd told me that he didn't care or even that he got off on killing the innocent. At least he would have a good goddamned reason that made sense in his own fucked-up mind. The human in front of me is nothing but a malfunctioning robot that's been programmed for destruction. And the earth would be better off without him. I stand and nod to my team leader.

"I have no more questions."

CHAPTER 5
AFTERMATH

WHAT THE HELL JUST HAPPENED? My brain is static. White noise. I lift my head again, trying to understand. The light is gone. No glow, no spinning, no swirling. Just darkness.

Then, it comes back in flashes....

The screaming woman.

The lollipops.

The wrong damn house.

The AK barrel pressing into my chest.

The hallway.

The walls exploding.

The vortex.

Arm. My right arm. Something about my right arm. It's there again, that signal, coming from far away. The absent feeling. I reach to my right side with my gloved left hand. I connect with something, but it's not my arm. There's no bone there, no muscle, no structure—only softness and liquid. I pull my glove back, and it's soaking wet. Another feeling comes, one so powerful that I feel overwhelmed—like an injection of stress in its most potent form, registering in every cell of my body, coursing through my veins. I pick myself up from the floor, and as I rise, my brain fires another train of thought: Something about a movie... *Saving Private Ryan*...A missing arm...*That's it. I need to look for my fucking arm. I need to bring it with me.*

With my left hand, I swipe at the ground, feeling around in the darkness, hoping to connect with an object that feels like a body part. I gotta bring it with me. But I can't feel anything, and I can't see anything, and now it's all registering: *I'm bleeding out, and I need to get the FUCK out of here. NOW!*

There is still gunfire exploding all around me, but I cannot hear anything. There is only silence and darkness. I'm on my feet now, running, feeling my way through the inky black until I'm out of the house and onto a small porch. A dim light casts a yellow glow over my skin. *Check and see if it's still there.* I turn my head to the right, but I'm not prepared for what I see. Shredded flesh hangs from my shoulder like fistfuls of raw hamburger meat. I see no bone—only a large flap of bloody skin flayed out, barely attached to something dangling beside my leg. *Maybe my hand?* Blood is spraying from the mangled flesh. Arterial bleed. Other thoughts are coming to me, simplistic in nature but in rapid succession. *You're going to be like one of those Vietnam vets without a right arm. And that's okay. You'll deal with it. But if you don't fix the arterial bleed, you're going to die. And that would just be stupid.*

It takes approximately sixty seconds to lose consciousness from an arterial bleed like mine, and two minutes to die. I estimate that I've burned at least twenty-five seconds looking for my arm and getting out of the house, which leaves about thirty-five seconds to get a tourniquet on and stop the bleeding. I move away from the doorway and walk into the back courtyard area. I keep walking until I touch a thick mud wall. I look up. *That's not going to happen. There's no way I'm getting over that thing.*

30 seconds. I turn around, press my back to the wall, then slowly slide down into a seated position. I need to get my tourniquet, which is attached with rubber bands to my belt on my right side. I reach around with my left hand, but the angle is all wrong, and I can't get a good grip on it. My hand is shaking as I fumble to rip it free. I twist, reaching further to the right. *Come on, come on, goddammit.*

25 seconds. I feel it, grab it, and tear it free. My brain fires instructions to apply the tourniquet—a sequence of movements I've practiced a dozen times. But nothing is happening. All the self-applied-tourniquet training techniques involve two hands. This isn't going to fucking work. I can't put on a tourniquet with one hand. I try again with my left hand. I try to loop it through the bloody mass of flesh that occupies the space where my right arm should be, but the wet pile of meat is slipping and flopping around like a fish out of water.

20 seconds. I need to get my morphine and the autoinjectors. I need to inject myself. I reach for them, and then it hits me: *They were in the pouch on my right arm…I have no right arm, no autoinjectors. I need to get to the other…the other…Wait, wait, what am I thinking? Shit, I'm losing my ability to think clearly. Too much blood loss.*

15 seconds. Suddenly, there is a face above me. It's my buddy Joe Brad McKenzie. He grabs the tourniquet.

10 seconds. Within seconds, I feel a tight squeezing sensation followed by intense, overwhelming pain. *MOTHERFUCKER, that hurts!*

5 seconds. McKenzie stops the bleeding. I don't die. And for the first time all day, I'm feeling intense pain. The tourniquet goes over the top of my arm, the part that's still capable of feeling something. And boy, do I feel. For a split second, I want to ask McKenzie to lay off the tension, until I realize that it's idiotic even to think such a thought. He's saving my life. But the pain is excruciating, and I'm aching for relief. I want to be outside my body; I need something, anything, to take the pain away. McKenzie grabs one of his own morphine injectors and prepares to jab it into my arm. I feel a burst of anticipation. Except for a swig of Pepto-Bismol and a couple of baby aspirin my mom gave me for a fever once, I've never taken any drugs, and I'm not sure how I'm going to feel. Never took pills, never did lines in the bathroom of a nightclub, never even smoked a joint. Hell, I'd just had my first glass of wine with Vanessa a few weeks earlier, and boy oh boy, did I have a whopper of a headache the next day. I tell myself to hold on. I can make it until the morphine kicks in. And so I wait. I wait for the feeling everyone talks about—that superhero I-can-conquer-the-world feeling, anything besides the pain. A minute passes. Nothing changes. The sharp edges have not dulled even a little bit.

"Any better?" McKenzie asks.

I shake my head. "Not a bit." Someone else is beside McKenzie now, looking at me. McKenzie shoves another autoinjector into my arm. "That oughta do something."

But it's still there, that unrelenting pain. I keep my face angled away from my right arm and tell myself not to look at it. Another thirty seconds pass, then a minute, but there's not even the slightest reprieve from the torment. I feel cheated. All that hype, all that drama in the movies about how strong morphine is—it's just a big load of nothing. Fuck this. (It will be two months before I learn that I'm morphine intolerant—my body just doesn't process it like most people's do. It turns out the movies weren't lying after all; I'm just weird.) Another wave of pain comes, and this time it's overwhelming. My body isn't just screaming anymore, it's surrendering. The edges of my vision grow dark.

I hear McKenzie say something, but the sound is floating somewhere above me, and I can't seem to find it. "Scott, I need you over here now!"

The next thing I hear is my troop commander's voice shouting for Scott, the medic. I'm not lying against the wall anymore; I've been transported to the muddy area where the whole night began. I must have lost consciousness. The pain isn't coming in waves now—there's no ebb and flow. It's acute and unrelenting. A strange feeling is overtaking me, swallowing me, and I don't want to be swallowed.

"I'm working on two right now. What do you need?" Scott radios back. My troop commander's voice is louder over the radio this time. "I NEED YOU TO GET OVER HERE!" When I hear his urgency, I understand that something is very wrong. For the first time all day, a surge of panic washes over me. Am I bleeding out? Am I about to die? It's all been logistics up to this point: stand up, look for the arm, get a tourniquet on the bleeder, wait for the morphine to kick in. *Details.*

I know the injury is bad, I know it hurts like a motherfucker, but now the dominos are falling in my mind when I see the alarm on the troop commander's face and hear him screaming for the medic. They're trying to save my life right now, which means there's a good chance I'm going to die today. I've seen dozens of men die before, watched medics work against time to save them, and slowly lose the battle. There's always a look of surprise on the dying man's face, the moment he realizes he isn't going to make it. *It's never you until it's you.* I've heard the quote many times, but I never really got it until now. I've always been on the other side, the guy looking down on the injured and dying. Fuck, it's me. It's me this time. I'm the poor sucker with the realization dawning in his eyes that I'm not going to make it. This is the bright-light-in-the-distance, come-to-Jesus moment. Maybe I should be looking up to the heavens and begging the Almighty to save my life. I've got a few minutes left to surrender into that divine light, to convert, to believe in God and the heaven above before it's too late. I wait to feel something. Nothing comes. *Absofuckinglutely nothing. What a scam.*

I'm actually proud of myself. This is the point when most people submit and compromise the beliefs they've held for a lifetime just to save their ass. They spend their whole lives not giving a shit about the Man Upstairs until they need to call in a favor. Not me. I'm staring death right in the face all on my own, and I'm still not going to believe in anything until I see some clear proof of its existence. No convenient drive-thru religion for me at the last minute to make sure I've got a ticket to heaven. I've said it before and I'll say it again: "If there is a hell, I'll go there in protest." I feel like I conquered a test. *What else have you got for me? Yeah, that's what I thought. Death was the last big move, right? Checkmate.*

Scott is here, and the moment he sees my arm, his eyes widen, and he starts working.

"You're going to be okay; everything is going to be just fine." His voice is steady and calm, but I'm not buying it. I roll my eyes. I know that's exactly what he's supposed to say. I've said the same to dying men plenty of times, just to offer them some peace of mind in their final moments before death.

"Don't bullshit me, Scott." I shoot him a look, a don't-you-dare-give-me-a-fucking-bullshit-line-right-now look. I know Scott well. He's a redheaded modern Viking who doesn't take shit from anyone. We went through specialized training together, and he beat the living shit out of me once while we were there, and he's a fucking medic. I mean, who gets beat up by the *medic*? Geez. We've spent pretty much every day together for over an entire year, which means this forced bedside manner isn't necessary. I look up at the concerned faces peering over me, and I suddenly switch gears. Fuck the Rapture and the bright light. *Geez, everyone needs to lighten up.* I grab Scott's hand and stare imploringly into his eyes.

"Scott, listen," I croak. "Tell my…my…my wife and kids that… that…" I swallow as if holding back tears as I speak my final words. "Oh yeah, I don't have a fucking wife and kids. Never mind." I laugh. No one else cracks a smile. *Tough crowd.*

"Look, I got the arteries clamped. I think you'll be okay, but the arm looks bad, really bad."

Scott hands me a fentanyl lollipop. "This should help."

I suck on the lollipop like my life depends on it. "Just bite into it and break it up into chunks and swallow," someone suggests. I crack my molars down, chomping the shit out of that thing.

After a minute, I feel the pain smoothing at the edges. The blade is still there, cutting into me, but it's duller this time. Scott hands me another lollipop and continues to work on my arm, fishing out pieces of shrapnel from the hamburger meat. "Goddamned shame, isn't it boys?" I say. "Best looking guy on target today, and look what they did to me." Scott snorts a laugh and then shifts his attention to my legs and starts unbuttoning my pants.

"What the fuck are you doing, man?" He's staring in between my legs, and now I'm concerned. I can figure out a way to live Vietnam vet style with no arm and still get laid. I'll figure it out. I cannot—will not—live without my dick. "Well, come on, man, is my dick still there?"

"Your dick is fine; your scrotum, however, is *not*," Scott says without looking up. Lance Armstrong flashes through my mind. Okay, if the dick is okay, I'm okay. The balls we'll figure out later.

The fentanyl lollipops finally begin working, and the next thing I hear is the sound of two Boeing MH-6M Little Birds overhead. They've come to transport me, but Scott tells them to wait. He's still working intently on my arm. My face is turned away from my right side, and I refuse to move it. I don't want to see the shredded flesh and handfuls of raw hamburger meat hanging from my shoulder.

"Okay, let's get him up," Scott calls after nearly twenty minutes pass. The lollipops are working, but the pain is still severe. Within a few minutes, I'm in the back of one of the Little Birds, squeezed into the hellhole—the small space reserved for minigun ammo or fast ropes, depending on the type of Bird. It's not a big space, hardly enough room for two grown men. Scott lays down on the litter, right on top of me, to prevent me from moving. His body is the only strap available to keep me in place for the trip. Within fifteen minutes, we're descending on the rooftop of the Baghdad cache with a landing flare. My body screams in pain as we do. The next thing I know, I'm being wheeled down a long hallway and into a stark-looking room with a bed, medical equipment, and a doctor and five young female nurses. One of them makes eye contact with me for a minute, and I smile, but she doesn't smile back. *Denied.*

The group surrounds me, and two of the nurses begin to remove my uniform.

"STOP! We have to get EOD [Explosive Ordnance Disposal]! He's got grenades on him!" one of the nurses shouts, and everyone freezes. I've still got three grenades and five chargers that I left with this morning inside my vest, and it seems they've found them. No one moves for a minute.

"Guys, come on, if they were going to go off, they sure as fuck would have when I got blown up," I say, trying to talk some sense into them. "Calm down, it'll be fine." The nurses look at each other and nod. My logic checks out, just as I knew it would.

"Let's just get the vest off and get it out of here," the screamer says. I know what's coming next. They're about to start cutting my vest off of me. I'll be damned if I'll let that happen. "HEY! Stop! You're not fucking cutting this off of me! I don't want it getting fucked up."

One of the nurses looks at me briefly. "We'll do our best."

"JUST DON'T!" I say, more forcefully this time. This is my breacher vest, and God knows I spent hours custom-designing it. Every pouch and pocket are made for specific functionality and custom-sewn to perfectly fit every inch of my body. I custom-made this myself, and

I'm going to need it again when I'm operational. I'm not about to lose it to a couple of scissor-happy nurses. To their credit, they manage to get it off without any cutting. They still cut right through my uniform, but I can live with that. Within seconds, I'm totally naked, junk on display for the whole room to see. "So, uh, you girls do know about shrinkage after getting blown up, right?" I laugh and wait for a reaction, but they don't so much as acknowledge the joke. Not even a smile.

"C'mon, don't act like you're not impressed." I try again. Nothing. *Very tough crowd.*

I can see the shock and horror on their young faces, and I know that I'm the reason for it. I hate it. I hate being the reason for another person's discomfort. I want to find a way to make them feel better, but my jokes seem to be making it worse. Only two of the five nurses are working intently on undressing me; the others are just standing there watching. I'm not sure if they're on standby, ready to swoop in and help, or if they just heard that there was an SOF operator on the floor and curiosity got the better of them and they came to take a peek behind the curtain. Either way, I feel bad. I forget all of that when I feel sudden, intense pressure inside my asshole.

"WHAT THE FUCK ARE YOU DOING?" I yelp and look between my legs. One of the nurses is shoving her finger up my rectum. Why the fuck is she sticking a finger in my ass when I don't have an arm?

"HEY! The injury is RIGHT HERE!" I yell at her and jab a finger in the direction of my right arm. "NOT THERE!"

She doesn't say a word; she just continues to feel around in my asshole for a minute and then pulls her finger out. Turns out that's how you check for internal bleeding. Would have been nice to know that bit of info before she just violated my anal cavity. I'm relieved, but that relief is short-lived. Within a second, another nurse begins shoving a catheter into my dick.

"WHAT THE FUCK ARE YOU GUYS DOING? Aren't you supposed to wait until I'm knocked out? You're fucking shoving fingers up my ass, shoving tubes down my fucking penis hole. JESUS CHRIST. What is going on here?" This is not the medical care I expected. One nurse in the corner looks at me. She's pretty. Young and pretty. Not deployment pretty but *pretty* pretty. But there's some kind of hollow sadness in her eyes as she looks at me. Like I'm a wounded animal. And I fucking hate it.

"We need to get you into surgery now, okay? We're just going to move you down the hall," one of the nurses says, her voice floating above me, and the room begins to move. I'm being wheeled down another hallway. The pain is almost more than I can take now. I want to escape it, but there's nowhere to go. It's inside me, all around me, swallowing me whole. I close my eyes. When I come to a stop, there's an anesthesiologist above me saying something about giving me a shot of Demerol. I watch as he slowly pushes the needle into my vein. I will pray to the Demerol gods all day if they offer me any salvation from the torment.

"This should help," the anesthesiologist nods at me. My face is tight with pain. That's what they told me about the morphine and the fentanyl, but they barely took the edge off. This time is different. A salty, metallic taste spreads through my mouth, and I feel relief from the pain, and it's the sweetest pleasure I've ever experienced in my life. I am superhuman, flying through time without a care in the world. A surgeon walks in the room and begins talking to me about the operation he's about to do. I hear his voice, but it's far away. I just nod my head. Up and down. Up and down. He pauses and looks at me like he's about to tell a secret.

"Listen, I want to prepare you for the fact that we are more than likely going to remove your right arm entirely," he says. "We are going to do everything we can to save it. I don't want you to be surprised if it's not there when you wake up." I nod again, considering his words, but the Demerol has got me jumping off the rings of Saturn right now.

No arm when I wake up. Okay. I got it. How nice of him to tell me. He's nice. He's a very nice man. And this bed is nice. The surgeon is nice, the bed is nice, and Demerol—the Demerol is fucking GREAT. No arm, no problem. Cut my fucking legs off if you need to. Do what you gotta do, Doc.

CHAPTER 6
TUBE OF MISERY

WHEN I BLINK MY EYES open again, the first thing I feel is pain in my throat. From the way it feels, the intubation tube they shoved down my throat was wrapped in barbed wire. I'm no longer in the operating room. My eyelids feel heavy and gritty, and my mouth is dry. In a split second, every event flashes through my mind in snapshots: screaming family, hallway, explosion, bright lights, vortex, porch light, raw hamburger meat, helicopter, vest, finger in my ass, Demerol, arm...*arm! Do I have a fucking arm?*

I snap my head to the right. What I see isn't exactly an arm. It's about twenty rolls of Ace wrap, medical tape, and an awkward metal external fixator propping up something beside me. That means my arm is still there—or at least some part of it. I feel a flood of relief, but the throbbing pain is back. A nurse walks around me, fiddling with the tubes and wires attached to my body. The surgeon comes in to speak with me a few minutes later. He says something about my arm and the surgery, but my mind can't seem to hold onto his words. I only understand that I have an arm, it's fucked up, and I need to get to Balad Air Base. I'll be on a Chinook to Balad today and then headed straight to Germany for more surgeries by tonight. I lay my head back on the pillow, feeling deeply exhausted. A light knock on the door wakes me a few minutes or hours later; I can't be sure. My entire team files into the room and circles around my bed. No one smiles. Their faces are solemn, serious, and reverent. I want to look away.

"Hey, bud, how ya holding up?" Scott asks and puts a hand on my ankle.

"I've had better days, but you know, it is what it is." I snort out a low chuckle, but I'm met with only somber silence. Mac, my team leader, steps forward and I see a flash of purple in his palm. Now I understand what's happening. He leans over and places a Purple Heart on my chest and nods with a look of respect. I love my team, and it feels damn good to see their faces again. But I feel royally pissed off at the sight of that Purple Heart on my chest. It feels so cheap, so trite, so wildly inappropriate for this situation. I got fucking blown up. My arm is a bunch of raw hamburger meat held together by metal pins and rods, and my government is giving me a pretty little Purple Heart like I'm a fucking child who earned a sticker at the doctor's office. I didn't get an award for valorous acts or some display of special skill. I'm getting awarded for being injured. *This is just fucked up.* The rest of the team doesn't say much, but their eyes speak volumes: respect, love, sadness. That much I can see, and I deeply appreciate it, even though I can't express it. My eyes grow heavy, but before I close them, I have one more request.

"Do not, under any circumstances, notify anyone about this. Not my parents. Not my girlfriend. No one."

They nod, my eyes close, and when I open them again, my bed is moving and I'm being loaded onto a C-141 Starlifter along with a whole group of other injured men. My body sits on the stretcher at a strange angle to allow my right arm to remain propped up by a large metal external fixator. It's heavy and cumbersome. They've administered a nerve block to make the flight to Balad more bearable, and it's definitely working; I can't feel my arm at all. But as the plane takes off, my heart begins to pound. That awful empty sensation is back, the same one I felt when groping around in the darkness, looking for my arm on the ground. I can't feel my arm, and I feel like it's gone completely, which sets off alarm bells throughout my mind and body. A deep anxiety takes hold of me, and as the minutes drag by, I feel like I'm going insane. My brain has triggered a state of total alarm throughout my body, and the anxiety and dread are overwhelming.

I need to feel my arm again, and I need to feel it NOW! Even the pain was a reminder that it was there. After a while, I feel a buzzing sensation, like I've been lying on my arm all night and it's fallen asleep. I'm bordering on a full-blown anxiety attack now. I fucking hate nerve blockers.

I'm in a small room in Balad when I open my eyes again. A nurse is beside me, a very beautiful nurse. A deployment ten, no doubt about it. What an angel.

"Hey there, how are you feeling?" She smiles when her eyes meet mine, and I don't look away. "I'll be taking care of you. I just gave you a little more Demerol, which should help with the pain. You just let me know if there's anything you need, okay?"

"Yes, Demerol," I reply with a smile.

As she moves around the room, I can't keep my eyes off of her. The Demerol is making me feel happy, very happy, flirty, and brave.

"I guess I'm lucky. Looks like I got the prettiest nurse in all of Balad," I say, flashing her a smile, and this time she doesn't look away. When her cheeks show a hint of pink, my confidence soars. *Still got it.*

"Only the prettiest in Balad, huh?" She puts a hand on her hip as if she's insulted, offering a trace of a smile. I throw out another line, and she hits it back with precision. The banter continues, line after line. It seems that Demerol and a pretty nurse were all I needed.

A few hours later, she knocks on my door and says I have a visitor. I have no idea who it could be. I haven't told anyone I know about the explosion, not even my parents, and I'm in fucking Balad.

Then General Stanley Allen McChrystal walks in. I'm shocked. The man is a legend, and he's here to see me. Turns out that Joint Command is in Balad, and when he heard through the grapevine that a few of his guys had gotten hurt, he decided to pay us a visit. His reputation is larger than life, and now I can see exactly why. As we fall into natural conversation, I feel myself beginning to relax. We talk about the 75th Ranger Regiment, which he took command of between 1997 and 1999, right around the same time I joined. We talk about life. We talk about the war. And we talk about them like old friends catching up. I'm on a Demerol high, but I feel like I'm keeping up with the conversation pretty well. It's only when I insert a quote from the movie *Aliens* into the conversation that he looks at me strangely. It makes perfect sense to me, but his reaction makes me feel like I'm off. That's the drugs talking, I guess. He smiles, and we keep going. After half an hour or more, he shakes my hand, thanks me, and leaves. The pretty nurse is back again, and the banter continues, but I'm not as quick on my feet to respond—I'm in more pain now. They say I'll be moving to Germany soon. For a minute, I think of my parents. I think of Vanessa. I know I should tell them what's happened, but I don't want to do so until I know whether I'll be keeping my arm.

The pretty nurse is walking around me again, preparing me to leave, and I push the thought out of my mind. I'm flirting again. Something about having met in a different life, something about the fact that she'll always be my "nurse from Balad." I definitely watched too many movies as a kid. Every time she grins, smiles, or throws an intelligent quip back at me with those pretty brown eyes, I feel a chemical surge of happiness, like an injection. We both know it's a game. She's married and I have no intentions toward her beyond our playful exchange. But it makes me feel alive, whole, like a goddamned man, not a helpless wounded animal. It helps me push away the looming thoughts about all I've lost, about who I was, and who I'm about to become. When we say goodbye, the pain is back. The Demerol doesn't seem to be taking the edge off like it had been.

I'm loaded onto a C-14, the medevac bird that will take me to Germany with the others: the four SEALs who were injured the same night I was and more than fifteen Marines who were hit by an IED. I thought they'd upgraded most of our birds to C-17s, but it seems they forgot about this one, and she looks like she's on her last leg. Every time my stretcher shakes, I feel shooting pain. I bite down on my lip. This is just the beginning—I've still got an eight-hour flight ahead of me, and I try not to think about it. I've been assigned a doctor from the unit who will make the trip with me, but I can't stop thinking about why the Demerol isn't working. I can't take eight hours of agony like this.

When the plane takes off, I enter into a hellish purgatory. There is only one nurse caring for the entire group, and five of the Marines are in critical condition. Their moans and cries echo off the old aircraft's walls—desperate and filled with suffering and torment. The nurse runs from one man to another, trying to do as much as she can, but there are too many of us. One of the SEALs, whose hand was shot, gets up from his seat and tries to help her by bringing water to one of the Marines who's mangled beyond recognition. Pain invades my body like I've never felt before. I thought I'd learned to embrace the pain, to allow it to make me stronger. I thought I'd learned to press into the suck and the suffering, but FUCK, this is different. I need to get out of my body. The doctor gives me another dose of Demerol, and I wait for relief, but it doesn't come.

"If you're okay for now, I'm going to try and help the others," the doctor says quietly.

"I'm fine. Just go."

I close my eyes and try to find a happy place to run to and hide. I have two happy places in my mind. I choose door number one. When I walk through it, I'm at Disneyland with my family. I see my parents and my little brother. I see sunshine. I see smiles. I am safe now. I am safe and I am happy. I am living in the only moment that my family ever felt like a real family. I stay for as long as I can, but outside that little corner of my mind, I feel a storm raging, banging on the door of my safe haven, overtaking me. The door isn't strong enough to hold it back. I open my eyes, and I'm in hell again. One of the Marines is moaning in agony. His cries are not the result of a decision to express himself; this is an animalistic howl, the instinctual, uncontrollable sound of pure human suffering.

I can't move. I can't even move an inch without shifting the metal structure holding the remains of my arm together. I try to find my happy place again. This time I have to battle my way through my stormy mind just to get there. When I do, I choose door number two. Now I'm in a bubbling hot tub with a beautiful, naked woman. The water flows over my body. I am safe. I am safe. Then comes a knife of pain, slicing through the warm water and plunging into my body. I am exhausted by the fight. I am losing control. Another deep, guttural groan comes from one of the Marines on the opposite side of the plane. The sound mirrors the pain I feel in every cell of my body. It's inescapable, it's everywhere. Maybe I don't believe in God or heaven, but I sure as fuck believe in hell. And it's right inside this tube of misery.

CHAPTER 7
PRAYING FOR TURDS

Fort Bragg, North Carolina, March 2005

I WAKE UP TO AN uncomfortable pressure between my ass cheeks. I'd like to say that the sensation surprises me, but it doesn't. A nurse is pulling shit out of my asshole. It's become a regular part of my day, just like pissing through a tube, being poked at by doctors, and staring up at the ceiling while screaming silently inside my skull. My right arm is mangled, skinless from wrist to shoulder. The bones are still blasted out, the tendons shredded, the artery severed, the muscles pulverized into ground chuck. It smells of shrimp, though no one has told me why. My entire arm looks like a shrink-wrapped slab of meat that came straight from the butcher. I'm a walking open wound, a ball of pain.

I hardly remember anything about my stay in Germany. Just a few fuzzy snapshots of uncomfortable consciousness in between multiple surgeries. I endured another long, uncomfortable flight, and then, after a quick stopover at Walter Reed Hospital, I was transported to Womack Army Medical Center here at Fort Bragg. Seems this will be home for the foreseeable future. A handful of the Unit's finest doctors are here at Womack, making it the obvious choice for my ongoing care, which, at the moment, involves pulling turds out of my backside.

The entire ordeal is uncomfortable, not just the sensations but the deep feeling of guilt that has gathered in the pit of my stomach as the nurses work. I'm the reason these perfectly kind women have to do this difficult job. I feel humiliated. I've apologized profusely a hundred times, and they continue to be polite about the whole situation and assure me that it's "all normal," given the number of antibiotics and painkillers swirling around in my body. Still, I want to disappear. I want to be anywhere but inside my body. My self-respect, built on my good deeds and heroic acts, is crumbling. Every act of service and sacrifice is slowly being erased with every hour that I sit here—I am nothing but a big waste of time, money, and effort.

I'd do anything to shit on the toilet like a goddamned man, but we've exhausted all other options. The stomach cramps and nausea from not being able to shit for a week have become almost unbearable. A team of three nurses came yesterday to help me out of bed and onto a portable toilet that they positioned beside my bed. I tried to make it happen on my own because I knew what was coming if I couldn't. *Nothing.* I just couldn't do it.

In a bid to get a better angle on my butt crack, the nurse rolls me carefully onto my left side so that I'm now facing the person in the hospital bed next to mine. Though he has been my neighbor for weeks, up until this moment I have only known him as a silhouette against the privacy curtain that is usually pulled closed between us. Seeing him now, for the first time in the flesh, I am shocked by how young he looks. Too young to buy a beer, for sure. So young that his clumsy, overgrown child's face is still in the process of being ravaged by puberty. Acne scars, ingrown hairs, and un-popped zits stubble his cheeks and jaw like a beard gone bad, while his hormone-engorged Adam's apple makes his skinny neck look like an ostrich choking on a basketball. If we met on the street, I'd assume he was just another unfortunate-looking teenager crying his way through high school. But seeing him here, propped up on an Army hospital bed with tubes in his arm, his sunken chest wrapped with bandages from nipples to navel, it's impossible to deny the fact that this teenager is an American soldier. At least that's what he's supposed to be.

There's something off about him, but I can't remember what it is. Maybe it was something I overheard him say, or maybe it was someone else who said something to him, I can't be sure. The drugs have made me stupid and slow on the uptake. The pizza-faced kid is ignoring me, that's for sure. Despite my staring and the admittedly shameful spectacle of a grown man getting his ass wiped just three feet away, the kid keeps his eyes glued to the blank television screen mounted on the far wall. Maybe he's just trying to be polite. Maybe he thinks that by ignoring me, I'll be able to hold on to what little dignity I have left. But I don't think that's it. It's coming back to me—the bits and pieces I've gathered over the past few weeks of listening through a drug-induced stupor. The memory is there, but retrieving it is slow.

"You did this to yourself, Private," I remember the voice saying. "What would your parents say?"

Snatches of the conversation I had with the kid replay in my mind. A couple of days ago—how many, I can't be sure, thanks to the pain meds—he decided to make me his honorary priest for the day and spilled his entire life story. I didn't ask for it and sure as hell didn't care, but he was determined to tell me everything. I kept asking questions, not because I actually gave a shit, but because I needed to understand how someone manages to accidentally shoot himself in the chest. And now it's all coming back to me. The kid isn't ignoring me to spare me any shame. He's doing it to spare himself his own. This neighbor of mine shot himself. Not in an effort to end things, mind you—he'd be on suicide watch if that were the case. This kid is either clumsy and stupid or he was trying to escape deployment and stay home.

I watch his pimpled jaw clench and I know that he can feel my eyes upon him. He still doesn't turn to meet my gaze, and I wish he would. I want him to challenge me, to ask me what the fuck I'm looking at or, at the very least, to raise a defiant middle finger in my direction. I would like him a lot better if he did. The destroyer in me loathes weakness.

I want to open my mouth and say something, force the little coward to face me. I know I'm being an insufferable prick and that mocking such a tortured soul won't do either of us any good. After a few more moments of staring at the kid, I finally give in to the angel on my shoulder and look away.

"You're all good, Sergeant," the nurse says to me, dropping her gloves and the last of the soiled wipes into a bedpan. I smile at her in gratitude, but she doesn't see it; she's too busy preparing to roll me onto my back. "Should I give you a little something to help you rest?" she asks when I'm staring at the ceiling again. I shake my head, but she has already turned away from me—fingers reaching for the control panel on the infusion pump. She clicks it a few times.

"Who wants the remote?" She looks from me to my unlucky neighbor.

"Give it to him," I say, throwing a glance in his direction. "Looks like he needs it more than I do."

"No, you can have it," the kid's voice cracks as he speaks.

"Nah, I'm good." We've been watching fucking *Seinfeld* reruns anyway. *Fuck TNT.*

The nurse hands the remote to the kid, and then it's just me and the drugs and the coward and the ceiling again—just like it has been for three weeks. The ceiling tiles are white, speckled with black, the dots printed in no discernible pattern. I wish I could see shapes or faces in them, but I can't. I pray for an interesting water stain or crack to form, anything to break up the monotony. The tiles remain pristine.

I still haven't told a single person about the injury. Not my mother, not my father, not my brother, and not Vanessa. No one even knows that I'm back in the United States. The doctors still can't say for sure whether I'm keeping my arm. I'd like to know exactly what we're dealing with before I tell anyone anything. I see no reason to get everyone's hopes up for recovery just to let them down again if we have to amputate. At least, that's what I keep telling myself. The truth is that I don't want to listen to their crying, and I hate the idea of them being sad because of me. I need to be strong enough to help everyone process this and feel okay. I need to be strong enough for them to lean on. But between the pain and the meds and the humiliation of having shit pulled from my ass, I've only got enough mental stability to keep myself sane. *Just a few more days and I'll call them.*

And then it hits me. Vanessa's number was saved in my phone, a phone that is back at my apartment. The only people I know are in Iraq. I don't have a single friend I can call and ask to go and get it. That means I have no easy way to contact her. I'll find a way; I know I'll find a way. I just need to think. I close my eyes, but I cannot focus. The kid is sniffing back tears now and I can't for the life of me understand why. He got what he wanted, didn't he? He's firmly on American soil, no deployment in sight. Mission accomplished. If putting a bullet in my body would get me where I wanted to be, I'd pull the goddamned trigger in a flash. No questions. No tears. Unfortunately, it's not that simple for me. I want to be with my team, and a lot of fucking good I'd be with half an arm and a bullet wound. I can't even squeeze out a good morning shit to save my life. The thought eats at me, gnaws in the corner of my mind until I feel like I'm going insane. I know my team has moved on by now and I'm missing everything. There's a gunfight going down right now and I'm not there. There's a door being kicked in by some other guy's boot that's not mine. I've been replaced. Now there's a stranger on the team, covering my teammates' backs when it should have been me. For a while, I wonder who he is, this operator who has taken my place. One side of me hopes that he's even better than I was. I want my teammates to be safe; I want them to succeed. Another side of me hopes he sucks. I want to be missed. I have to get back. I'm going to get back. Even as the drugs do their work and I begin to fade into a familiar oblivion, I hold onto that thought: Find a way back; you've got to find a way back.

These days, I don't really sleep; I just exist in that middle purgatory between sleep and wakefulness, full of thoughts that never conclude and memories that never stay long enough to truly remember. When the drugs fade, my body throbs until I pass out. The man in the hospital bed next to me shot himself to stay home, to be here. I would shoot myself to be there. Find a way back; you've got to find a way back.

I'm a knuckle dragger, a goddamned superhero. And no matter what happens, no matter what they say or how hard this gets, I will find my power again. As the dreamlike madness of opioids floods through me again, I let my eyes close.

I feel my chest growing heavy as the poison seeps into my veins. My breathing becomes shallow and anxiety builds and builds until I feel like I'm going to hyperventilate. I could ask one of the nurses for a paper bag, but then they'd know I was having these attacks and would probably just sedate me. I need to get out of my head, but there are still no new cracks on the ceiling to crawl into. I need something besides fucking daytime television—that utterly grotesque dogshit that has, after these many days of unwilling viewership, shaken my once ironclad faith in this country, its people, and our future to its very core. For a moment, my silent rant is enough to help me forget about the anxiety. I try to hold onto it, feed it. I need a problem to solve, a torch to carry, a cause to stand for. Fuck this mind-numbing stream of meaningless entertainment, fuck the stupid, lazy, complacent people who have nothing better to do than sit in their oversized La-Z-Boy chairs and stuff their faces and minds with junk.

The feeling of indignation is tasty, and I try to feed it, try to strengthen the resolve of my resentment, but it's a false hope. No matter how much I loathe *Dr. Phil*, *Maury*, and *The View*, the shows are so shallow that there isn't anything left to say about them. Without the lifeline of my own bitterness to hold onto, I feel myself falling back into a world of nothingness. The anxiety is back again. Eventually, I sleep. Then wake. Then sleep again. The cycle of utter useless existence continues. Days pass in a blur, hours stretch into eternity. I am floating face up in a vat of cold, dulled, perpetual pain. My dreams are unchanging, nothing but images of the ceiling swirling above my head. The waking world is distinguishable from my sleep only by the periodic conscious realization that I am peeing.

When I wake again, there are two doctors at my bedside. They have arrived, wearing their white coats, to discuss the upcoming operation with me. I understand they are sharing crucial information that will impact my health and future significantly. However, I'm struggling to concentrate on the specifics of their words. It could be the medication or perhaps my mental state deteriorating, but I can't seem to comprehend their message or string coherent thoughts together. Since my arrival at this hospital, I've undergone two or three operations every week, each thoroughly explained beforehand, yet none have seemed to improve my condition.

"If you look just there," one of the doctors says, pointing his pen at my right arm now, "you'll see where the extensor tendons are…" He stops in the middle of the sentence. I've turned my face away, refusing to look where he's pointing.

"Umm, Sergeant?" He's being polite. Too polite. He doesn't understand. He doesn't understand that I can't just "look right there" like he wants me to. The truth is I haven't really looked at my arm since I saw it under that yellow porch light in Sadr City. I cast a quick glance in that direction when I tried to attach the tourniquet to the bloody mess, but I didn't really look. I still haven't. And why should I? I don't need to stare to know it's there on the periphery of my vision, a lumpy, orange blur of shrink wrap. A big, gaping open wound on display, unmoving, like roadkill flung to the side of the highway. Looking directly at the thing now won't make it heal any faster.

"Are you with us, Sergeant?" the second doctor asks, sounding dickishly annoyed.

"I'm with you, sir." I lie to him. "So, how long is this going to take?"

"The operation?"

"No, sir. The whole thing."

Neither doctor responds immediately, though the nasally one takes the time to slowly look up and away before sniffing the air in the most perfect display of arrogant incredulity I have ever witnessed. I'm impressed but also offended. I'd like to throw something right at his smug little face and see what happens.

"You have to understand, Sergeant," the first doctor interrupts. His voice is nice and pleasant-sounding, not at all like Dr. Dick's. "Your arm has lost at least one part of every essential piece that makes it function," says Dr. Pleasant. "Tendons, bone, muscles, fat, the skin, your brachial artery. We have to fix each of these, one at a time, and from the inside out."

"Right," I nod sagely, as if I understand the depth of meaning behind his words. "That makes sense. So what's left to fix?"

"We've had this conversation before," sighs Dr. Dick, most dickishly.

Yeah, and I've been on so many fucking drugs that I can't even shit properly, and you're surprised that I haven't logged in every detail of your little medical spiel, you asshole.

I think it, I don't shout it out loud, though God knows I want to. The white-coated cocksucker is still a captain, after all. "Is there no one we can call?" asks Dr. Pleasant. "A family member or a girlfriend? Someone who can be with you when we brief you next, perhaps? Fill you in when you wake up and keep you in the loop?"

"Nope," I say at once. I say it without any hesitation.

They just gape at me and then exchange meaningful glances with each other. Dr. Dick looks down at me in pity, and Dr. Pleasant seems to be drawing his breath to gently segue into some sort of impromptu therapy session. Both men look like they come from money, the types who probably had a dad who was a doctor and a mom who sat on the front-row bench at every little league game with a Tupperware container of nicely peeled oranges. People who grow up in that kind of environment are always overly interested, fascinated even, to learn more about your sad, dysfunctional childhood. *Condescending assholes.*

"What's left to fix?" I cut in fast before they say anything else about family. They look at each other again, and I watch as a wordless debate takes place over which of them is going to deliver what I can only assume, by the look on their faces, is bad news. Dr. Dick wins. He's off the hook.

"We've only really just begun," Dr. Pleasant begins. "With all the shrapnel, dirt, bone chips, not to mention the decaying flesh, the cleaning process alone has taken multiple surgeries. This is going to take some time."

"How long?"

He doesn't answer immediately.

"Tyler?" Dr. Pleasant's voice is back. "So, you asked me how long. Five years."

He keeps talking, but I only catch those two words. How could I hear anything else over the roar of reality's chainsaw as it chews its way through my hopes and dreams, spitting chunks of my life this way and that?

"Five fucking years until I'm operational?" I gasp, interrupting Dr. Pleasant.

Dr. Dick shakes his head.

"I'd say your chances of being operational are less than one percent."

Now it's Dr. Pleasant's turn to interrupt.

"I would give you about a fifty percent chance of being operational again."

I feel sick. Dizzy. I need to throw up or scream. In a year, the war will probably be over. In a year, my team will be back home. In five years, I will still be here, rotting away. I will have missed everything. I will have nothing left to give.

"Tyler?" asks Dr. Pleasant, obviously concerned.

"We are discussing your future, Sergeant," says Dr. Dick, obviously annoyed.

I shake my head at them. I shake my head at their idea of the future. I won't accept it. Not after all these weeks of madness, pain, and purgatory. No, I refuse this.

Find a way back; you have to find a way back, the voice in my head whispers to me. I will find a way back. I look up at the doctors. "Five years?"

"Five years," Dr. Pleasant sighs. "And even then, there is a good chance that you won't…"

"Never tell me the odds," I interrupt him, quoting Han Solo with as close an approximation of Harrison Ford's roguish grin as I can muster. Dr. Pleasant can't help but chuckle. Dr. Dick doesn't even try to hide his rolling eyes. He's probably a stupid Trekkie anyway.

"But thank you, sirs," I say, though I feel no gratitude at all. "Let's try to make it months, huh?"

"Right," Dr. Dick nods. He's ready to finish the conversation. "A nurse will be here first thing in the morning to prep you for surgery."

"We are going to make this happen, Tyler," says Dr. Pleasant. And he says it with such feeling, such genuine compassion, that I smile just to make sure he doesn't burst into a big bout of manly tears.

Thankfully, in an effort to curtail his discomfort at such an emotional display, Dr. Dick tugs Dr. Pleasant by the sleeve and leads him toward the door. As their white coats disappear, so does my fake smile.

"Five years. Fifty percent chance…" Dr. Pleasant's prognosis plays back in my mind, over and over, like a bad song. I have gone into dark places full of men with guns who desperately want to kill me. I've leaped from airplanes in the dead of night, fast-roped from helicopters, stormed buildings while under fire, and waited silently in a hide site as armed enemy combatants passed just inches away from my face. I never felt afraid then. But as I stare down the barrel of five years of uselessness, my breath catches in my lungs. The anxiety begins like a sharp prick, a needle breaking the skin and plunging into my body. Then I feel it, the poison pumping its way toward my heart. My chest tightens. My head begins to buzz like a hive of angry bees.

"Don't think about it," I say to myself. "Do not think about it. Go somewhere else. Go anywhere else." *Disneyland.* But I can't move an inch, and the smell of shrimp is back. I still don't know why.

CHAPTER 8
MY SCROTUM IN SADR CITY

I LEFT A PIECE OF my scrotum in Sadr City. I kept the balls, praise be, and the fact that a little sliver of my nutsack is lying in some Iraqi fella's courtyard six thousand miles away strikes me as funny. I realize that by now some stray dog has probably lapped it up with the rest of my blood and gristle, made a meal out of that most intimate part of me. But then again, who knows?

Maybe some sort of Al-Qaeda super scientist has discovered it and is currently in the process of cloning an army of little shriveled, hairy Tylers. The thought makes me smile, and for a minute, that anxious poison slows down its steady march toward my heart. I have too much time on my hands; that much is evident by the fact that I'm entertaining myself with the thought of Al-Qaeda in an underground lab doing experiments with a fragment of my nutsack. The only thing that seems to help me mentally is excavating the shit I've been through in an attempt to unearth little relics that I can piece together into some sort of morbid joke. The humor helps; it's always helped. It's a shield, an antidote, a wall of protection against the other feelings, the ones I'm not sure I'm ready to experience. I lean back and rest my head on the stark white pillows behind me, looking for more relics in the pile of shit that has become my life. I find another one. *Who knew that lying in a bed would be the most challenging part of your military career?* Now that's fucking irony at its best right there.

And here I thought I'd done it all. I graduated from the toughest schools the military has to offer. I completed operator selection on my first attempt and was selected for the most elite anti-terrorist unit in the world at the age of twenty-six. I willingly signed my body away to be tested and tortured until I proved myself worthy of the job, and boy, did they give me their best. Still, I didn't break, not even once. I thought I'd done it all. But as it turns out, the most physically and mentally challenging thing I've ever had to do is sit in a bed and stare at the ceiling, trying to fend off another panic attack.

The thought has lost its humor now, and I run back to Al-Qaeda and the scrotum army. Maybe the average person wouldn't find the humor in taking a piece of white-hot shrapnel in the junk. But here and now, stuck in this bed with this stinking, skinless arm, listening to the soft, mournful weeping of my pimply teenage neighbor who shot himself, it seems hilarious. Anyhow, the docs had it sewn up in a matter of minutes—just a tuck, a couple of stitches, and I was good to go. If it were my only wound, I'd still be with my team right now, fending off gags about my short sack while prepping for an op. I flick my eyes open when I hear heavy footsteps.

A man in khakis and a tucked-in navy-blue polo shirt struts into the room and comes to a halt at the foot of my bed. The big bastard looks down at me with small, beady eyes bulging with what appears to be pure hatred. At first, I'm taken aback by his sudden appearance in my room and his obvious display of aggression, but then I feel a light turn on in my dark mind. I'm alert again. Vigilant. Ready for action. He's a challenge. I'm ready to take it. You want to give me a death stare? Just watch the daggers I can shoot from my eyes, you little fuck. I meet his angry look with one of my own, still wondering who this business-casual gorilla is. I rack my brain, trying to remember if we've met before and why he's so angry with me. Did I offend him? Sleep with a girl he liked? Had to be something major for him to show up in a hospital room and pick a fight with a man whose right arm is hamburger meat propped up by a big metal rack. Nothing rings a bell. I don't think we've ever met before. His glare intensifies. *Shit. Is he about to attack?* I begin to form my defense strategy.

I'm lying down—not ideal. My dominant right arm is pinned in its cradle—useless fucking thing. My legs are trapped under the bedsheets, and I'll have to spend precious moments kicking them free once he strikes. My left arm is the only appendage I'll have at my disposal during the initial exchange, and I'm going to have to use it to block blows to my head. So I'm screwed. Two months ago, I would have liked my chances. Now? I'm crippled, defenseless, weak. A fucking superhero without his powers. The gorilla's eyes flick down to my arm, and suddenly, his glare mellows. He clocks my chart, squints, and then grunts, shaking his big dumb head with something approaching self-deprecation. He nods to me, maybe in respect.

"What's up?" I ask. He doesn't bother answering. Instead, he moves past my bed and on to my neighbor's, his glare returning with full force. It's not directed at me anymore. The curtain between us is closed, so I can't see the kid, but I have to assume that he's shitting himself right now.

"Private," snarls the gorilla in khaki and navy. "I'm with Fort Bragg's Criminal Investigation Division. I'm here to ask you some questions."

It's clear from the moment he begins to talk that he believes the kid shot himself to escape deployment. That's what everyone thinks. But as I sit listening to this CID agent interrogate my neighbor, I'm more and more convinced that I was all wrong about the kid. It's true that, back in the day, guys who had no stomach—or lost the stomach—for fighting would sometimes shoot themselves in order to escape the horrors of the front lines. This was a real problem for armies during the later years of World War I and a much publicized but rather rare phenomenon during America's adventure in Vietnam. The difference between then and now, between those wars and the ones we're fighting today, is that all our soldiers are volunteers. There was no mass conscription in the run-up to our invasion of Afghanistan. No draft to dodge to escape the fighting in Iraq. Every single American soldier dressed in digital camouflage today is wearing it because they signed up for it.

As for my neighbor, he probably didn't even have hair on his balls back when those planes hit the towers on 9/11. Our country has been at war for some two decades since then, about twice as long as we were fighting in Vietnam. That kid would have known what he was getting himself into when he joined the Army. He had to have known they'd be sending him to war. Then again, maybe he assumed that he'd be posted stateside. Maybe he didn't understand the risks. Maybe he saw something or heard something that spooked him so much that he actually did decide to take the plunge and fire a bullet into his own body in order to escape deployment.

But then again, who shoots themselves in the torso? No one, not if you want to survive. The premise doesn't make sense because fear of getting shot in the chest (or head or nuts) is the very thing that makes a young soldier resort to self-harm to stay home. If you're going to shoot yourself for any reason other than suicide, you go for the hand, the foot, maybe even the meat of the butt. Not the fucking torso, not where all the important bits are. No one could be that dumb. The CID agent thinks otherwise. I can hear the bullying condescension in his tone as he asks his questions.

"If it wasn't on purpose, then how did it happen, Private? Go on. I'm all ears."

The kid explains that while he was at home checking his sidearm, the slide got stuck. He moved the gun to the side of his body to try and create a little leverage, and somehow a shot got fired. I still don't exactly know how that's possible, but I suppose it's just a chucklefuck move, eminently feasible for a nineteen-year-old fresh-faced private. Luckily for him, the bullet skirted around his ribcage and exited his side, never penetrating his chest cavity. That's a one-in-a-million shot. A goddamned miracle. There is no actual way he could have pulled that off on purpose. How is the CID agent not seeing this? The injustice of it all is making me sweat. The sheet covering my lower half feels like an electric blanket turned up too high. My left hand is clenched in a white-knuckled fist. My mind is on high alert, but my anxiety is gone. That's something. I let myself revel in righteous indignation as I listen to the agent poke nonsensical holes in the kid's sensible story.

For an hour or so, I am free of my own drama, outside my own head, consumed with frustration and a bit of pride in myself for cracking this case wide open. It won't do this kid any good, of course. This isn't the movies where some random bystander's unsolicited insight can change the course of an investigation. No, this is the Army, where the surest way to keep a self-important fool like this CID man on the path to disaster is by warning him of what's ahead. It's sad, but this kid is fucked and was fucked the moment they put this particular gorilla on his case. It doesn't matter what the facts may be; this CID man will find a way to fit a square peg into a round hole, and his piggy little eyes will see nothing but symmetry.

"You'll be hearing from us soon," he tells my neighbor, and I can hear the shitty, self-satisfied smile in his voice. As he struts towards the door, the agent nods to me again. I glare daggers back, but he doesn't notice. How could he? He's too far up his own ass. Dumb and proud, there's no more dangerous combination. The kid starts crying once the CID man's gone, and this time I understand why. At a minimum, he's got a dishonorable discharge in his future. That's not something you want to take home to mom, dad, or prospective employers.

There's some part of me that wants me to say something to him, to reach out and be a comfort in this trying time. Another side of me says that I could be wrong, that I am on a lot of pain meds right now, and that my Holmesian powers of deductive reasoning might very well be tainted. Shit, he could be guilty as sin and I'm just way too high to see it. The thought begins to eat at me. If there's one thing I've always been able to count on, it's my mind and ability to judge people and situations fairly. That internal justice system has been with me for as long as I can remember—a courtroom, judge, and jury that work around the clock. Every situation, every person, every action is carefully analyzed and measured by the letter of the law. The guilty are judged, and the innocent go free. I despise injustice.

But as night falls and the kid's tears turn into snores, chaos has erupted in the courtroom. The facts are jumbled now, the jury is split in disagreement, and the judge is full of self-doubt. Did I convince myself he's innocent because I'm drugged? Or is it because the CID agent made me feel weak? Bound to this bed, I subject myself to another self-examination. I hate it, but I cannot escape it. Take the goddamned mirror away, enough staring at myself. Give me a gunfight. Give me a thirty-mile march through the snow with a full pack. Give me an adventure. Not this staring at the ceiling, asking "Who am I?" horseshit.

Hours later, three nurses come into my room, and shame fills me again, worse than the cramping in my stomach. As I teeter on the portable toilet, I look up and catch a glimpse of my naked self in the mirror. I look like a skeleton, my arm held by the nurse—as pathetic a sight as I've ever seen. I'm a shadow of my former self. I was one of our nation's top commandos, and now here I stand, naked, humbled, and ashamed. I hardly recognize myself. Who am I? When I lie back in bed, one of the nurses presses the button on my infusion pump, and I welcome it. Within minutes, my mind begins to feel fuzzy, and a smile creases on my face. *Who am I?*

What a silly question. I know who I am. I'm Tyler Grey. A member of the Unit. A ninja, a superhero, a Jedi, a goddamned warrior supreme. Not some useless, self-doubting cripple, not some sad and broken thing. No. This is temporary. A hurdle to hop over. I'm going to get better. I'm going to be fine. I know that I have another surgery in a few hours, but I can't for the life of me remember what it's for. Did the doctors tell me? They usually do. For a minute, I wonder if I should call my mom or dad. Maybe Vanessa? An image of my mom's face covered in hot tears and my dad's hollow stare flashes through my mind. I see Vanessa's green eyes pooling with wet sympathy. Nope. I try to remember my mantra, but it's lost in the tide of painkiller-induced stupidity. I'm excavating again, searching for a thought, an observation, anything to escape the mental path I have accidentally stumbled upon. The ceiling offers me nothing. The snores of my neighbor have faded into silence. I sniff the air.

"My arm smells like shrimp," I say to myself, grabbing hold of the sentence and making it a mantra of convenience.

"My arm smells like shrimp," I repeat again and again until I feel my eyelids getting heavy. I am going to fall asleep now, crisis averted. I am going to fall asleep now, and tomorrow I will start to get better. When I'm conscious again, Vanessa comes to my mind. I still don't have her number, but I'll get it. I'd like to see her again, but I'd very much like for her not to see me, at least not like this.

A few days later, I receive a visit from my buddy Dan. He strides into my room with a serious look on his face and says hello, but it's clear he has something on his mind. It's not just something he wants to say; it's something he's planning to do. He's on a mission.

Dan is one of my best friends in the Unit and one of the greatest soldiers I have ever known. We met in Fallujah, where his acts of heroism earned him the Distinguished Service Cross, the second-highest medal any serviceman can receive. He was a medic at the time, a Doogie Howser of sorts—the youngest honor graduate to ever pass the Special Forces medical course, at the age of nineteen.

Dan takes one look at me and leaves the room after saying hello. I hear low voices in the hallway as he speaks quietly to the head nurse. When he returns, he leans close to my ear and whispers, "I'm busting you out." He grins. "Look, I told the nurse that I need to escort you to the front entrance to see your dog, whom you haven't reunited with since, *you know*." He glances at my shoulder. "I told her that the psychologists at the Unit thought the dog would be good therapy." He winks and nods encouragingly at me.

We both know I don't own a dog, but the head nurse bought the story hook, line, and sinker. Dan helps me into a wheelchair. We go down in the elevator, through the hallways, and finally out a side door. He grabs another wheelchair stashed in the bushes just outside the entrance.

"The hospital wheelchairs have a tracker, so the alarm goes off if they leave the perimeter," he says. "Hop into this one." We head for a work van parked at the curb. Another buddy of mine, Brandon, is inside. He's also a medic and quickly helps Dan load me into the van. He hangs my IV and pain drip on the coat hook on one side of the van and my right arm, now in a cast, on the opposite hook. Dan's operational precision does not disappoint. I find myself smiling, really smiling, for the first time in ages. We're on a covert mission, and it feels great.

I ask where we're going, and Dan grins. "Sightseeing." He doesn't elaborate. "Oh, and I have a surprise." He pulls out a hookup with two canisters—one filled with pure oxygen, the other with pure nitrous oxide. Go to a dentist's office, and they'll give you a generous 10 percent dose of nitrous that will get you high. This tank, which delivers 50 percent, will have you emerging from a black hole and touching the apex of the universe's butthole.

"Fuck it," I smile at Dan. Those two words have preceded every crazy thing I've ever done. Within twenty seconds, my body starts to tingle. Then it happens. Total relief. I feel no pain at all. You could cut off both my legs and I wouldn't notice. My buddies nod with approval the moment they see the euphoric expression on my face as I pass them the mask so everyone can partake of the goodness.

Over the next two hours, we drain the nitrous tank and bask in its glow. We drive onto the parade field, spin brodies in the dirt, and laugh until we're sick. I look at Dan and Brandon and feel something I haven't felt in a long time. I feel like I'm part of a team again. I feel like I'm finally home.

The guys help me sneak back into the hospital, and we barely make it before the nurses grow suspicious. The operation is a complete success, and I have no words to adequately thank Dan for what he did. He put me back in the game, gave me a little taste of action and relief from the pain. I bask in the glow of Dan's visit for several days. It was exactly what I needed. I'm going to beat this; I'm going to get through this and bounce back stronger. I'm going to be the greatest comeback story ever told. No matter how long it takes or how hard it gets, I'm going to make it back to my team.

But first, I probably need to call my parents and Vanessa and rip off the Band-Aid. They're going to find out sooner or later anyway. Better to get it over with.

Mom's phone rings a few times before she answers. "It's Tyler!" she says to someone who I can only presume is my father. Sure enough, my father's low voice comes on the other end of the line. "How's it going?"

I take a deep breath. It takes just three sentences to tear their world apart. Mom instantly becomes hysterical, just as I knew she would. Dad starts asking questions. I hate hearing the sadness in his voice. One of my dad's lifelong regrets is that they wouldn't let him go to Vietnam because of a hernia. The day I joined the military, he lit up with one of the few proud smiles I'd ever seen on his face. I can't see his face now, but I can hear the disappointment in his voice, and it's excruciating. I try to downplay the incident, minimize the damage, deflect it with humor—anything to soften the news—but it hardly helps. After an hour, I hang up the phone, exhausted.

Vanessa comes next. As the phone rings, I feel nervous. It took me days to track down the number, and I hope it's the right one. "Hello?" It's her. "Hi, Vanessa." Before I say it, even before my lips form the words, she knows. Somehow she just knows. She cries, and I tell her it's all going to be okay. What else can I say?

"I want to come and see you," she says when she can speak again.

"You'll see me soon enough," I say, trying to play it off, but she insists. I won't budge. I need to get through this part alone. I came here alone, and that's how I'll walk out of here. I don't want her to see me like this. I don't want an image of me lying in this bed to be imprinted on her memory. When she realizes that protesting is futile, she insists no further, and we fall into easy conversation. For three hours, we talk just like we did before. And it feels good. I feel relieved when I hang up the phone. It's not the end; it's just the beginning. Maybe things are going to be alright after all.

But days later, I'm not so sure. The pain in my arm is killing me, and my stomach feels like it's going to explode.

"Tyler, it looks like you have a visitor." Nurse Latonya is on duty tonight. Boy, did I hate her for weeks, and boy, did she hate me back. She was like a drill sergeant with a stethoscope, and I was her least favorite recruit. But somewhere along the line, her tough love and relentless nagging grew on me, and now she's my favorite nurse. Who knew a woman with the bedside manner of a cactus could have such a soft spot? I shrug my shoulders at her announcement. I have no idea who the hell it could be. But I recognize the tall man as soon as he enters the room: Baldy. His serious expression relaxes as he spots me, and I can tell this visit is more than just a courtesy call.

Baldy is a legend, a sergeant major who's been in the Unit for what seems like forever, the epitome of a true operator. He was also the sergeant major in charge of the course when I went through selection. I respect the hell out of him, which is why I feel mortified that he decided to show up on one of the worst nights I've had in the hospital so far. The pain is more intense today than usual, and no matter how many times the nurses assure me that I'm being given plenty of drugs, I still question whether the IV drip is full of painkiller or just water.

"How are you holding up?" Baldy asks and takes a seat on the chair opposite my bed, spine straight and smile full of professional sympathy. I can hardly breathe without wincing.

"Good as can be expected," I say, trying to make my voice sound strong and casual, but it's almost more than I can muster. In an effort to make conversation, Baldy launches into a full explanation about what my team is up to in Iraq. I nod and try to throw in a comment here or there to show that I'm engaged in the conversation. But the more we talk, the more I feel emotion building inside me. The worst part is that tonight I seem to have no ability to suppress it. I feel my jaw clenching in an attempt to contain the emotional vomit that's rising and threatening to spew out. But the pain is building, and my stomach is cramping, and I know that those three poor nurses will be back to put the toilet under me, and I'll sit in agony, trying to force my body to do a basic human function that it's forgotten how to do.

All I can think about is my team and what they're doing and the fact that they're doing it without me. I don't want to break down in front of Baldy. It'll be the end of my self-respect. But no matter how hard I try, I cannot even find a shred of humorous armor to shield myself from the onslaught of emotion. My mental barriers are crumbling, leaving me without protection. It's hitting me all at once. *I just want to go back. I want to press rewind and start over. I want all of this to have never happened. I want to wake up from this bad dream and be myself again. I just want to be who I was, not who I'm becoming, not this shrimp-scented waste of space that can't even shit by himself.* He keeps talking, but I feel tears pushing at my eyelids, and with every ounce of strength I have, I am pushing back, willing those tears not to fall, not in front of Baldy, not like this. But I'm not strong enough, and I do the last thing I could ever imagine doing in front of a man like Baldy. I begin to cry.

Even worse, I begin to talk, a torrent of pent-up thoughts and feelings. *I just want it all to go away. I don't think I can take it anymore. I'm sick of it. I just want to feel like myself again.* Baldy reaches out and takes my hand. I don't refuse it, but I feel like a child, crying in front of this distinguished veteran. My self-respect is long gone; it disappeared with the first tear, and now I've given way to self-loathing. And after the loathing comes the anger. What a worthless piece of shit I am. Sitting in front of me is a highly decorated, respected warrior who's listening to me whine about my problems. I'm unworthy to break down in front of someone who has been through so much more than me. I'm not even dying, for Christ's sake. I didn't lose my legs. So many people have it worse than I do, and I'm crying here like a coward. *I'm pitiful. Worthless. Weak. What the fuck is wrong with me?*

Baldy is kind, polite, and compassionate, which only makes it worse. Hours later, after the lights are off and visiting hours are over, I cry again. I'm not crying because of the pain or the loss. I'm crying because I am broken, and I cannot seem to piece the fragments back together to form the man I used to be. If the challenges of my training and job have taught me anything, it's self-reliance. I can always count on myself to stay strong and pull through, no matter what. But it seems that I'm not as strong as I thought. I can't rely on myself because I don't know who I am anymore. And that realization shakes me to my core.

CHAPTER 9
JUST THE BEGINNING

"SO, I GUESS YOU'RE FINALLY getting rid of me." I smile at Nurse Latonya as she scribbles something on the top sheet of paper attached to her clipboard. I can't understand why more paperwork is needed for one bum arm than for buying a house, but that's how things are. The day I've been waiting for is finally here. Today is the day I will walk out of the hospital.

"Take care of yourself, Tyler, ya hear?" Nurse Latonya gives me a warm smile and squeezes my good arm. I wish there were a way to thank her and all the staff who've taken such good care of me. I do my best, but thank-yous seem inadequate.

The walk down the hallway is surreal. After so many months of staring at the ceiling, eating pre-portioned microwaved food on a brown tray, and nearly driving myself to the brink of insanity with hours of uninterrupted mental analysis of nearly every single part of my life, I am free. The whole world is shining as I walk out the door—even the fucking trees are greener—and I feel like a new man. I lunge forward to open the door handle when my buddy Dave pulls the car around. I'm ready to fly my cage and never return. But the door doesn't open. When I look down, I see why. My casted arm is hanging limply beside the handle, unable to complete the task my brain has assigned it. *Fuck, so this is it.* This is the new normal. In the hospital, surrounded by the nursing staff, I hadn't experienced real life without an operational right arm. *It's not the end; it's just the beginning.* I repeat the line in my mind as I open the door with my left hand. I've got a long road ahead before I will be ready to rejoin my team, and I can't afford to lose hope now.

Half an hour later, I'm sitting in a small café with a cup of coffee in front of me. I've already scanned the entrance four times now, waiting to see a glimpse of Vanessa's shiny blonde hair. I take a sip of the coffee and focus on another part of the room, but my eyes cannot help but dart back to the entrance every few seconds.

Then I see her, just as gorgeous as I remember. Her eyes glide across the room and then lock onto mine, and it feels good. I'm the guy that beautiful girl is looking at. I stand to greet her, and she pauses for a blink of an eye as she looks me over from head to toe. I know I look different than the man she kissed goodbye six months ago. I've lost nearly 45 pounds and haven't lifted more than a cup of water to my lips in weeks. But her eyes haven't changed. She's still staring at me with the same starry look as the day she handed me her phone number on that street corner in downtown Dallas. She wraps her arms around me gently and doesn't move. Face buried in my chest, she cries softly, her fingers tightly grasping the back of my shirt, pulling me close. She doesn't let go for a while. When she does, she wipes away her tears and a smile breaks out on her face.

"I'm so happy to see you," she says. Her eyes shine with the sincerity of her words. "You have no idea."

I pull her close again, feeling nearly euphoric with happiness. It's not the end; it's just the beginning. I am a free man with a beautiful girl on his arm, and nothing else seems to matter now. "How about I take you out for the finest dinner that Fayetteville has to offer?" I grin, even though we both know that Fayetteville embodies every cliché of a city outside a military installation.

It's a boring place with boring chain restaurants that close early. But I'm too happy to care. At 6:00 p.m., I walk through the doors of the Samurai Japanese Steakhouse & Sushi Bar feeling like a champion. We take a seat around the teppanyaki grill, and the chef performs his entire repertoire of tricks—the flaming onion stack, the cracked egg on the metal spatula, and the catapulted shrimp onto our plates. I'm making jokes, Vanessa is laughing, and for the first time in a long time, life is good.

I notice the teppanyaki chef sniffing the air as if he's trying to hunt down a strange smell, and then I notice it too. There is a strange burning smell, and it's not the flaming onions. That's when I notice the pinky finger of my right arm resting on the hot grill.

"Hey, man, I think your—" The teppanyaki chef notices it the same moment I do, and I see the horror register on his face. I yank my hand back and look at Vanessa, whose expression mirrors the chef's.

I still can't feel a thing. My arm is nothing but a numb lump of flesh and bone attached to my body. My hand is burned now, and I hate myself. I'm uncomfortable with the spotlight that has shifted on me, so I do what I always do. *Deflect with humor.*

"Side of seared pinky finger, anyone?" I crack a grin, and then the chef and Vanessa begin to laugh, and the others around the grill follow suit. I feel relieved when everyone stops looking at me. *This isn't the end; it's just the beginning.*

Ten days later, I'm lying on my couch looking at the ceiling. Vanessa is gone now, off to another Beach Body event and then back to her home in South Beach. She'll be back in a few weeks, but until then, it's just me and this empty apartment. I shouldn't complain, really. I've got an arm, or at least some version of it. I'm not stuck in the hospital anymore. *Hell, I'm alive.* That's something. But there's an emptiness inside me, a black hole that swallows the space that something like joy or happiness should occupy. I'm thinking of my team and what they're doing tonight halfway across the world. I check the time and do the math to account for the time difference. It's 09:00 now, which means that it's almost 17:00 for them—they're probably waking up and preparing for another long night. I look down at my arm and the finger I burned last week. It's hard to believe that this numb, useless lump of skin, bone, and tendons was once one of the most highly trained arms in the world. Now, I've got a second-degree burn from a teppanyaki grill because I can't even feel the goddamned thing. It's going to take time to get my strength and reflexes back, that's clear. But I'm going to do it. I'm going to make it back to my team and be even better than before.

I look at my watch again. It's time to take my morning dose of pain meds: 60 mg of OxyContin in the morning and another 60 mg at night, plus my Dilaudid pills, Gabapentin, Neurontin, and a few others that are hard to pronounce. God, who names these drugs anyway? I grab the bottle of OxyContin and shake out a pill into my palm. I feel disgusted with myself as I look at it. How pathetic I've become.

"Oh, gotta take my morning pain pills..." I'm that guy. *Weak-ass bitch.*

I swallow the pills and try to distract myself from the uneasiness festering inside me. I turn on a movie and microwave a chicken teriyaki Lean Cuisine for lunch, but I'm only half focused on what I'm watching. I'm too preoccupied with being disgusted with myself. I've never taken pain meds in my life. Now, I've got bottles of pills lining my countertops and special reminders for when to take what. If I had a dollar for every time some idiot, buzzed on one too many beers, looked at me and said, "I don't trust a man who doesn't drink," I'd be rich.

No one seems to fathom why a grown man doesn't want to drink, but that's me. I only drink on special occasions. The smell of alcohol reminds me of the blue light of my childhood television, my father erupting in rage, and the vow I made to myself when he made my mother cry: *I'm not going to be like you when I grow up.*

I don't even touch caffeine or pop pills. Even if I've got a whopper headache, I won't so much as take a baby aspirin. I've always been able to stick it out on my own—until now. I think it's time for a change. It's time for me to get back to basics. I'm not one of those weak people who needs booze, religion, or pain meds to get by. Never did, never will. In the hospital, I didn't really have a choice; I followed the doctor's orders. Now I'm home, on my own turf, and it's time for me to take control of my life again.

I stand up, walk to the counter, and gather all the little bottles full of pills in my hands. *"Oh, I've gotta take my evening pain meds..."*

No, I do not. Pain doesn't scare me, not after what I've been through. *Yeah, it will hurt for a little while, but so what? I'll get through it. I'm ready to get my life back.* Hovering over the toilet, I unscrew the lid of the OxyContin and turn the bottle upside down. *Plop, plop, plop.*

All those little pills are swimming in toilet water now, and I feel great. The Dilaudid team soon joins them, and then the Gabapentin, Neurontin, and all the others. Maybe the black hole inside me has swallowed the space that joy or happiness should occupy, but it hasn't swallowed my rebellion or stubbornness, which I'm relieved to find. I feel fucking great as I watch the toilet water swirl around and flush away all those little tablets of weakness. Back to basics. A new chapter starts now.

I settle back on the couch to finish my movie, feeling like a piece of my old self has returned. I'm now living life on my own terms, in control, back in the driver's seat, and it feels amazing. But I'm unlucky. An hour later, I begin to feel like I'm getting the flu. *Fuck, that's the last thing I need right now.* I can't catch a break. Not even two weeks out of the hospital and I've caught the flu. Where the hell would I have caught it anyway? Fayetteville is about as exciting as boiled rice, so it's not like I've got a vibrant social scene going on. An hour passes, and I feel even worse—now I'm starting to think it's not the flu at all. Maybe it's somehow connected to my arm. An infection. Or swelling. I'm not sure.

For a minute, my mind flashes back to the time I had a cyst removed from my wrist as a teenager. The doctors put it in a cast and sent me home, but then one of the stitches broke, causing the wrist to swell. *God, did that hurt like a motherfucker!* My wrist was swelling, but there was nowhere for it to go beneath that cast. They rushed me back to the hospital, cut the cast off, and discovered my arm was bleeding and swollen. That pain was a sign. Maybe this pain and the sick feeling are also a sign. Or maybe it will blow over.

I lie back and try to focus on the movie, but now I feel like I'm dying. My stomach hurts, and every single fiber of my body is registering intense pain. Something has clearly gone wrong with my arm.

I pick up the phone and dial Dr. Pleasant, waiting for her to answer. I'm frustrated and angry. I just made it out of the hospital, and I don't want to deal with any more complications. And to make things worse, I'm getting sick on the very day I decided to take a significant step in my recovery. Now I have to deal with whatever the hell this new issue is with my arm.

Dr. Pleasant answers, and I tell her how I'm feeling. She asks several questions, trying to understand what's going on, but we're both puzzled. I haven't changed my routine at all, haven't done anything out of the ordinary. I try to explain my symptoms, but I'm aware of how poorly my description matches the extreme sensations in my body.

"Tyler, based on what you're saying, it's hard to pinpoint exactly what's going on. I'm going to call Dr. John and chat with him about it and see if he has any ideas. In the meantime, since you're in a lot of pain, try upping your dose of pain medication just for tonight, and hopefully it will give you some relief while we sort this out. Okay?"

I let out a low chuckle. "Well, I can't exactly do that."

She pauses for a moment. "Why not?"

"Well, this afternoon I decided to flush all my medication down the toilet. I'm just done with it."

Long, awkward pause.

"Tyler, are you telling me that you flushed ALL YOUR MEDICATION down the toilet?"

"Yes."

I snicker at the indignation in her voice. Her fiery red hair about matches her personality, and we've always had a unique sort of sassy doctor-patient relationship. She keeps me in line, and I respect that. But now she's overreacting. Probably worried about my ability to cope with pain—she clearly doesn't know how much I can handle. It's this flu or infection or whatever the hell this is that's the real problem. I don't need a scolding about taking my pills; I need some answers about what's wrong with my body.

"Tyler, what the hell? You are a fucking idiot!"

I'm surprised by the tone of her voice.

"Tyler, listen to me. You need to go knock on your next-door neighbor's door. Tell them to bring you to the hospital immediately. If they are not home or if they won't take you, you call 911 and go by ambulance. Either way, get to the hospital as fast as you can. I am driving there now and will meet you there. Do you understand?"

I don't understand at all. What happened to consulting Dr. John and diagnosing my problem?

"What? You want me to go next door and ask my neighbors to drive me to the hospital? Why?"

She snorts impatiently.

"Look, you can't just get off that many pain meds cold turkey. It's stupid, dangerous, and you could die. You need to get to the hospital right now."

After she hangs up the phone, I sit for a few seconds before moving. She's a great doctor, but I'm not sure she got it right this time. I guess I didn't do a good job explaining my symptoms, which gave her the wrong impression. It seems a bit overdramatic to go knocking on my neighbor's door, someone I've never met, and ask them to drive me to the hospital. But I'm not going to defy Dr. Pleasant. And truth be told, I'm feeling worse and worse by the minute. I do exactly as she instructed.

"Hi, hello, I'm your neighbor Tyler Grey; it's nice to meet you. Can you take me to the hospital?"

I feel like an idiot doing it, but the pain is getting worse, and now even standing in the doorway is tiring. My neighbors are good sports about the whole thing, and within ten minutes, we're on our way. The pain is increasing, not only in my arm but across every single part of my body. It's more than achy now; I feel like death is slowly spreading through me, like every function of my body is shutting down. My hands are shaking and mucus is pouring from my nose, and I don't even have a fucking Kleenex to wipe it. My friendly neighbor pulls one from the glove box and hands it to me. I'm counting down the minutes until we get to the hospital. I'm panicking now. Something is really wrong, and I need answers.

When we arrive, there is a wheelchair waiting for me. Dr. Pleasant must have called ahead. An hour ago, I might have refused, but now my legs feel unstable, and a cold sweat breaks across my body as I get out of the car. I don't think I can hold myself upright without passing out. When I feel the wheelchair beneath me, I'm relieved. The same walls that lined my victory walk to freedom just a week ago pass by again as I'm wheeled back to the exact same room that had held me for months. When I stand up from the chair and fall into bed, a horrible sort of déjà vu washes over me. I know every inch of that room—the small generic piece of art on the wall, the position of the window, the feel of the mattress. I should be angry that I'm back here again, but I'm too sick to care. I feel like I'm going to die.

Is this really because I didn't take my stupid pain meds today?

It still doesn't make sense to me that a few little pain meds could cause this fucking black-death feeling. I feel tiny needles prick my wrists as the nurse attaches an IV, and I think it's time for an experiment. I take note of every sensation in my body. This will be my data for comparison. When nothing changes an hour from now, everyone is going to realize that they've got this whole thing wrong. Turns out I'm the one who got it wrong. As I turn my head and watch the nurse slowly push the syringe full of Dilaudid into the IV line, it feels as though God himself has breathed the breath of life into that line, and it's coursing through my veins. The pain disappears, and my mind feels relaxed and clear. The feeling is so strong, it's surreal. By the time she finishes pushing the last drop into the IV line, I'm fairly certain I could stand up and run a marathon.

So this is what heroin addicts feel like, I think when the nurse smiles and leaves the room.

My experiment has provided me with conclusive results. I am physically addicted to my pain medication. Not by choice or intentional dependency; this is purely physical. Even if my mind says I don't need this stuff, my body has become a junkie. The thought doesn't make me feel sad or angry; I'm hormonally incapable of feeling either at the moment. I'm just aware, deeply aware, that things are different now.

I feel like someone should have told me about this. They briefed me about my arm and all the potential outcomes and complications. Dr. Dick and Dr. Pleasant stood in my room, explaining every procedure in painstaking detail, my recovery process, and what to expect.

Oh, and you're officially addicted to drugs now. Drugs which, by the way, are pretty much a legal version of heroin. It seems like kind of a big thing to leave out. Not sure how they missed that one. At least now I know. All my disgust, righteous rebellion, and indignation have been washed away in the river of Dilaudid, flowing through my body, and I just don't care.

It's not the end; it's just the beginning.

CHAPTER 10
YOU SHOULD BE A THERAPIST

PSYCHIATRISTS ARE FULL OF SHIT. And psychologists, for that matter. And who fucking knows the difference between the two anyway? I'm sitting on a couch, staring at one right now as she arranges a neat little stack of paperwork in front of her and takes a sip from her pristine little cup. Just watching her makes my blood boil, but I keep a fake smile plastered on my face. I'm not here of my own free will; I'm here because I'm following orders, and I need to get through the next hour as smoothly as possible. Over the past few months, there's been an uncommon surge of injuries inside the Unit, and Command seems to think that this unfortunate trend might be fucking with our heads. When I was in the hospital, there were fourteen others there, and since my release, they've received even more. It's a brutal world out there, and the target packages are more dangerous than ever right now. In an effort to help, Command implemented a blanket policy to force all of us to see one of the Unit's psychiatrists.

The woman in front of me looks nice enough, I suppose. She's got that overly calm voice and a polite, borderline patronizing smile. She's already made it clear that she's just sooo happy to meet me. Oh boy, she must really care about me. I should just spill all my dirty little secrets and cry about the time my dad yelled at me when I was a little boy. *Sheesh. Crock of shit.* I hate it. These con artists with a few letters beside their names ask questions to make people get emotional for forty-five minutes and then dole out some generic, pre-canned answers and solutions that aren't even really solutions in the last fifteen minutes before the clock runs out, and waltz home with a paycheck for doing nothing.

I've hated therapists, counselors, psychiatrists, and the like since I sat in a dreary room with my family when I was nine years old for family therapy. It was Mom's idea. She dragged us there two weeks after she pulled me aside to ask my opinion about whether she should divorce my father. My mom liked getting a good second opinion before making any major life choices, and since I had a front-row seat to their ongoing fights and arguments—and on most occasions helped to mediate them—I was in a perfect position to offer solid advice on what she should do. At that age, I was still a sensitive kid, a sponge that seemed to soak up the emotions, tension, and feelings around me, and I genuinely wanted to help. It took me a minute to consider what she said because my stomach sort of twisted in knots when she hit me with the big *D* word. But I found my composure and offered her the very best unbiased advice and life guidance that a nine-year-old can: she should stay. I offered many compelling reasons that backed my firm opinion, and she listened, thanked me for my sage advice, and did exactly as I suggested. She stayed. But she also dragged the entire family to a counseling session. There in that stuffy room, I sat with both my parents and my little brother. My dad looked terribly uncomfortable. My mom spoke for a little while, and then my dad mumbled a few things under his breath, and then the counselor looked at me. "And how do you feel about all this, Tyler?"

I was so happy and relieved to finally have a chance to speak. I'd saved up years of data, listened to every argument and conversation, and done my best to help my parents understand each other. Finally, here was a real professional who could help. I took time to carefully explain my mother's point of view and then my father's—the cause of their arguments and the effects they had on the family. I laid it out neatly and clearly and waited for the counselor to jump in when I was done.

When I finished, the counselor sat back and smiled, "Wow, you should be a therapist when you grow up." Then he shifted the direction of the conversation and began to recite a list of recommendations for our family. I sat up, all ears. I was shocked at what he said. "Do activities together, try to compromise, and say nice things to each other…" The more he spoke, the more deflated I felt. Nothing he said was going to help my dysfunctional family. I wasn't even sure he'd been listening. He was supposed to say something that we hadn't thought of before, offer some solution or clue that we wouldn't have discovered on our own. I wanted him to help my family, but nothing he said was even remotely applicable.

"You should be a therapist when you grow up."

His words kept ringing in my ears, and I felt lonely and hollow inside. What the counselor didn't realize was that I'd been forced into being a therapist against my will long ago and I hated the job. What I really wanted to be was a kid. I've never liked therapists, counselors, or psychiatrists since.

At last, the papers have been neatly stacked, the glass of water on her desk has been sipped, and it's time to get through my compulsory little visit with the psychiatrist. She begins with a few simple questions, and I answer them without much elaboration. Then she asks another question, and by her slightly furrowed eyebrows, I can tell that she's expecting to facilitate a little breakthrough moment for me. *"Aha! What a question, how have I never thought of this before? How in the world did I not put that together?"*

I answer skillfully, serving up a perfectly sculpted platter of bullshit just for her. She gladly accepts it and nods encouragingly as I speak, as if we're really getting somewhere. Inwardly, I scoff. She's a psychiatrist at the Unit, and yet she has failed to realize that I'm using all the classic counter-interrogation techniques I've been taught to maneuver through the session. She seems to have forgotten that little detail of my training. I'm running circles around her, throwing out small tests along the way to check her intelligence, and she's none the wiser. I'm being a smartass, I know, but I didn't ask for this, and she's too dumb even to notice what I'm doing. It's pathetic and entertaining, the way she's furiously writing all my bullshit answers with that pleased look on her face, congratulating herself on a job well done. I check my watch. Eight minutes to go. She draws in a deep breath and looks up as she closes my folder. "Tyler, it seems like you are doing really well."

She's giving me a professional stamp of approval, a winning smile that she knows will make my day. I'm mocking her in my mind. I've just spent an hour brushing the dust off my counter-intelligence techniques and entertaining myself. She never figured out that I'm officially addicted to pain medication, likely clinically depressed, and feel next to no motivation to do anything. If she only knew what was going on inside my head, she'd have me committed to the fourth-floor mental ward on the spot.

"Doing the best I can," I say, mirroring her winning smile. She thanks me and sends me on my way with a big good-luck wish. Thank God I'm not paying for this shit.

I head home. My apartment is as silent and depressingly beige as when I left this morning. I open the refrigerator, even though I know exactly what's inside. I remember when days used to pass like minutes, with a clear sense of purpose, mission, and objectives providing structure to my time. I used to go to sleep with the satisfaction of knowing I had accomplished what I set out to do that day. I miss being able to quantify and measure the use of my time, the success of my efforts, and the outcome of my performance. Now time seems to flow without direction. My days feel meaningless and insignificant. I don't feel like I'm contributing anything to the world, and that makes me deeply uncomfortable. I feel worthless, like a waste of space, nothing but a useless guy on pain meds, waiting for my arm to heal so I can get back in the game. *"The most important thing you can do is just focus on getting better."* I've heard that one about a hundred times, and it makes me want to scream. The truth is, I could be focusing on much more important things. I could be with my team right now, utilizing my skill set, taking out the meanest bullies on the world's playground. But I'm here. And the emptiness is back again. That black hole suffocates the little light I have left until it's nothing but darkness. I feel disconnected from myself—from the man I used to be and the way I once experienced life. Like there's been a fracture in my identity. That's the part that shakes me to my core. I'd try to get help if I thought it would do any good, but today proved to me once again that therapists, counselors, and psychiatrists aren't worth the time.

I sit for a while in the darkness, feeling numb until a strange memory pops into my mind of a documentary I once saw about a man with multiple personality disorder. He would film himself and talk to the camera like it was a diary, then watch it later to understand more about each of his personalities. This eventually helped him fit the puzzle pieces of his condition together and improve his life. It's got me thinking. What if I filmed myself when I'm in one frame of mind and then watched it later in a different frame of mind? It would be kind of like two different people talking. Then I could compare, contrast, analyze, and diagnose. Sounds crazy, but then again, I kind of feel crazy.

By the time evening comes, I've set up a video camera and pressed record. Unsurprisingly, it feels awkward at first—talking to the camera like it's a diary. I knew it would. I ramble on for nearly half an hour and then press stop. I'll do it again tomorrow and the next day, until I have enough data to work with. Then I'll analyze, compare, and look for clues about what's going on with me, because I know it's more than just a bum arm. *"You should be a therapist when you grow up." Looks like I'm gonna have to be.*

CHAPTER 11
AUGUSTA

IT TURNS OUT I LEFT more than just a piece of my nutsack in Iraq. The doctors tell me that the explosion also blew off all my extensor tendons—the ones that control my hand's ability to straighten my fingers. They probably got mopped up along with the rest of the Tyler-flavored human smoothie that sprayed across the hallway that night.

I have a surgery scheduled in Augusta, Georgia, to reconstruct and repair these extensor tendons. The procedure is going to be challenging. The doctors plan to reroute my still-working flexor tendons, which are responsible for closing the hand, to serve as my new extensor tendons. Essentially, they'll be reengineering my hand from the inside out.

I have no idea what to expect. I've had so many operations that I've lost track. These days, I just follow the doctors' orders and try not to think about it too much. But sometimes I can't help it. I just want to press fast-forward, skip ahead, and rejoin my team.

Vanessa offered to join me on the trip so I wouldn't have to drive and face the surgery alone. The idea of having someone with me is strange; I've always been a loner. As I settle into the passenger seat, I feel awkward but happy. She grins at me as she ramps onto the freeway and turns up the music. Her fingers tap the steering wheel to the beat of the song blaring through the speakers, and I lean back against the headrest, watching her.

Her lips move with the music, and her face glows with the same energy I noticed when I first saw her across the street in Dallas. Every so often, she turns down the music when a new topic pops into her mind and starts talking a million miles an hour. She's a river of momentum, and I am swept into her current. As the miles pass, we begin to talk about our lives and the future.

We brainstorm, dream, and strategize. We finish each other's sentences. I like the way her mind works, and I can see exactly why she's a top earner in her company. The feeling is electric as we plan for all the things we'll do together. For the first time in a long while, I feel a sense of hope and excitement about the future. When I see the sign that reads WELCOME TO AUGUSTA, I'm surprised at how quickly the drive has passed.

When the surgery is over, Vanessa is waiting for me, and I crack a few jokes to wipe the sympathy from her face. She laughs, and we keep right on talking until I'm released. Vanessa carries our bags and races to open the door when we walk back to the car. I'm not exactly sure how to respond to her care and attention. This is all so new for me—but I like it. I don't say much besides thank you, but I make note of each act of kindness, good deed, and sacrifice. I record them in my mind's ledger, one by one, and promise myself that I will find a way to make it up to her.

Once I settle into the passenger seat, I position a white bed pillow on my lap so I can rest my arm during the drive. It hurts a lot, but I've got a fresh round of pain meds running through my system and a beautiful girl beside me. Vanessa checks on me frequently, adjusting the pillow and asking if I'm comfortable. When she stops at a gas station, she runs inside and grabs two bottles of water, handing one to me without me asking. As the hours pass, I feel relaxed. I think I'm going to be just fine.

"OH MY GOD, OH MY GOD, TYLER!" A few miles shy of the North Carolina border, Vanessa is shouting in panic. I look down at my lap and see the white pillow is soaked in blood—too much blood. The blanket over my arm must have covered the fact that my hand has been bleeding heavily since we left.

Calm turns to chaos in a matter of seconds, and suddenly, my mind is clear. My senses are now on high alert, clearing out the fog of medication in my body as I form a plan of action.

"Hey, hey, Vanessa. Calm down. It's all good. Just hand me my cell phone, okay?"

My voice is soothing and calm. It's after midnight, but I know just who to call: Dan. If there's one person on the planet I can trust to help me solve this situation, it's *Dan*.

"We need to do something! You're bleeding out, Tyler. This isn't good," Vanessa says, talking a million miles an hour again, this time with fear and concern in her eyes.

"Just hand me my cell phone—I've got a plan."

Vanessa doesn't look entirely convinced, but she hands over my phone. I dial Dan's number and give him a rundown of the situation.

"How far out are you?" He's straight to business.

"Navigation says forty-eight minutes to Fort Bragg."

"I'll meet you at the gate, and we'll get you fixed. No problem."

Vanessa doesn't ask for an explanation when I hang up. Her gaze is fixed on the road ahead now, and there's a steely determination in her eyes that I've never seen before. No panic, just execution.

"Sit tight, baby," she says, giving me a brave smile. "We'll be there in no time."

With one hand on my thigh and the other on the steering wheel, she presses the gas pedal and we are flying down the freeway. Dan and his wife are waiting for us beside the entrance gate at Fort Bragg just as promised when we arrive.

"C'mon, let's get you fixed up, buddy," Dan says and motions us toward the Med Shed, a small but well-equipped medical facility with a red tile roof.

I can tell that he and his wife have each had a few drinks—they were probably enjoying a night out before my phone call. Inside the Med Shed, Dan removes the bandages and looks over the damage. Within minutes, he diagnoses the mistake that caused the excessive bleeding and goes to work. There in the Med Shed, with more than a few beers in his system, Dan outperforms the entire hospital staff. He told Vanessa he'd had three, which definitely means he'd had at least six.

While he works, I smile and crack jokes to distract myself from the pain, and Dan plays right along like a champ. But as I stare at my bloody, disfigured hand, a slow, sickening realization settles in.

My body will never be like it was. No matter how many thousands of dollars, hours of surgeries, and years of rehab I invest in my recovery, I will never have the same function that I used to. I will never handle my weapons in the same way, never be able to breach a doorway or clear a room or hit a target with the same speed and precision I once did. This construction of bone and grafted skin and rerouted tendons that I now call a right arm will never perform the same way the old one did. Even if I kill myself to rehabilitate, even if I give everything I have, my best will never be what it was. Dan is stitching, mending, and pulling me back together, but I feel myself ripping apart at the core. *I'm never going back. It's over. It's all over.*

The finality of it is so unceremonious, so anticlimactic, so quiet. All the years of investment, sacrifice, focus, and effort just wadded up like a paper napkin and discarded. I feel empty and worthless. The pain is back again, like a familiar friend. I'm about to close my eyes and find that iron will inside the darkness to disconnect from my body and block out the pain when I see Vanessa staring at me from the corner of the room. Her steady gaze catches my eyes, and I don't look away.

She looks so pretty, too pretty to be standing in a Med Shed watching her boyfriend's bloody arm get patched up. But her eyes don't speak of discomfort or a desire to run away. She's not looking at me like I'm wounded or injured. She's looking at me like I'm the last man on earth. She's looking at me with a devious *"We've got this"* look in her eyes. Like we're Bonnie and Fucking Clyde and we're ready to face the world, guns blazing. Something is unfolding between us that is beyond romance. This connection is far stronger. We're coconspirators, allies, partners. Or maybe we're just two kids trying to surf the chaos of life—arm in arm as we face the trauma of a cruel world. At least we're riding the waves together.

Everything I've trained for, bled for, worked for, and sacrificed for is gone now. I taste confusion, loss, grief, sadness, and anger. I hate the flavor. Every remnant of the man I used to be is broken and shattered, and the approval in her eyes is holding me together. When it's all over, and we're lying side by side in the early morning hours, my mind races with somersaults of possibilities in the space where the walls and barriers of my military service used to be. I need a change. A BIG change. We both do.

"I think it's time for me to move on," I whisper into the darkness. She's silent for a minute. She knows what I'm trying to say.

"I need a fresh start too." She saves me from having to name it, having to taste the finality of the words on my lips. "I don't want to do what I'm doing forever, Tyler. I don't want to spend my life traveling and running one event after another. I don't know what's next, but I'm ready."

"How about Vegas?"

Even I'm surprised by my words.

"To live?"

I know she's ready to leave South Beach, and without a future in the military, I remember just how much I absolufuckinglutely hate living in Fayetteville. Vegas is action. Vegas is a party that never ends. Vegas is the perfect place for a couple of good-looking kids to get a house and enjoy being young and in love.

"Why not?"

"Vegas. Wow. Imagine us. We'd be great."

We talk and dream until the sun rises, and I cling to her like a life raft. She is the only one who remembers who I was, who still looks at me and sees a warrior and a goddamned superhero. I'm losing everything, but at least I still have her.

CHAPTER 12
BEAUTIFUL CHAOS

"I LIKE IT. WHAT DO you think, Tyler?" Vanessa's gaze is fixed on the gleaming kitchen cabinets as we trail behind a cheerful Las Vegas realtor.

"I think this might be it." I whisper it quietly so the realtor doesn't hear and hit us with an overly eager sales pitch. The house is in a great location, has four bedrooms, a nice kitchen, and plenty of living space. It's perfect. I just landed a job as an outreach coordinator for a large nonprofit organization that helps veterans connect with job opportunities. It will require a little bit of travel, but I can work from home most of the time, and it pays pretty decently. Combined with Vanessa's income, we're in a great position to buy.

This would make a great office, I think to myself as I look inside one of the empty upstairs rooms. I can already envision my desk in the corner. When Vanessa and I lock eyes again, we both know—this will be our first house together. We celebrate Vegas-style with a nice dinner and then visit a nightclub afterward. I gulp down another sip of my drink as a few dancers come out on stage—a parade of long legs, heels, and hips that sway to the music. Suddenly, an idea pops into my mind, and I turn to Vanessa.

"Have you ever thought about becoming a dancer? I mean, you're gorgeous, you want a new career, we're going to be living in Vegas, and it pays well."

She looks surprised at my suggestion, but I see the wheels turning. Her business mind works fast.

"You think I could do it?"

"Look around. You're prettier than anyone in here. You'd be great."

The idea begins to germinate, and by the following night, it's sprouted to life. Vanessa has already begun calculating how this new career path might be able to replace her current position as a top earner at Beach Body. The more we talk about it, the more excited we both become. A new home, new jobs, and a whole new city to enjoy—we're creating our dream life. I can make great money from my home office during the day, and then we can go out and enjoy all the wonders of the Las Vegas nightlife while she dances at night. What more could we ask for?

The next evening, we decide to do a little market research. We head to one of the nicest clubs in town and book a couple of dancers—not to watch but to pick their brains on the ins and outs of the business. We've come prepared with lots of questions, and they seem happy to answer. When our time is up, we head to another club and do the same thing. As the night is drawing to a close, I notice a man who appears to be the nightclub manager standing in the corner.

"Look over there." I nudge Vanessa. "Looks like the manager. You should ask him what the requirements are for getting hired."

"Great idea." She grins and her hand connects with mine in a subtle high five as she stands up. She's gone for several minutes, and when she returns, she's beaming.

"Tyler, you won't believe this! He gave me his card and told me to show up tomorrow. I think he might actually want to hire me."

We leave the club feeling on top of the world. I can see the excitement building in her eyes as she considers this new career path. Vanessa is one of the hardest-working people I've ever met, and she's devoted every ounce of herself to her career, which has certainly paid off. What's more, she has cared for me and supported me through the most challenging time in my life without hesitation.

She's been patient with me as I've had to navigate a tough legal battle after ending my "military marriage" to a woman I hadn't lived with in years. Through it all, she keeps sticking by me, loving me, and defending me. If anyone deserves to let their hair down and enjoy life, it's her.

After returning home to pack our things, we make one more stop before leaving California: *Disneyland*. We arrive by 10:15 and walk hand in hand through the park. After a while, we stop at the bench on

Main Street at the entrance right across from the fire station and I sit down, pulling her next to me. She laughs and talks a million miles an hour like she always does.

The last time I sat on this bench, I sat for hours waiting for so-called friends to come who never did. It was one of the loneliest days of my life, a day when I questioned myself and then decided to make my peace with being alone forever. But here I am again, with a beautiful girl beside me who loves me for who I am. And I'm starting to think that maybe there isn't something wrong with me. Maybe I'm not a bad person after all. The fact that a beautiful girl like this wants to be with me must mean I've got *something* worth *something*.

We sit for a while before I work up the courage to tell her why I wanted to bring her to this particular bench. She's quiet for a while after I tell the story and laces her fingers through mine.

"You're not alone anymore," she says softly. "You're not alone."

We sit in silence, hand in hand, and I can't help but think, *Is this it? Is this the big, epic love story I always hoped I'd find?*

Later that afternoon, Vanessa rests her head on my chest as we wait in line for Splash Mountain. A couple about our age stands a few feet away, each holding the tiny hand of a brown-eyed little boy. Vanessa turns her head, watching them, and then looks back at me with a smile. When I catch her eyes, I feel panic constricting my chest. *Oh shit.*

I know exactly what that look means—that nurturing, glowing, let's-have-a-baby-together-someday look.

"Wouldn't we make the cutest babies?" she whispers.

Shit, I should have known Disneyland was a contagious breeding ground for baby fever.

"Oh no, no kids for me." I'm emphatic. "I'm just not cut out to be the soccer dad type. I mean, big props to the dudes that are, but it sure ain't me." I laugh and change the subject, ignoring the deflated look in Vanessa's eyes.

No suburban family life for us. It's time for Vegas, baby.

◄►

"Ready to go?" Vanessa asks as she peers around the corner into the bathroom. It's a few months later and we're back in Las Vegas, this time for good, and tonight is her first night working at the club.

"Almost," I say, flicking my eyes to her and then back to my reflection in the mirror. My chest is lean, my shoulders are thin, and my arms are uneven. Flaming red scars coil around my right arm, and I'm starting to call bullshit on the doctors' prediction that they'll eventually fade. For a second, a vision flashes before me—a memory of the goddamned superhero I used to be: chest strong; arms thick with experience, action, and performance; my confidence sky-high. He stares back at me with a gleam in his eyes. But the memory fades as quickly as it comes, and it's just me again—scar-painted, gimpy-armed, and skinny. *Pathetic.*

Suddenly, I feel Vanessa's fingertips gliding across my right arm, tracing my scars. I look up, and when my eyes meet hers, I don't see compassion or pity—I see desire. She's still looking at me like I'm the last man on earth.

"Your scars are sexy," she says, her lips curling into a smile. I turn away from the mirror and face her. My reflection in her eyes is the only one I want to see.

"Come on, let's go," I say, flipping off the bathroom light and grabbing her hand. "I hear there's this club in town that hired the hottest new dancer, and I don't want to miss her opening performance tonight."

Vanessa giggles and follows me to the car.

A buddy of mine and his girlfriend have decided to join us for the occasion, and the mood is high as we take a seat and the drinks begin to flow. Vanessa looks amazing in her outfit, and I can see that her confidence is soaring. She sits next to me for a little while as the club begins to fill up. When I take a sip of my third cocktail, I hear the first few notes of my favorite song beginning to play. *I guess the DJ has good taste.*

Now Vanessa is standing up, and her eyes are set on me. As her hips begin to move, I understand. This is her first dance, and she's dedicating it to me. As the song plays, she lets herself go. There is a new Vanessa in front of me, one I have never seen before. She is wild, free, and fierce. She's a natural. *Holy shit.*

As she dances, I find myself shocked, proud, and uneasy all at the same time. I'm shocked that this woman on display has been inside her all along. I'd seen glimpses before but never knew that so much was lying dormant within her until tonight. I feel proud that I'm the man she wants to be with, the one who's taking her home tonight. But I also feel deeply uneasy, though I'm not sure why.

Vanessa dances and the lights flash. My favorite song reverberates throughout the room and alcohol flows through my body. This is a whole new world, that much is clear. A whole new world full of beautiful chaos. *Just how I like it.*

CHAPTER 13
TABLEFUL OF STRIPPERS

2006

"GOOD MORNING."

I hear Vanessa's voice behind me, but I don't turn around—my eyes are glued to the three screens in front of me. A pack of thieves has just attacked two traders, and it's up to me to take them down.

"Good morning!" I call out without breaking my focus.

"What?" my buddy's voice comes through my headset. "You talking to me?"

"Nah, sorry. Just saying good morning to Vanessa."

"Ah, gotcha."

Five months ago, Vanessa's brother introduced me to *Silkroad Online*, a multiplayer video game set in the seventh century AD, along the Silk Road between China and Europe. I've been hooked ever since. Vanessa gets home after I'm asleep—usually at 4:00 or 5:00 a.m.—and sleeps until midday. That gives me plenty of time to knock out my day's worth of phone calls and meetings with hours to spare for *Silkroad*. Never really thought of myself as the gamer type, but I probably play at least four or five hours a day now. Truth be told, the black hole is back these days and I don't feel much of anything. There's just a big cavern of nothingness inside of me. No motivation. No excitement. No fear. No happiness. No anger. Just…*nothing*.

"So there's this party across town tonight," Vanessa's voice is there again.

"Yeah?"

"So do you want to go? It'll be fun."

I know she's trying to pull me out of my little nest here in my office. Truth be told, I'm spending a lot more time in here than I used to. Idleness is my worst enemy these days—my work and *Silkroad* help keep me from walking to that mental ledge in my mind and staring off into the great abyss.

"I don't think so. Rather just stay in tonight."

There's a brief pause.

"Hey...hey, right behind you!" I suddenly blurt out. We're just about to gain the upper hand on the thieves.

"What?" Vanessa asks.

"Oh, sorry, babe. Not talking to you."

When there's another long silence, I wonder if she's left.

"Do you want to go out to dinner at least?"

She's still in the doorway.

"Maybe, I don't know. You go ahead. I'll just stay here."

Another long silence, and this time I'm sure she's gone.

"We'll have a great time," she breaks in again. "Just think about it, okay?"

This time, I hear the door click as she leaves.

A great night, a fun night, a wild night—seems that's all anyone talks about around here. Vegas is full of tales about what a "good night" it was or is or will be. At first, I thought people were just exaggerating all that hype and emotion, but I can see the sincerity in their eyes—that spark of anticipation and excitement as the alcohol flows and the music picks up.

It's not that I don't like being out. Hell, I get to spend the night with six strippers at my table, and my girlfriend is the pack leader of them all. I know I'm living the life most guys dream about. But I feel disconnected from it all. Like I'm there but not really there.

Even in the moments when I'm supposed to relax or have a good time, I feel like my mind and body are on high alert, vigilant and ready. But there's nothing to do. Nothing but sit in my office or in a club or in a car. And sometimes it fucking drives me nuts. I'm drinking more these days, and I guess it's all part of the lifestyle. Alcohol is about the only thing capable of making me feel blissfully numb. And when I'm lucky enough to black out from it, at least it saves me from one night's battle with anxiety.

I tried Ecstasy for the first time just a month ago. Never thought I'd ever be open to trying any type of illicit drug in a million years. I never even smoked weed in high school. The moment that tiny little pill touched my tongue, I could hardly believe what I was doing. *This isn't me. This isn't me. This isn't me.* But then again, I had the opportunity to spend the night dancing with six strippers all on Ecstasy. I mean, I'm mentally strong, but I'm not *that* strong. *Hell yes, I'll take the blue pill. Time to see how far the rabbit hole goes.*

Like I said, I'm living the dream. I'm surrounded by smoking-hot women, have a girlfriend who adores me, a job that pays well, and a video game to pass the extra time. If I complain, I'm sure there'd be a lineup of guys ready to shoot me and take my place. But a *great night*? A *fun night*? A *wild night*? I don't know. Everyone uses these words and I find myself doing it too. But I feel nothing, empty. Even worse, I don't feel like myself.

I still record myself every day and watch the videos later to look for clues. I'm always surprised when I see the man on the screen looking back at me. That guy is scrawny, his eyes are fuzzy like he hasn't slept in a long time, and he doesn't look happy at all. But it's not the lack of happiness that bothers me so much. I was never the happy-go-lucky, isn't-life-just-a-pile-of-cotton-candy type anyway—not as a kid or an adult. And why would I be? The world is a cruel place, and it's hard for me to believe that anyone could be really happy without lying to themselves at least a little bit.

No, the part that bothers me is that I can't find that motivating force inside myself that used to drive me to push, conquer, expand, and achieve. No matter how tough things got, I always knew that I had that little switch inside me that I could flip and overcome anything. When that switch was on, all the pain, suffering, and pure suck of a challenge only added to my resolve. But these days I can't seem to find the switch. God knows I'm looking for it and waiting for it to come back—that feeling of power, aggression, and pure burning desire to succeed. But the switch just isn't there, and I continue to feel disconnected from myself and the world around me. I'm not the man I used to be, and that's the part that bothers me the most.

Vanessa returns to my office and wraps her arms around me as I stare at the computer screen, sweetly begging me to go with her. She's not going to take no for an answer. But there's something behind her big smile and high energy. She's worried about me, I think.

Six hours later, I'm sitting in a booth with Vanessa and four other strippers. "We've got a new girl tonight," Vanessa whispers as a long-legged, bleached blonde approaches our table and takes a seat.

"Oh my Goddddd! What happened to your arm?" she asks as soon as she lays eyes on it. Those bright red scars jump out at everyone; you can't miss them.

"Shark attack," I say solemnly, pulling up my sleeve to let her get a better look. Vanessa smirks. I've created a few good answers when people ask about my arm—talking about my military service is not something I'm ready to do. "Just a workplace injury" is my typical go-to response and, technically, not a lie. But when I'm feeling particularly spicy, I go with shark attack.

"Oh my Goddddd, nooooo. That's terrible. Where did it happen?"

The blonde honestly looks like she might shed a tear for the poor shark-bitten stranger.

"Well, I'm sure you're familiar with bucktooth sharks that live off the coast of Australia..."

She bobs her head approvingly. Of course she knows about bucktooth sharks in Australia. Vanessa looks at me and we laugh with our eyes even though we don't crack a smile.

"Unfortunately, that bucktooth bastard got me while I was shark surfing off the Gold Coast."

Her eyes, weighed down with fake eyelashes that look more like tiny witch brooms, are drawn in an expression of deep sympathy. She offers her deepest condolences, and I order another round for the table.

Humor seems to be the only thing capable of surviving the black hole.

"Yesss…it's gonna be a great night!" the blonde bubbles and thrusts her glass forward. "Cheers, everybody!" And there it is.

"Cheers…" I mumble along with the group. But is it a great night? A fun night? A wild night?

Not really, not for me anyway. I feel anxious. Despite the fact that I'm surrounded by happy people, I still feel like every cell of my body is on high alert and I can't turn it off. I reach for my glass and take a gulp. When the alcohol blurs the edges of my mind, I fall into a hazy space of nothingness, and it's a relief. I've got a nice house, a good job, a girlfriend who's crazy about me, and a tableful of strippers…but I don't feel anything at all.

CHAPTER 14
GARGOYLE

Just another day in the office...

I'M SITTING IN MY CHAIR, looking at the same wall and screen I've looked at for the better part of a year. I hear Vanessa somewhere across the house, preparing to leave for work. She came to the doorway twice this morning, asking how I was doing and if I needed anything. "Fine," I said, and she left me in peace. I know she's trying to sweep me up in the current of her happiness and high energy, hoping that it will be strong enough to carry the both of us. If I had a choice, I'd dive in with both feet, maybe even sweep her off her feet for a change. But I'm not fine, and the hollowness inside me isn't there by choice.

Nothing about my surroundings has changed, but today I feel different. Maybe it's the fact that nothing has changed that's bothering me so much. My eyes wander from the wall to the edges of the desk to the black armrests of my office chair. This little room has become my whole world, and I'm disgusted by it.

I guess some people spend their whole lives in a predictable little hamster wheel: wake up, drink coffee, sit in an office, work, play video games, eat, repeat. But I'm not one of those people. I used to be a goddamned superhero. I'm the guy who used to wake up, eat breakfast, and head to HQ for a briefing on the day's mission. *Who are we after today? What's the strategy? How many chargers will I need to bring to breach the doorway of the target's location? Will we go by heli or by vehicle transport?* I used to have these thoughts daily when my world was big and I was a real player in the game. I was sharp then, and my mind felt clear and calm. My skill set was honed and ready. Now, I'm sitting in a goddamned office chair in a room I've hardly left for an entire year.

I feel like I'm living someone else's life—as if the Man Upstairs accidentally mixed up the scripts for the main character and the absolute nobody they'll bill as the "guy in the home office" at the very end of the movie credits because he's so pathetic and insignificant that his character doesn't even deserve to have a name. This isn't how it's supposed to be. I'm not "depressed guy in the home office" who gets one scene with no lines. I'm the goddamned superhero who jumps out of airplanes, rescues hostages, and sweeps the beautiful girl off her feet. But here I sit in my same stupid office chair, making the same stupid phone calls, playing the same stupid game, looking at the same stupid wall.

I'm the lucky bastard living with a woman that every man would die to take home from the club, and yet here I sit…in my same stupid office chair, making the same stupid phone calls, playing the same stupid game, looking at the same stupid wall. I'm starting to feel like an NPC in one of my games, trapped at the fucking blacksmith shop, here to service the other characters and nothing more.

The disgust and self-loathing are back until another thought cuts through the dull haze: *You need to get your fucking shit together. This isn't the life you want. This isn't you.*

For a moment, I hear it—an echo from deep inside that vast empty cavern that seems to eclipse all the light and goodness in my life. I recognize the voice, though I haven't heard it in a long time. The voice of the Warrior begins to echo inside of me, and it feels damn good.

"You are a warrior. You've never given up, backed down, or surrendered. You've always found strength and resilience to keep going, no matter how tough or painful things got. This will be no different. You will rise up and fight back."

This voice used to be so loud, strong, and clear, but these days I'm so disconnected that I hardly even hear it anymore. I know I'm meant for something better than this. I know I have a higher purpose to fulfill and a mission to accomplish beyond this hamster wheel of suburban life. But then the Destroyer's voice roars back at the Warrior.

"Rise up? Fight back? Stand up to the darkness? Who are you kidding? You're not a goddamned superhero, you're a worthless piece of shit. Look at you, sitting in this office like a loser. You don't even deserve the life you have. There's no silver lining here, no changing this dark, cruel world. It's fucked up, and you're fucked up, and you might as well stop giving a fuck about it and ride the fucked-up chaos while you can."

Now I'm beginning to think that the terrible emptiness, numbness, and feeling of total disconnection I've lived with are far better than witnessing this war raging inside me—a conflict between the two fractured parts of myself. But then I hear the Warrior again, echoing through the halls of my foggy mind, and I welcome the sound.

"Get out there and fight for the life you deserve."

It's back. That raw aggression to fight, that determination to win, that unwavering focus on the mission at hand, and that dedication to succeed. I've found the switch inside me—it's turned on and I don't dare waste time. I know how strong the darkness in me has become, and I can't afford to let it overtake me again. I pull out a sheet of paper and begin to write out a list of goals that I want to accomplish. I need structure and I need a plan. My hands move furiously across the paper, and I know exactly what I'm going to do: I'm going to start my own security business. I know plenty of guys with my type of background and skill set who run major security contracts, and they are killing it. Why not me too? I've been kicking around the idea for long enough, and it's time to do the fucking thing. I'm aware of an online course that is widely regarded as the top training program in this industry. I've considered signing up for it many times but never have. When you complete the program, you become eligible to join an alumni network consisting of prominent players in the industry. This is exactly what I need—more connections in the field.

As I fill out the signup form, I notice a banner at the top of the web page announcing an upcoming convention for all the program's alumni. I click on the itinerary for the event and notice that it's scheduled to take place in Las Vegas in less than two months. I also recognize most of the names on the list of speakers, and they are all A-list power players in the space. An overwhelming feeling hits me, some deep sense of knowing that attending this event will open doors for the future I want. But there's a catch. The event is for alumni only, and the estimated time to finish the course is four months. I'll have to finish it in six weeks to be eligible to attend, and there's a shitload of information and coursework to be done. *Challenge accepted.*

I spend the rest of the day organizing my office and then head for bed early. Vanessa won't be home until morning, and I've got a big day ahead of me tomorrow.

When my alarm goes off, everything in me wants to roll over and keep sleeping, but I force my eyes open anyway. I slip out of bed so as not to wake Vanessa, scarf down breakfast, and then get started on the course. By the end of the day, my mind is swimming with information, and I feel tired, but it's the I-worked-hard-and-accomplished-something-today kind of tired. The feeling is great, and it just adds more kindling to the fire.

Six weeks later, I'm at the event as an official alumnus—connecting with a handful of the major leaders in the security space. It's a tight industry, and everyone seems to know everyone. New conversations and connections flow easily, and I feel alert and on my game. I'm in my element, and it seems that the fog is finally lifting. I feel more like myself than I have in a long time.

Two months later, I receive an email from one of the biggest security companies operating in the region, offering my new company a contract to provide security at a MAC Cosmetics store in Las Vegas. *And so it begins.* I thank him and accept the job on behalf of my company, which at the moment consists of exactly one person: me. It's gonna be my ass on the floor until I find, hire, and train a team, and that's going to take time. Working as a security guard for a MAC store isn't exactly an ideal job for someone with my qualifications, but I see it as an opportunity to gain visibility. Who knows, it could be the initial step toward securing a national partnership with MAC in the future.

Three weeks later, I'm standing military-style in a full suit as two MAC employees buzz around the store preparing to open for the day. I feel like a fish out of water. Sure, I've seen makeup before, even kept a girlfriend or two company as she shopped, but I never took the time to really study a cosmetics store before now. Every shelf seems to be lined with a different version of the same product. At 10:00 they unlock the doors. A middle-aged woman walks in, dressed in khaki capri pants and comfortable shoes, holding a faded leather purse. The blonde ends of her hair are a color that can only come from a box or a bottle, and the roots are dark brown. The woman begins to browse, picking up one item and then another. The model pictured on the display case stares at her without a smile—arms crossed over her naked body, chin jutted out, and bright red lips drawn in a seductive pout. The woman glances up at the model and then back down at the products in front of her before selecting a tube of lipstick and turning it over. Her movements are slow, painfully slow.

As I watch her, I can't for the life of me understand what she could be looking at for so long. There's no writing on the tube except for the label. Is she imagining herself wearing it? Wondering if the lipstick will make her look like the model on the wall? Envisioning some new red-lipped version of herself? She replaces the tube and then selects another shade. Again, she stares, turning the tube over so slowly that I feel my nerves screaming. What could possibly be so interesting? And why do I even care?

After what seems like an eternity, she places the lipstick in her plastic basket and makes her way slowly to the counter. As the cashier taps on the register, the woman looks fondly at her purchase. Her face is serene, occupied with pure happiness. I find it both fascinating and disturbing. The simplicity of her happiness is hard for me to grasp, and the emotion I see painted on her face is so foreign to me that it's hard to believe it's real. But it is. She has no one to put on an act for. Her back was turned to the cashiers, and she hasn't made eye contact with me once since she arrived. I'm nothing but a fixture in the building to her. However unbelievable it seems to me, that happiness has got to be real. Truth be told, I'm not sure if I envy it or am disgusted by it. I guess a little of both. I don't know if I've lost the ability to feel happiness like others do, or if I was never capable of it anyway. Either way, I just don't get it.

Two more people come in: a well-dressed woman who seems to be in a hurry and a mother pushing a baby stroller. One of the employees plasters a smile on her face and walks straight to the well-dressed woman and offers her assistance. The mother browses alone. I keep my eye on all of them, but there is nothing unusual to see.

By late morning, the store is filled with customers, and my legs are beginning to feel fatigued. I check my watch and am surprised that only a few hours have passed since I arrived. It's been months since the injury, and I haven't done any physical exercise since then, and it shows. I'm surprised by how achy and exhausted I feel. I adjust my weight in an effort to find relief, but none comes. At 13:00, I leave for a fifteen-minute break. I take a quick piss and then sit down to eat lunch, and it's a huge relief to be off my feet. I had no idea how taxing it would be to stand for so long. My legs are already swollen with fatigue.

After lunch, three teenage girls browse aimlessly through the store, breaking out into sporadic spurts of hysterical laughter. A woman with bleached blonde hair circled into a giant nest on the top of her head walks to the cashier with a basket full of products. Her mouth never stops moving as she smacks her gum like a teenager, even though she's definitely over thirty-five and holding a designer bag. The cashier scans the items and the woman scans her phone. When all the items are in the bag, the cashier waits awkwardly for several seconds while the woman continues to smack the gum and brush her thumb over the glossy screen of her phone. When she finally realizes that she's the one holding up the line, she lets out an exasperated sigh and makes a production of setting down her large iced coffee, rummaging through her oversized bag, and finally producing a credit card. Her total is $358.

A young, shy-looking girl in an old, oversized sweatshirt and long ponytail waits patiently behind her and sets four small items on the counter. Her total is $39.50. She carefully counts out two ten-dollar bills and hands them to the cashier, then pulls out a credit card to cover the remaining balance. Her face is kind, her expression almost too polite—

perhaps a cover for the fact that she's nervous about the money she's spending. But the cashier appears more annoyed with the girl in the old clothes than she was with the gum-smacking blonde, even though the girl is nothing but kind. The injustice of it all annoys me.

Not a single customer looks me in the eye or seems even to notice that I'm here. I'm just the guy in a black suit playing mall cop in a makeup store. The more I stand, the more I feel intensely ashamed of myself. All those years of training in counterterrorism, hostage rescue, and sniper tactics, and here I am in a stupid suit making sure no one steals a tube of lipstick. *What a waste.*

I'm a highly trained operator guarding a MAC store on a Tuesday morning. I'm nothing but a gargoyle, one of those grotesqueries on a Gothic cathedral, a symbolic figure standing guard over this little haven of consumerism. I think of all the skills I spent years acquiring, testing, and honing that I'll never use again. I think of all the information stored in my mind that will rot there without reason. Decades of sacrifice and effort to optimize my mind and body to be an elite warrior, and here I stand in a fucking makeup store, guarding mascara, checking my watch to see how long it will be until my break. I hate myself. I hate what I have become. *Fucking pathetic.*

Another customer passes me without looking up. I take a deep breath and do another sweep of the store, looking for anything out of place, any behaviors that might indicate that someone is planning to do something wrong. I'm hoping for a terrorist attack, a jewelry heist, even a fucking active shooter. *Nothing.* A large woman with a phone sandwiched between her ear and shoulder bumps into my leg and doesn't even notice.

Sure, move along. Don't mind me. I'm not a human or anything, just a pathetic gargoyle.

At first, I'm angry at her, and then I'm angry at myself. Why am I acting like a judgy, arrogant asshole when it's not her responsibility or anyone else's to know who I am and what I'm capable of? I may have proven myself in the military world, but I'm nobody here in the civilian world, at least not yet. In the civilian world, I'm unproven, a beginner, only capable of guarding a MAC Cosmetics store until I prove myself worthy of more. No one in the civilian world will ever understand what I'm capable of. No one will ever know what I've seen and done. They don't know what they don't know.

Even so, I'd let them blow my other arm to raw hamburger meat if it would give back even a shred of the dignity and self-respect I used to have for myself. The voice of the Warrior in me is still there, telling me to keep going, put one foot in front of the other, and build a new life for myself. But the voice is quieter than it was before. *"Pitiful. Worthless. Pathetic."* The Destroyer is louder now.

I look around the store at all the happy faces and suddenly feel like an outsider in the very society I call home. I see a woman sitting on a tall black chair, smiling as the makeup artist brushes her cheeks with blush, preparing her for a night out. I see the two teenage girls giggling in the discount section. I see a mother, grandmother, and small toddler listening intently to a sales pitch about a new line of products. All of them are blissfully unaware of the dark, cruel world that exists beyond their own.

It's stupid that I'm irritated by it, and now I hate myself for that too. After all, isn't that why guys like me exist? To face evil so that others can live their lives blissfully unaware? I hate my own righteous resentment. *Geez, I'm an asshole.* I can lay down my irritation, that I can do. But I cannot escape the feeling that I don't fit in, can't relate, and feel like an outsider in the very country I've devoted my life to. And I'm not sure that I ever will. I hear people say all the time that it takes time to "reintegrate" into civilian society, but I don't think I ever integrated in the first place. Even as a kid, I'm not sure I ever felt blissfully unaware. The world was always a dark and dangerous place in my eyes—a place where catastrophe lurks around every corner, a place where only the vigilant survive.

I joined the military when I was a teenager, and it's been my entire world since then—my social life, my metric system of success, and the deciding factor in every major decision I've ever made. I'm not resentful; at least, I don't want to think that I am. No one asked me to make the sacrifices I did or devote myself to public service. I went into that recruitment office and signed my name on that sheet of paper. I willingly made the decision to do what I did. So why am I angry? Nobody owes me shit.

Still, I can't escape the feeling that I've stepped into a world I will never fit into. People always assume that I feel better, safer, and calmer now that I don't have to be in the high-stress environments that I once inhabited. The truth is that I miss it. Because this environment, filled with suburban houses, chain restaurants, cotton-candy talk shows, and happy, blissfully unaware people—it makes me feel like I want to pull my hair out. I feel like an alien in my own country, like a superhero who's lost his powers and his home. The worst part is that I know I'll never get to feel what it's like to use my superpowers again. I feel like an alien whose home world has been destroyed. No one will ever know the man I was or the life I lived. It's gone, all gone. But I already knew that. I knew it was gone that night in the Med Shed when I saw just how damaged my arm was. This isn't new information; this isn't breaking news. I'm such an idiot. Why can't I just fucking put all this behind me?

I'll build a new life; I know I will. I'll get my shit together. I'll be the gargoyle in the MAC store until I can prove myself in the civilian world. I'll stand in roomfuls of happy, blissfully unaware people and force a smile on my face. I'll nod along in conversations that seem meaningless and talk about the bucktooth shark that ate my arm. I'll play a happy character that everyone wants me to play. I'll do it. *But will I ever stop feeling alone?*

CHAPTER 15
THAT'S NOT HOW IT FEELS

2008

WHEN THE EARLY MORNING SUNLIGHT hits my eyes, I immediately feel a surge of panic. I grab my phone from the nightstand. It's six o'clock on Sunday morning, and I still haven't heard from Vanessa. We both agreed that she's supposed to text or call if she's going to party after her shift or get home late. That was the deal. We made that deal so I wouldn't have to worry. And in all the years since she started dancing, she's never missed the cue.

I dial her number and hold the phone to my ear. On the third ring, a knot forms in my stomach. I'm worried. Maybe there's a good explanation for everything. Maybe she just forgot her phone, didn't charge it, or put it on silent. I try to calm my mind, but I can't shake the uneasiness. I turn over on my side and close my eyes, but I damn well know I won't be able to sleep. I sit up and call again. Time passes, and I'm not sure how long it is before I hear the door click and light footsteps approaching. *She's here. She's okay.*

The bedroom door opens quietly; it's clear that she thinks I'm asleep.

"Where the fuck have you been? It's six a.m. and you didn't call?" I waste no time in asking.

She looks tired; she's obviously had a long night. She tells me something about needing to go somewhere, about her phone, and why she couldn't call. It makes sense, *sort of.* But something isn't right. There's a look on her face, an emptiness in her eyes, a tone in her voice that's different than before. I ask another question, and another.

"Look, I'm exhausted. It was a long night. I just want to sleep," she says after explaining everything. I know she's right. She's had a long night, and I've been grilling her since the moment she walked in. I leave her to sleep and head to the kitchen to make breakfast and take my daily dose of pain medication. I head to my office and try to work, but my mind is distracted. Something is different. I feel a shift taking place—almost imperceptible but major nonetheless. I replay every word Vanessa said, every detail of her story, searching for discrepancies. Something is not right. In fact, something is very *wrong*.

When she wakes up hours later, her expression is serious, almost sad. "Tyler, I need to tell you something," she says, and the hollow look in her eyes makes me dread whatever is coming next. She drops one puzzle piece and then another, and I begin to fit them together until I understand the big picture. She left the club with a guy, and something happened between them. She's crying now, and I'm trying to process what I'm hearing. It takes a minute for the truth to sink in. *My girlfriend cheated on me.*

My hands begin to shake, and my whole body feels intensely cold. People always talk about having physical reactions to stress, and I've never understood what they meant. In all my years in the military, in active combat, and even on the day my whole damn arm was blown off, I'd never felt my palms sweat or my heart rate skyrocket. I'd never had tunnel vision or shaky hands. The closest I ever got to that feeling was during that little Fallujah traffic jam.

Back then, I hardly noticed any difference in my body whether knocking in a door or grabbing a burger. Now, I can't seem to stop the shaking, and it's pissing me off. I stand and begin to pace the room, hoping it will help. The movement is enough to distract her from seeing my shaking hands, but I still can't make them stop. I need a drink. I need to take a pill. I need *something*.

Vanessa apologizes profusely and says she never meant for any of it to happen. She tells me she loves me, wants to be with me, and I can see the truth of her words reflected in her eyes. As she talks and cries, a floodgate opens, and the current that is unleashed carries so much more than just the events of the previous night. The dam that has held back years of pain is broken, and for the first time, I see it. I see *her*. While I was at war with the voices in my head and the emptiness in my soul, she lost the man she loved.

I am barely a fragment of the man who chased her down on the sidewalk in Dallas and flew across the country just to take her on a date. I'm not the Warrior out conquering the world, pursuing and protecting her. I'm the loser playing video games in my home office, so stuck in my own depression that I haven't really been able to see her in a very long time. I'm angry that she cheated on me. And I'm angry and disgusted with myself, because I know I've done very little to be a man worthy of her love or attention.

As I stare at her tear-stained face, I think of all the times she has cared for me when I wasn't capable of caring for her. She never once made me feel like an inconvenience for my injury or less of a man for my scars. She accepted me, helped me, and loved me. She was attentive to my every need. More times than I can count, she threw a life raft into that vast sea of depression when I was drowning.

I hate her for what she's done, but how can I blame her? I don't say much as I look into her eyes. I don't know exactly what to say.

"Listen, maybe this could be good for us in the end," she says, with a little light in her eyes. "Maybe we both need the freedom to explore ourselves more. Maybe we should have an open relationship for a while."

I don't know how to respond. It's all too much to process at once. She's waiting for me to say something, to react to what she's saying, but with so many thoughts in my head, I can't seem to form a sentence. I feel angry, helpless, worthless—and desperately afraid of being alone. When I look into her eyes, I can still see the reflection of the man I used to be. She knows that man; she remembers him like I do. And she believes that I will be him again. She is the last shred of evidence I have left that proves I haven't become obsolete and useless, that I still have some worth and value, at least enough to earn the beautiful woman by my side. I don't want to lose that. I *can't* lose that.

I hate her for cheating, hate the thought of another man enjoying her as only I have since we've been together. The thought makes me want to punch a hole through the fucking wall and maybe through that bastard's nose—but I can't do that. The woman in front of me stayed strong and didn't give up on me or stop caring for me when she had every right to. The woman in front of me had a sheltered childhood and didn't have the chance to explore the world and herself or collect experiences like I did before meeting me. She lived her whole life caring for others, especially me. She spent her whole life living inside the restraints of expectation, and she's finally shedding her skin, experiencing a new, wild, and free version of herself. I know I need time to put myself back together. Maybe we both need time. We're partners, we're coconspirators, we're Bonnie and Fucking Clyde, right? She'll sow her wild oats, I'll get my shit together and hook up with other girls in the process, and we'll come back stronger than before.

By the time night falls, we've agreed to have an open relationship. We finish talking and head to bed, but I lie awake for hours, unable to sleep. No matter how many times I tell myself that I owe this to her after all she's done, that we'll be better and stronger for the change, and that I should be happy to have a beautiful girlfriend who cares for me, plus the potential to bang as many hot girls as I want, I don't feel good at all. My world is upside down, and I can't find the strength to right it again. A deep lethargy settles over me. I feel exhausted and drained, yet sleep eludes me.

The worst part is that I was just beginning to feel better. I was starting to find my way and piece together the fragments of my identity—at least, I thought I was. I know I can be the man she needs me to be. I *am* that man, I know I am. Over the past few months, I've been trying. Really trying. But perhaps it's too little too late. The damage is done, and I need to find a way to salvage things.

The next morning, I stuff a handful of T-shirts and two pairs of jeans into a backpack and hug Vanessa goodbye. I'm going to stay with my parents for a few days. I know she'll be going out with the same guy she saw Saturday night. This is our new reality, and I can't be angry about it now. But I also can't stay in our house, lying in our bed, thinking about her being with another man. I'll go insane.

When I arrive at my parents' home, they chat about the weather and the rising price of gas. I nod along but can't focus on a word they're saying. I feel like I'm losing control, that everything is changing and spinning around me, and I can't find a way to stop it. I have no idea what to do. For the first time, I think I need help.

◄►

The waiting room of the VA hospital is filled with balding heads, white beards, and liver-spotted skin. This will be my first time seeking help from a mental health professional, and as I wait for my number to be called and my appointment with the therapist to begin, I'm not feeling particularly comfortable with my decision. It's Tuesday morning, and Vanessa will be spending the night with him two days from now. Even the thought of it makes me feel lost inside. I still hate therapists, counselors, psychiatrists, and the like, but I'm desperate.

The man beside me blows his nose into a Kleenex the way my grandpa used to. It seems that all old men develop the same set of noises at some point in life. He's wearing a hat that says VIETNAM 1967, covering what I can only presume is a mop of gray hair, judging by his sprouting ears.

Another man exits the office, wearing a worn yellow polo shirt. He's stooped over and walking with a cane, causing the overhead fluorescent lights to reflect off his shiny bald head. I'm the youngest person in the waiting room by at least thirty years. Mr. Yellow Polo pauses and stares at Mr. '67 Hat for a moment.

"You were in there in sixty-seven, huh?" he asks loudly, though no one seems to mind. The man beside me leans forward, sizing up Mr. Yellow Polo.

"Yes, sir, I was," Mr. '67 Hat responds with a nod.

That nod turns into a full-blown conversation. "Which area were you stationed? The whatchamacallit Firebase? Me too! What a coincidence, what a small world. Were you involved in blankety-blank firefight? Did you ever meet Colonel So-and-So?"

I know I'm supposed to feel warm and fuzzy watching two old veterans connect and reminisce, but I don't. The more they talk, the more disgusted I feel. An image plays in my mind: me slowly shuffling out of that office, only to see an old man with a hat that says AFGHANISTAN 2004 on it. *"Which area were you stationed? The whatchamacallit Firebase? Me too! What a coincidence, what a small world. Were you involved in blankety-blank firefight? Did you ever meet Colonel So-and-So?"*

The more I listen, the angrier I feel. But then irritation gives way to something else—a deep sense of fear that begins to gnaw at me. I've tried to put my military career behind me, but even if I don't talk about it, it doesn't change the fact that it happened. I'm not scared of turning into one of these old vets; I'm afraid that maybe I already have and just haven't faced up to it yet. I am a veteran now. *Fuck.* I've known that for three years, but the reality of it never really settled in until this very moment. The more I think about it and the more I listen to the old men talk, the emptier I feel.

"Number twenty-nine?" That's my cue. The nurse beckons, and I get up to follow her down the hallway to the counselor's office. Behind the desk sits a tired-looking woman, likely in her late forties. She stands as I enter, offers a polite hello, then drops back into her chair, which squeaks upon impact.

She begins our session with a few routine questions. This is my prompt to start talking, and I comply. If she's really going to help me, I might as well give her all the key pieces of information she needs to do her job effectively. As I launch into the forty-five-minute version of my life story, I notice her eyes shifting more than once to my arm—those blood-red scars snaking around it are hard to miss. I know it's distracting, but I want her to focus on what I'm saying. I tell her about the injury, my relationship with Vanessa, and the affair. *"My girlfriend had an affair…"*

As I say the words for the first time out loud, I feel emotion rising in my chest. When I finish talking, I feel naked and exposed. It's unpleasant to hear your whole life summed up in a forty-five-minute elevator pitch. Tears begin streaming down my face, and I can't control them. I'm too overwhelmed to be angry at myself, and the worst part is that I don't know what to do. I've always known what to do. Give me a problem, and I'll find a solution. Give me an obstacle, and I'll get around it, over it, underneath it, or fucking through it. But I can't seem to find my way through this one. I've never doubted myself or lost faith in my ability to think clearly and logically until today.

The therapist nods and takes a few minutes to digest what I've said. Then she asks several questions, all related to my injury. I answer them, but the line of questioning seems pointless. I need help with my relationship. I need to understand why I don't feel like the man I once was. This isn't about an injured arm; this is about a fractured identity.

"Tyler, I believe you are dealing with the side effects of PTSD," she says, leaning back in her chair. I know what she's talking about, or at least I think I do. I've seen *First Blood* and *Rambo* before and heard people talk about it, but I'm not exactly sure what it is, how it works, or what it feels like.

"Can you tell me exactly what it is?"

She nods briefly and takes a breath.

"Post-traumatic stress disorder, or PTSD, is a psychiatric disorder that often occurs in people who have experienced or witnessed a traumatic event. This doesn't just happen to veterans; it happens to anyone who goes through a traumatic event. It could be combat, sexual assault, a natural disaster, a car accident, or many other things. After the event, many people develop symptoms like acute stress disorder, adjustment disorder, disinhibited social engagement disorder, and reactive attachment disorder."

I nod, processing everything she's saying.

"Okay, so can you tell me what PTSD feels like?"

"Well, typically, you'll have flashbacks," she begins.

"And what's the difference between a memory and a flashback?" I've never heard of anyone having a flashback before.

"Well, you might feel like the event is happening all over again. You may have trouble sleeping or experience nightmares, angry outbursts, or other extreme reactions. You could have frightening thoughts, trouble concentrating, avoidance of memories or thoughts related to the traumatic event, problems remembering things, and startle easily. It varies from person to person."

She smiles kindly.

"But that's not my problem. What I'm dealing with doesn't match what you're describing."

She smiles politely again. "Like I said, PTSD can manifest a bit differently for each person."

I'm not satisfied. "But I don't have any of these symptoms. I know my arm looks bad, but I've never had a single nightmare about it, never experienced a flashback. I don't startle easily or feel the need to avoid memories from combat. I'm not lying awake at night reliving some intense firefight and getting all bent out of shape about it. Honestly, I fucking miss it! I know I'm dealing with something; I know I'm at a low point right now, but I don't think it was caused by one traumatic event."

She pauses and listens, then begins again, patiently explaining why she thinks I'm wrong. But I'm still not convinced. Frustrated, I push back.

"Look, you keep telling me what it's supposed to be, and I keep telling you what it is. I know what I'm experiencing, and it doesn't match what you're describing. It just doesn't add up."

She smiles at me with a look that seems to say, "You'll understand someday; you're just too traumatized and hurt to see the truth."

"I'd like to schedule an appointment for you to see our psychiatrist tomorrow afternoon. I think it would be helpful," she says, bringing the session to a close. I nod in agreement. I don't feel like I got the help I was hoping for, but I figure I might as well follow through with the entire treatment plan before making any judgments. "Sure, put me down for the psychiatrist too."

The moment my eyes crack open on Thursday morning, I'm already done with the day. Today is the day Vanessa will be spending the night with him. I try not to think about it or indulge in images of what they might be doing, but I can't stop. The worst part is that it's not just anger I feel rising in me. I feel weak, worthless, and exhausted by the thought of living through the day. It will be my first time taking the medication the psychiatrist prescribed yesterday. The psychiatrist talked with me about PTSD, echoing just about everything the therapist had said the day before. This time, debate was a luxury beyond my reach, and I sat there like a prisoner of my own torrent of emotions and cried fat, ugly tears of shame and sadness.

I feel deeply fatigued as I get out of bed and walk to the kitchen. Eight orange bottles of medication sit on the counter, and I just stare at them for a while. Eight bottles. Seems like a lot, especially on top of all the pain meds the doctors still have me on. But then again, I'm no expert. I read the labels carefully, pull out the recommended dosage for each one, and swallow them.

Vanessa and I are going to get through this. We are going to be okay. I try to reassure myself, but I don't feel confident. At least I'm getting professional help now, which is a huge step in the right direction—the first step toward making myself healthy, strong, and capable of caring for the woman I love. Within an hour, I feel dizzy and sleepy. I can hardly think. I lie down on my parents' couch, still counting down the hours until I know she'll be with him again. Another hour passes, and I doze in and out of sleep. When I wake, there's a puddle of drool on my chest, dribbling down my chin. I lift my arm to wipe it away, but it feels so heavy that I can hardly move it. I stare at the ceiling, feeling nearly paralyzed. I slowly reach toward my phone and tap the screen. It's 8:00 p.m., which means she is with *him*.

And why wouldn't she be?

I'm no superhero, no warrior. I'm a drugged-up, crippled veteran, drooling on a couch, thinking about the woman I love being in the arms of another man tonight. I told myself that I was agreeing to this whole open relationship thing to pay her back for all the years she cared for me, but the truth is I'm just too weak to say no. I wipe the drool from my face and stumble as I try to stand up to get a glass of water from the kitchen. The room is spinning, my coordination is all off, and I feel like a walking zombie. *So this is the cure for PTSD? This is the professional prescription? Fuck no. I'm going to fucking stand up and fight. Tomorrow, the pills are going in the trash, and I'm never stepping foot in the VA hospital again. This isn't me... This isn't me... This isn't me...* The room swirls and then everything goes black as my weary eyes close. *This isn't me...*

CHAPTER 16
INTO THE FIRE

TICK, TICK, TICK.

The turn signal echoes through the dark car as I prepare to turn onto Sunset Boulevard from Beverly Hills, continuing for several seconds before I realize how idiotic I am. It's 2:45 in the morning and there's no one behind me to signal to. *You idiot.*

I mentally kick myself for my own stupidity, though I know it's less about stupidity and more about exhaustion. I've been on my feet for fifteen hours straight, bodyguarding yet another celebrity—something I've been doing for the past year. It's a step up from guarding MAC stores, that's for sure, but it's still just as tiring. Tonight's "person of interest" was an A-list musician, and now she's safe and sound in her hotel after a long performance and hectic after-party. I'm relieved that the day is over.

The streets are empty, not a car in sight. It's strange to see Sunset Boulevard this way, like a scene from a post-apocalyptic movie, where the remains of a famous landmark linger long after humans have disappeared. Sometimes I think the world would be a lot more beautiful if it weren't for the particularly destructive species known as the human race.

My eyes and mind wander, but I'm too tired to focus on anything. I know Vanessa is still working, so there's no point in calling her at this hour. I'll reach out in the morning when I wake up—it's not like I have anything important to say now anyway. I'm sure she'll stay the night with that billionaire she's been seeing a lot lately. She doesn't need the money—she earns more in a single night than my entire monthly income—which makes me think she might actually really like the guy. Good for her, I guess. You'd think I'd be used to this whole open relationship thing after a year, but it still bothers me. Another night, I might be tempted to fan the flames of my irritation, but I'm just too tired to care right now.

My buddy has offered me his couch as a crash point when I work late in LA, and with the increase in bodyguarding contracts, all I can think about is how good it will feel to be horizontal after being on my feet all day. The empty road has a hypnotic effect, as vacant as my mind.

My eyes are heavy, and my head droops as I drive until a loud noise jolts me wide awake. The silence is shattered by the wailing of sirens. I look out the window but see nothing—no vehicles, no flashing lights, just dark buildings, and empty roads. As the sirens grow louder, I realize I'm getting closer to the source of the noise, but I still can't see a thing.

Then, out of nowhere, a fire truck hurtles into my lane, heading straight for me. Although there's ample time to pull over and avoid a collision, the unexpected appearance of the fire truck is startling. I quickly survey my surroundings. To the right, an orange glow and thick smoke capture my attention. They're coming from a restaurant nestled among a row of shops in a mini mall at the intersection of Crescent Heights and Sunset. I'm transfixed by the sight of the orange flames consuming the building, dismantling the structure before me. *Holy shit.*

The ground is moving beneath me. My feet hit the pavement, legs pumping, propelling me toward the rapidly intensifying orange glow ahead. It grows larger and more vivid with every second. I keep my focus dead ahead, eyes locked on the source of the chaos. Smoke and flames billow from a shattered window, clawing their way into the darkening sky. I'm almost there now, about fifty to seventy yards to go.

Movement in my peripheral vision catches my attention. To my left, a trio of firefighters orchestrates their response beside the fire truck. To my right, another firefighter falls into synchronized step with me. Despite his cumbersome load—a heavy hose dragging behind him—our strides are almost identical. For a fraction of a second, he turns his head and locks eyes with me. His expression is one of confusion.

But why would he be confused? We're in this together. We're both running toward the…fire. *I'm running toward a fire! Why the hell am I running toward a fire?* My mind is catching up to a scene that my body has already entered. The realization hits all at once. I'm not in my vehicle anymore. I'm running toward the fire, and I have no memory of even getting out of my car. Something isn't right. I stop dead in my tracks, and the firefighter keeps running.

I'm rooted in place now, but my mind is blank. I'm only aware of the sensations in my body—my chest rising and falling, the rhythm of my heart. Every inch of me is on high alert, ready to act on pure instinct, but my mind is completely calm.

Then another feeling washes over me, more a memory than a physical sensation. I've been here before. I've lived this moment, or at least some variation of it. Everything about this moment is familiar, but I can't quite place why. I hear the unmistakable sound of the quickie saw and watch as sparks fly like confetti as its blade cuts through the door. From the tone, I can tell we're almost through, we're almost inside. But wait, there is no *we*. There are three firefighters about to breach the doorway to put out the fire, and then there's me, standing in the middle of a parking lot in my bodyguarding suit, just listening.

What the hell am I doing here?

It's all coming together now—the orange glow, the confused expression on the firefighter's face, my pumping legs, the rapid breathing. I shouldn't be here. Not in this place, not in this situation. So why does every fiber of my being scream with an instinctual sense that I belong? Not in a mini-mall parking lot, but in *this* body, *this* mind, *this* environment. As my heart rate begins to even out and my breath slows from sprinting, my conscious mind returns. *What the hell am I doing here? I need to leave. I need to get back in my truck and get the fuck out of here.*

I catch a glimpse of the firefighters attaching a hose to a hydrant as I turn and walk away from the scene. The sounds muffle as I shut the truck door and click my seatbelt into place. The clock reads 3:00 a.m. I lean my head back and draw in a deep breath. The rush of excitement and anticipation still courses through me. The feeling is strong and familiar, and every part of me is drinking it in.

Then, all at once, a wave of deep sadness washes over me, mixing with the excitement and morphing into a new emotion I've never experienced before. I shift into gear and drive away from the fire, then pull into an empty parking lot just down the road.

Something is trying to connect inside my brain, but I don't know what it is. The feeling is consuming me, and I need to concentrate. When the vehicle is in park and everything is still, I stare straight ahead into the dark sky, deep in thought.

I don't need anyone to tell me that what I just did isn't normal. I'm acutely aware that suddenly waking up to find yourself running toward a burning building is not a typical experience. I acted on automatic pilot, as if my body and will were separate entities. I need to understand what just happened and why, because I have a strong feeling that whatever I'm about to discover about myself is important. I'm embarrassed by my strange behavior—being the weird guy running next to a firefighter in the middle of the night—but I need to get past that to grasp what's going on. It's a clue. I know it's a clue.

The truth is I've been searching for clues ever since I went to the VA hospital. There's an unknown, faceless enemy I'm up against, a force greater and stronger than I've ever faced before, destroying me from the inside out. I feel disconnected from myself and the world around me. I feel broken. If I could just see it, name it, and understand it, I know I could find a way to overcome it.

"Post-traumatic stress disorder..." The VA counselor's voice rings in my ears. *"Tyler, I believe you are dealing with the side effects of PTSD."* That's what everyone seems to think this unnamed beast is. *"So can you tell me what PTSD feels like?"* I just want to name the beast and understand its power so I can overcome it.

"Frightening thoughts, trouble concentrating, avoidance of memories, thoughts or feelings associated with traumatic events, problems remembering things, startling easily..." She, along with everyone else who specializes in veteran care, is handing me a puzzle piece, expecting the diagnosis to match the contours of my experiences, and I want it to. God, I want it to fit. But it just doesn't. No matter how hard I try, I can't make it fit.

"Look, you keep telling me what it's supposed to be, and I keep telling you what it is. I know what I'm experiencing…" It's close now, and I can feel it. The naked truth is becoming clearer. *"You keep telling me what it's supposed to be, and I keep telling you what it is. I know what I'm experiencing…"* I replay the events of the last few hours in my mind. There's a clue here, something big I'm about to understand. *Concentrate.* I close my eyes and I feel myself running toward the fire again. I see the orange glow and hear the roar of the quickie saw. I feel it again. *Alert. Awake. Alive.*

And how did that make me feel? *Fucking fantastic.*

Then another thought hits me like a bolt of electricity. Running toward that fire was the best I've felt since getting blown up. If I were traumatized by a stressful event, wouldn't I want to avoid everything associated with that life? Wouldn't I feel a deep aversion to the sights, smells, and sounds related to those memories?

"This doesn't just happen to veterans; it happens to anyone who goes through a traumatic event. It could be combat, sexual assault, a natural disaster, a car wreck, or many other things."

But the girl who was raped in a bathroom stall at a club feels anxiety when she smells alcohol or hears someone enter a bathroom after she's inside, so she avoids bars and crowded places. The guy who was in a car accident feels anxious when his wife drives fast or slams on the brakes suddenly, and avoids getting behind the wheel. The man who survived an earthquake experiences anxiety when he feels shaking or vibrating. *That's* PTSD. So it must also stand to reason that combat veterans would feel anxious when experiencing reminders of the past. But when I saw that fire and heard the sound of the quickie saw, every part of my body turned *on*. I felt no fear, aversion, avoidance, or resistance; I felt just the opposite. *I loved it.* With every cell in my body, I loved it—and I miss it.

I ran to that fire because I knew I could help. I was built for that moment, designed for that environment—the chaos and high stress like oxygen to my lungs, a reminder of the world I was built for, the one I lived and thrived in, not this place that leaves me feeling like a shell of the man I once was.

But I'm not averse or resistant to the events of my past or the high-stress environment. I miss them.

That's why PTSD doesn't fit.

I'm not struggling because I'm trying to avoid the memory of the stressful environment I used to operate in; I'm struggling because I desperately want to be back in it again. I don't have PTSD; *I have LTSD (lack of traumatic stress disorder)*.

I *need* "traumatic" stress to feel comfortable, and when I don't have it, I feel the need to create it.

That's why the puzzle piece doesn't fit. Maybe it's because most therapists, counselors, and psychiatrists have never experienced active combat like veterans have. Maybe their framework for understanding these experiences can only be compared to traumatic events like a car crash or an assault. No one wants to relive an assault or a serious collision. "It was the worst day of my life," they say. But the worst day of my life wasn't the day I got blown up. My worst day wasn't fighting to survive a firefight or breaching the doorway of an Al-Qaeda member's house. These aren't the memories I'm running from or lie in bed at night wishing I could forget. These are the moments that lit me up and made me feel alive, when I acted with clarity and instinct, the days when I felt I had purpose and passion, the days when I felt like my existence mattered and I was a part of something bigger than myself.

But now I'm digging for more clues, probing into the recesses of my mind to understand.

I miss more than just the environment—there's more to it than that. I miss who I was within the environment. There's something about a chaotic environment that activates something inside of me, like a superpower. Now, it's all coming together…one piece after another. Chaotic environments make me hypervigilant. When I'm hypervigilant, I feel safe, protected, and invincible. I feel alive. I can think clearly and act aggressively, and I can take control of any situation.

Give me a stressful, chaotic environment, activate my superpower, and I become an island of calm amid the chaos. I'm not afflicted by haunting memories of high stress and chaos, I'm experiencing withdrawal from it. I'm addicted to chaos. I'm addicted to the man I was capable of being amid the chaos. I have no idea what this means, and I have no idea what the implications of this strange night will be. But for the first time, something is clicking into place, a puzzle piece that fits the contours of my feelings and experiences. I haven't solved the mystery, but I've discovered a key that is opening a new world of understanding.

I notice a light shade of pink gathering behind the dark, empty buildings in front of me. I look at the clock again, and it reads 06:00. I've been sitting here for three hours.

CHAPTER 17
COLLATERAL DAMAGE

"TYLER, WHAT THE HELL IS this?"

Vanessa is holding my phone, pure rage shooting from her eyes. I'm confused. We arrived in LA a few hours ago and are unloading our bags at my buddy's house, which he offered to let us use for a few days. This is our chance to have some alone time, and I've been looking forward to it. I study Vanessa's face before glancing at the phone. Anger, hurt, and betrayal are all evident in her eyes, but I can't for the life of me think of anything on my phone that could cause such a reaction.

"TYLER!" This time, she shoves the phone into my hand. A text message exchange between me and a girl she used to dance with is on the screen. I scan the messages, then look back at Vanessa.

"So?"

"So? What do you mean SO?? You two hooked up, it's clear."

I nod, still not fully grasping the situation.

"We've been in an open relationship for more than a year. This isn't a big secret."

But her anger doesn't subside; it intensifies. Within minutes, we're in a heated argument, and I feel my blood boiling.

"Why didn't you just tell me about you and her? I thought we were partners! I tell you EVERYTHING!"

A look of pain and betrayal flashes across her face.

"Yeah, you do tell me about you and all the guys you're hooking up with, but guess what, I DON'T WANT TO KNOW. And I did nothing wrong. WE ARE IN AN OPEN RELATIONSHIP. We have been FOR OVER A YEAR!"

My brain feels like it's about to explode.

"Tyler, I can't do this anymore. I am done. And I mean DONE. I'm breaking up with you."

My mouth drops open in shock.

"Are you fucking serious? After everything we've been through, you're just going to throw it all away?"

I can't wrap my mind around what's happening. I thought we were bulletproof by now. I know our relationship has changed since we started seeing other people, but we're still best friends and partners in crime. We're still Bonnie and Fucking Clyde, just in a different way. She's stuck by me through every low point, and I've stuck by her as she discovered new sides of herself, even when it made me deeply uncomfortable. We moved across the country together, cried together, built together, bled together. We stay together no matter what. Now anger and pain rise in my chest like vomit.

She looks down at the floor and then back up at me.

"Tyler, I'm BREAKING UP WITH YOU."

It's not her words that hit me first; it's the look in her eyes. I've seen countless shades of color and feeling in those eyes over the years we've been together, but I've never seen this before.

Holy shit, I think she's actually serious.

"I need you to drive me back to Las Vegas, NOW!" she says firmly, starting to reload her things into her bags.

"ARE YOU FUCKING JOKING? You're just going to show up here, break up with me over some stupid text messages, and then ask me to drive you all the way back to Las Vegas?"

The injustice of it all eats at me. It can't end like this, not after everything we've endured, not for this reason. Bitterness and resentment spill into my voice as I protest against her request, but she's insistent. To be honest, I'm not sure what else to do but get in the car and start driving.

The tension in the air is so thick it could be sliced with a knife and served up with all its bitterness and anger. We drive in silence for no more than sixty seconds before another round of toxic accusations spews from Vanessa. It becomes clear she's been keeping a hidden ledger of her own—everything she dislikes about me, complete with graphic descriptions of *what kind of man I am*. She intends to use our uninterrupted four-hour drive to go through every single fault—one by one. Each sentence is another piece of kindling on the fire. *Jesus, this day couldn't get any worse*, I think, until a blinking light catches my eye. The car is low on gas, very low. I look at the road ahead. *Fuck*. Not a sign of civilization in sight—just open road, trees, and Vanessa's voice eroding my patience with each angry comment.

"And you never...and you always..."

Another five minutes pass. Still no gas station. I clear my throat, preparing to stick my head into the lion's mouth. "We need to find a gas station. Looks like we're almost out."

She pops her head across the console to see for herself.

"ARE YOU FUCKING SERIOUS RIGHT NOW? YOU DIDN'T EVEN CHECK? YOU SHOULD HAVE FUCKING KNOWN THAT WE WERE ABOUT TO DRIVE FOUR FUCKING HOURS. MY GOD!"

My face feels hot with anger, and my hands shake with adrenaline.

"THIS is exactly the kind of thing I'm talking about! I need a man who will take care of me, Tyler. I don't want to have to worry about everything all the time. I just want to be taken care of!!"

The empty tank of gas has become Exhibit A in the Museum of Tyler's Fuckups, and we're taking a long tour through it. I'm about to lose my shit.

"So let me get this right. Is the problem that I hooked up with a girl WHILE WE WERE HAVING AN OPEN RELATIONSHIP, or is it that I'm not the *'kind of man'* who remembers to fill a gas tank? The issues shift every thirty seconds, and logic seems completely unnecessary in this discussion.

"I need a man who handles things and knows how to LEAD! I need a man who—"

"THEN WHY DON'T YOU JUST SHUT THE FUCK UP?" My voice is raw from screaming, my veins pulsing with hot rage. "IF YOU DON'T WANT TO BE IN CHARGE, THEN STOP TRYING TO BE IN CHARGE AND JUST SHUT THE FUCK UP!"

I've never shouted at a woman before, not like this, but I've lost the ability to hold back any longer. Vanessa falls silent for a few minutes, looking at me with pure hatred, but the silence doesn't last. Within minutes, we're back on the tour of the Museum of Tyler's Fuckups. I shut my mouth, hoping that by some miracle we'll make it to a gas station. I seem more shaken by my loss of control than she is.

When I see a sign for a town ten miles ahead, I feel a flicker of hope. I just want to get through the day, get this over with. I need silence to hear myself think because I'm reeling. How could we have been so close to the end and not seen it coming? How did we miss the warning signs? How could we endure so much and break up now? I really thought we were stronger than everything. I see a gas station up ahead. We're either going to make it, or I'll push us the rest of the way. *Somehow, we'll find a way.*

When the tank is filled, I go inside and buy two bottles of water. I return to the car and toss one to her without a word. She catches it, unscrews the top, and takes a sip as we start driving again. That's when it hits me: This is the thing that's about to change. This won't be a two-bottle life anymore. There will be no more *us*, only *me*. I don't feel sad exactly; I'm still too angry and indignant for that. But I'm deeply aware that everything is about to change, and I really, really don't want to be alone.

When we arrive at our house, Vanessa exits the car immediately, grabs her bags, and disappears inside. I put the vehicle in reverse, back out of the driveway, and begin the four-hour drive back to Los Angeles. Now the silence I so desperately craved is finally here, but when it settles in, I feel empty and exhausted. Maybe the road signs were there, maybe we just didn't want to see them. My mind wanders, veering this way and that, pausing to formulate winning responses to her arguments and accusations, only to realize that it's all pointless anyway. She's gone. We're done.

There are so many implications to this new development—both big and small. We own two houses together: the one we live in and another rental property. Both will need to be sold. Our lives are so intertwined that it seems nearly impossible to unravel them without ripping apart at the seams. After all the pain, jealousy, hardship, and changes we've been through, after all the chaos we've weathered together…*Chaos*. What do you know? There it is again. *Chaos*.

Maybe, somewhere deep inside me, I needed the highs and lows, the ups and downs, the crazy and the chaos in our relationship. Maybe I didn't realize how much I'd neglected her for so long. Maybe I just couldn't get my shit together fast enough. Maybe I pushed her away because I didn't feel like I deserved to be happy anyway. Maybe it's all of the above—I still don't really know. What I do know is that this war inside me runs deep, and there is no part of my life that hasn't suffered collateral damage from the battle.

CHAPTER 18

SQUARE ONE

I WAKE UP TO THE sound of moaning. At first, it's just a woman's voice, barely more than a breathy exhale, but it quickly builds into a high whimper of pleasure. A low, throaty, masculine grunt mingles with hers, and then both voices grow louder. I'm wide awake now. This isn't a porno playing on somebody's DVR; this is the real deal. Someone is having sweaty, passionate sex on the balcony next door and they don't care who knows it. I grab one of the decorative couch pillows beside me and shove it over my head, trying to drown out the noise. My buddy is probably sleeping through the entire ordeal in his bedroom, but there's nowhere to escape from my spot on the living room couch. The woman's voice rises higher, and the pillow isn't doing much to block the sound.

Shut up, you inconsiderate freaks.

Images of naked bodies flash in my mind, and I'm disgusted by it. I don't want to think about sex, hear someone having sex, or be reminded that I'm not having sex. I don't want another reminder of the fact that I'm completely alone. I roll over and close my eyes, hoping it will help sleep come, though I know damn well it won't. *God, just finish already...*

I crave the silence so I can hide in it and forget that I'm back to square one. It's hard to believe. For a while, it seemed like I was building something in life...like everything was actually coming together. I had the girl, the houses, the career. Not everything, maybe, but something. Now, I'm living alone on a couch in my buddy's house, taking bodyguarding jobs just to make ends meet. Square one. Actually, worse than square one because I'm up to my eyeballs in debt. The recession is in full swing, which means the resale value of the houses Vanessa and I bought together is worthless. So technically, I'm at *negative square one*.

The room is quiet now, and the couple next door has presumably drifted into euphoric sleep, unaware that they've stolen my chances of doing so. The thought only adds to my deep irritation. The only thing worse than standing for fifteen hours on your feet is standing for fifteen hours on your feet without having slept the night before. It's going to be a long day tomorrow. I roll over again, but the new position is even worse than the last. The lumpy pillow beneath my neck is awkward, and my back presses into the crack of the sofa. I roll again. Anxiety snakes through my body, and my mind races. Every cell is on high alert. My thoughts hover between sleep and wakefulness, prompting a stream of memories, snapshots, and random information to flash through my mind. I see every pocket and stitch of the customized vest I made for myself. I see doorways and human shapes moving in a world of NOD green. I see one mud-caked boot and then another propelling me forward on a long ruck, though I'm not sure which one. I see a black and gold Ranger pin pressing into my uniform. I see a gun. I see chargers. I see the shrink-wrapped vomit called MREs (Meals, Ready to Eat). I see helicopters. Vivid images and seemingly useless information swirl inside my tired mind. *I used to be a goddamned superhero, and now look at me.*

How is it possible to sweat, bleed, and train your way into the world's most elite class of warriors and have it count for absolutely nothing in the civilian world? Ten years, ten fucking years, and millions of dollars built my mind and body into a human machine specializing in counterterrorism, direct action, hostage rescue, and reconnaissance. I pushed myself to learn more, do more, reach the top of my game. I mastered specialized skills, completed courses, and acquired knowledge. I did it. I fucking did it, and thought I'd gotten through the hardest part and earned my spot at the top. Now, I'm lying on a couch in another man's house like a college dropout, listening to two people fucking, up to my balls in debt, and it feels like I'm starting over. It just seems wildly unfair.

"And do you have any other special skills you want to list here?" I can still see the face of the perky girl behind the desk at the office, helping me write my resume. Fuck yeah, I have special skills—hundreds of them. Skills I spent years cultivating, honing, and improving through

severe discipline and repetition. I came from a world where it all meant something, where my qualifications made me someone others respected and wanted to be. But her eyes glazed over as I listed my top skills and credentials.

"Okayyy, so I think I'm just going to write 'excellent leadership skills,'" she says when I finish speaking. All those years of investment amount to nothing but leadership skills. I could scoff at her naïveté for not understanding the value of what I've done, but the truth is she's right. Sift through all the qualifications and skills, and the only thing of value I have for the civilian world is leadership skills and the ability to be a mere bodyguard. *Such a waste. Such a fucking waste.*

Nobody sees me for who I really am—an elite warrior. I'm just the slightly depressed—okay, moderately depressed—guy with a weird arm who's living on his buddy's couch after his hot girlfriend dumped him. *Goddammit, I'm such a loser. Such a pathetic loser.*

Vanessa was the last shred of proof I had pointing to the man I used to be. And that counted for something. When I had her, it didn't matter that no one knew who I was. One look at the beauty on my arm and they knew I was somebody. Maybe my uncommon skill set doesn't earn points in the civilian world, but having a hot girlfriend sure does. But now, even that's gone. Every shred of validating evidence that I have any worth in this world is gone. The chicks are really going to love me now.

"I'm glad it's over. That girl is your kryptonite," my buddy Mike told me, and maybe he's right. Now that it's over, everything is so clear—the tender love and innocent connection we once had has transformed into a toxic mix of jealousy, revenge, and hate. Mike might be right; maybe she was my kryptonite. The closer we got, the weaker my ability to think clearly became. How many things have I agreed to, passively complied with, and found myself entangled in that go against who I am at my core? I even agreed to an open relationship. That's not me. The mere thought of another man touching her gnawed at me, made me angry, hurt, and uncomfortable. I'm just not cut out for it. Kryptonite… sounds about right. Kryptonite wasn't just radioactive material; it was a piece of Superman's home planet. I clung to Vanessa because she was a remnant, a reminder of where I came from and who I used to be, but somewhere along the way, it became toxic. So maybe it's a good thing that I'm starting over.

Square one. Scratch that...*negative square one.*

I stare at the ceiling in misery, disgusted at my own self-pity, lying here like a martyr on his deathbed, whining about how nobody understands my special skill set. Of course they don't get it, and it's not their fault. Nobody asked me to do what I did. I made that decision all on my own.

Jesus Christ, haven't I had this same conversation with myself before? The very fact that I'm back here again at this same fucking mental crossroad means I'm not learning anything. Or if I am learning something, I'm sure not changing anything.

Maybe this whole square one might be a blessing in disguise. I need to get back to basics and focus on myself for a change. As much as I'd like to blame Vanessa for my unhappiness, I know that the wreckage of my life is just collateral damage from my own internal war. I've got a lot of work to do. I've lost myself in every way. My body isn't the same, my mind isn't the same, even my personality has changed. I need to start reading, researching, and finding myself again. But haven't I been saying that for years now?

The sound of my cell phone ringing jolts me awake. At some point, I must have fallen asleep. Sunlight bounces off the coffee table and hits my gritty eyes. It's morning now, and Vanessa is calling. I answer with a polite but monotone voice, not just because of the lack of sleep but because I want her to know just how meaningless her call is to me. Tone of voice is everything in the battle for the upper hand after a breakup. Secretly, I'm relieved to hear from her. She gets straight to the point: my half of the monthly mortgage payment on the house needs to be paid. I respond with a one-word reply and hang up as quickly as I can. I'm working my ass off every day, but the debt is piling up faster than I can track.

Just hearing her voice and the reminder of the mess my life has become makes me want to slip back into another round of self-loathing.

My issues and problems are swirling together—my mental state, relationships, career, finances, you name it. So much collateral damage, but from exactly what battle? Square one or negative square one…*who the fuck cares?* Now's the time to sort it out. Now's the time to get back to basics. But haven't I been saying *that* for years now too?

CHAPTER 19
DON'T MISS A DAY

BACK IN 2002, I WAS stationed in Afghanistan as an Army Ranger at a newly established outstation near the Pakistan border, which we built from scratch. Rumor had it that a village just over ten kilometers away was harboring Al-Qaeda fighters and weapons. Most of our missions centered around tracking how and where Al-Qaeda forces were coming across the Pakistan border. Life at the outstation was as low-tech as you could get. If we wanted eyes on an area, we had to hike there—state-of-the-art equipment and drones were a distant dream. We assembled two four-man sniper teams for the trek: one team leader, one shooter, one spotter, and one JTAC (Joint Terminal Attack Controller). We estimated it would take about four days to reach the village, conduct reconnaissance, and return to base. We planned our departure for the night of the new moon, moving under cover of darkness and staying put during the day. Our advanced weaponry gave us a significant edge, but once we strapped on our NODs, we were like gods of the night. The open, arid desert terrain was our playground. A single shot from any of our weapons could reach distances our adversaries could only dream of—poor bastards would never see it coming.

On the day of departure, we geared up and formed a single-file line. As team leader, I had two primary responsibilities: navigation and avoiding Soviet land mines still scattered throughout the area. We always walked in single file to minimize the risk of triggering an explosion that could wipe out the entire team.

The first ten steps felt like a cruel joke. With over 100 pounds of gear, batteries, food, and water—our four-day supply of essentials—our loadout was fucking heavy. But we were strong. Maybe not mega-bicep gym-bro strong, but definitely pack-mule strong. Still, it sucked. About an hour in, my body started sending signals up the chain with a clear message: "Hey, this is miserable." And my body was right; it *was* miserable.

The thing is, though, I thrived on suffering. Not in a cut-your-wrist-with-a-razor way, but in pushing my body to the brink of collapse through deprivation to see if I had what it took to come out alive. That love of suffering got me through the toughest parts of training. When the guys around me showed signs of suffering—tight faces, tense muscles, barely audible groans of pain—a sick part of me came alive. The ability to control your response to pain and suffering is a powerful feeling, and I became the mightiest.

That's the thing about the military. You can be a worthless piece of shit; you can come from nothing; you can be an absolute nobody and become a hero if you're willing to sacrifice yourself for the sake of the team and endure a lot of pain and discomfort. Your value is measured by the extent of your ability to sacrifice yourself for others. You can become somebody by becoming nobody. People often focus on the glamorous parts of being an Army Ranger—conducting raids and assault missions deep inside enemy territory. Hell, I did too; that's why I signed up. But beneath the surface, it's a lot of repetition, practice, and physical suffering.

You suffer in training, and if you make it, you're stamped as *suffer-ready*. I liked feeling like one of the superheroes from my childhood comics. I liked possessing the skills I once idolized. But I also liked to suffer. It was my self-development catalyst of choice. It made me better, stronger, and feel like a goddamned man. So when my body started sending signals about an hour into the trek, saying, "Hey, this is miserable," it felt like welcoming back an old friend.

"Three, two, one, GOOOO!" The trainer's voice echoes through the room as twelve sets of hands curl around twelve barbells lined up in neat rows. Loud heavy rock music blares through the speakers, and eleven barbells are soon thrust into the air. Eleven CrossFit athletes begin a series of overhead squats. The twelfth barbell is in my hands, but

I don't raise it. My arm won't allow that without serious pain and risk. Instead, I place it across my shoulders and squat along with the class.

At first, our movements are synchronized, but that changes quickly. The big guy at the front finishes fifteen burpees in record time, and I'm surprised at how fast he's moving. *Damn.*

This is my first CrossFit class. I promised myself I'd get my act together, starting with getting back into shape. I arrived at the gym just as dawn was breaking and was greeted by a group of enthusiastic early risers from the morning class. The coach outlined the day's workout, detailing every movement, the number of reps, and how quickly we should finish. I was surprised by how short it seemed—maybe it's just an off day or something. Fifteen minutes? It should be a piece of cake. I knew right away that I wouldn't be able to do a couple of the moves on the whiteboard due to my arm, so I gave the coach a quick heads-up. With a glance at my arm, adorned with those bright pink scars, he offered several modifications without asking any more questions. I appreciate a guy who can respect a man's privacy.

After completing fifteen squats, I let go of the bar, which makes a satisfying clang as it hits the ground. I drop into a burpee position, then back up again, jumping laterally over the barbell into another burpee, careful not to stress my right arm. I'm winded by burpee number ten, with fourteen more to go. By the time I finish the last rep, my legs and arms are exhausted. I glance up at the clock—only three minutes and five seconds have passed. Now, fifteen minutes feels like an eternity. Half of the group has already left their stations for a 400-meter run in the early morning light. I follow and am trailing the pack. *Time to hit the gas.* I might not be able to keep up with the barbell movements like the others, but I sure as hell know how to run, and it's the only part of today's workout unaffected by my injury. I've always been a good runner and quickly whiz past two, then three people. The big guy is still up ahead with a significant lead. I don't overtake him, but I'm right on his heels by the time we return to our barbells. My body isn't used to this much activity, and nothing feels good, but I'm loving every minute of it. Even the suck—*I love the suck.*

After pushing myself on the run, the second round of burpees is even harder, but I keep going. My body starts sending signals up the chain: "Hey, this is miserable." And it is. But I remember that I thrive on this. I look around at the other athletes—tight faces, tense muscles, barely audible groans of pain—and I feel energized. I'm controlling my response to pain and suffering, and I relish this mighty feeling. I haven't suffered like this in a while.

There are only fifty seconds left on the clock when I finish the third round of burpees. "Come on, guys, push it—you can finish up this run if you hurry!" the trainer calls out.

The big guy left at least fifteen seconds before me, and two other guys around my age are heading out the door. I know the finish line is in sight, and I give it everything I've got. My lungs expand, and I feel my feet flying. I round the corner, and a new surge of energy takes over my body; The Warrior is stirring, and I love the feeling awakening within me. I pass the other two guys, and that gives me another boost. I'm the skinny guy with the weird arm who can't overhead squat, but I'm still a great goddamned runner. Right now, I want to prove to myself that I still have it in me. I sprint back into the building and glance up at the clock, surprised to see there are eleven seconds still remaining. I was even faster than I thought.

"Come on! You've got time for at least one more rep!" the trainer shouts.

I stare at the barbell, winded and fatigued. I hadn't planned for needing energy reserves after the run—I've spent them all. But I feel the eyes of the other athletes on me. I set the barbell on my shoulders, lower into a squat, and feel the lactic acid burning in my legs. The squat feels twice as heavy as the first one, but I push through. I glance at the clock. Three seconds.

I lower again and push up just as the trainer counts down, "Three, two, one...and stop! Nice job, everyone."

I drop to the ground, breathing heavily, sweat dripping onto the floor.

"Hey, man, great job out there." A hand enters my line of vision, ready for a high five. I'm flat on my back, trying to regain control of my breathing. I sit up as the room fills with sweaty high fives and chatter, everyone basking in the exhausted euphoria. High fives, fist bumps, and a few pats on the back follow. I wipe sweat from my forehead with my arm; my shirt was discarded long ago, as was most everyone else's, as the temperature rose along with the sun. I feel alive. I feel strong. I feel like a man again. There's sweat, teamwork, and aggression.

As I look around, it strikes me that since retiring from active duty, this is the first place I've found that offers an outlet for the raw masculine energy inside me. It's still hard for me to believe that it's been five fucking years since I've been able to work out, and a part of me that felt like it had died has been resurrected. For years, my days were filled with extreme physical exertion, long treks, and manual labor. We were running, lifting, and shooting almost daily. We navigated the wilderness, created hide sites, and breached doorways. The government invested untold thousands to train and build my body and mind into an organism designed to adapt to natural elements, survive without food, thrive in harsh conditions, resist fatigue, traverse long distances, overpower the enemy, and think outside the box.

My body and mind adapted to this way of life, learned to love and excel in it—not unlike my ancestors. Then, everything changed in a single day. Instead of sunlight, wilderness, and active combat, I was thrust into a world of climate-controlled rooms, office chairs, suburban houses, convenience food, and a society that really likes *nice guys*. Or thinks it does, at least. It dawns on me that there are very few spaces left in modern society where masculinity and aggression are given a healthy outlet. I miss it more than I realized—and I know I'll be back again.

"Hey, Tyler, a group of us are hiking Mount Baldy on Saturday. Want to join us?" the trainer asks three months later. I haven't missed a single day since my first CrossFit workout and have become a regular in the morning class. I quickly accept the invitation, and a surge of happiness accompanies my decision. At 10,068 feet, Mount Baldy is the highest peak in the San Gabriel Mountains and the highest point in

Los Angeles County. The hike spans about 6.5 miles and ascends 2,300 feet. We gather at the base of the trail just before sunrise and start off. Half an hour in, my body remembers. It all feels so familiar. While I still have a long way to go before regaining the muscular definition I once had, my body is still pack-mule strong, honed by more long rucks than I can count. The miles pass quickly as conversation flows among the group—jokes and friendly jabs exchanged, questions asked, lives shared. When we reach the summit, everyone falls silent for a moment, collectively absorbing the beauty and grandeur around us. I take a deep breath, savoring the moment.

This is all so new to me. As a kid, I was always a loner—not the first to be invited to parties or activities. Then I joined the military as a teenager. The only civilian life I've known was with Vanessa. But reflecting on it, our life in Las Vegas and our social circle weren't exactly normal. My "social circle" as an adult often revolved around women—trying to get close to them, engaging in activities I thought they would enjoy, all in an effort to get even closer. But this group seems different; they just like me, Tyler, the guy who shows up for the early morning CrossFit class and cracks a lot of jokes. *So, this is what it feels like…*

"So, you really like it, huh?" Vanessa asks the next morning. Although our relationship ended a few years ago, we still talk frequently. After I finish telling her about the hike, she fills me in on a new guy she just met. "I really like him, Tyler," she says. I have mixed feelings hearing this, but I'm genuinely happy for her and relieved that we're still friends. When we hang up, I head to the kitchen to make breakfast. My buddy won't be up for another hour or so. When my plate is piled with eggs and protein pancakes, I pull out a book I recently picked up from the bookstore and open it to the page where I left off. It suddenly occurs to me that it's been months since I've taken any pain medication. With my new morning CrossFit routine, I'd fallen out of the habit, not wanting to risk compromising my workout performance. I've also been reading more lately, and I enjoy the clarity it brings to my mind. The book I'm reading is about health, wellness, and cultivating a strong mindset. A line toward the bottom of the page catches my eye, discussing the effects of testosterone deficiencies in men, such as trouble concentrating, fatigue, and sleep disturbances. I wonder if I might have low testosterone. Initially, I dismiss the thought, finish making breakfast, and keep reading. But later, as I drive to a location for a bodyguarding job, the thought resurfaces.

Three days later, I track down a clinic that offers hormone testing and request a full panel. The results are shocking. The doctor tells me that the average man's testosterone level should be between 265 and 923 nanograms per deciliter (ng/dL). Mine is 320, which is extremely low. I also read somewhere that traumatic brain injuries from impact or blast exposure can cause hormone disruptions, so this checks out. Instead of feeling shame or embarrassment, I feel relief.

Knowing that there's something physically imbalanced in my body gives me hope that I can change it. It's not an abstract feeling; it's tangible, physical, and quantifiable. I've identified a problem, and now I have a target. This I can work with. The next morning, I'm back at the clinic for a testosterone injection. As the nurse administers the shot, I have a gut feeling that my life is about to improve. I thank her, pay for the injection, and step outside into the sunshine. It might be too early to feel any real results, but even as I leave the building, I feel changed.

Within two weeks, I'm an entirely new man. I have energy, my mind is clear, and the anxiety that was my constant companion—the low-level hum of white noise—is gone for the first time in years. I'm stronger and faster in my workouts, and I can think and reason with precision. But the most noticeable change is how I see everyone around me. I've regained the confidence I once had—the feeling that no one can hurt me. For the first time since my breakup with Vanessa, I'm reclaiming my dignity, self-respect, and identity. I'm proving to myself that I still have the ability to push my body past its limits and ignore the pain. This tenacity, the drive to earn respect through self-denial and sacrifice, was ingrained in me from the first day of basic training. I needed it then, and I need it now. I never had a natural reservoir of self-esteem or self-love; instead, I earned it through sweat, pain, and blood. And that's what I'm doing again—day by day. This is working for me. I just fucking wish I'd figured it out sooner. I think back to those days in the beige office, seeing Vanessa trying to pull me into her current of energy and momentum. I now realize just how hormonally deficient and chemically depressed I must have been. How many years I fought through fog, exhaustion, and disorientation, desperately searching for the aggression, motivation, and energy I used to have.

I'm glad I've figured it out now, but it saddens me to think about how things might have turned out differently if I had just known a little sooner. I lost the essence of my masculinity and my ability to properly love and fight for the woman I cared about because I couldn't even properly love and fight for myself. I want to go back, press rewind, and do it over, but I can't. I can only move forward. I just need to stick with what I'm doing. Even if I'm sick or don't feel like it, I can't stop. *No excuses. No compromises. Don't miss a day.*

When night falls and I close my eyes, my mind drifts back to Afghanistan, to the end of that long trek from the outstation to the village where we suspected Al-Qaeda fighters were hiding. I can still see the wilderness bathed in night-vision green as I kept my eyes trained on the ground, constantly searching for signs of land mines left over from the Soviet invasion. Reports of land mines exploding in our area were frequent, and it was my job to ensure my team avoided them. Our pace was steady, but progress felt slow. The terrain was mostly sharp, jagged rocks, making trekking in Afghanistan akin to climbing mountains and hills with teeth—it took immense effort just to stay balanced. Every step mattered, and we moved in silence.

After six hours, I spotted a couple of large trees ahead and decided to stop. Morning was approaching, and we needed to create a hide site to stay out of view while we waited for nightfall and caught some much-needed rest. Ideally, hide sites are dug into the ground, providing enough space to stand up and shield your head. But digging was not an option—I'd learned that the hard way. One of our first tasks in-country had been to help build one of the first outstations near the Pakistan border. I was tasked with helping dig a 120 mm mortar pit, which seemed like an easy job. The pit only needed to be about four feet deep, and we figured it would be a quick job. I grabbed a shovel, swung it back to gain momentum, and thrust it into the ground—which responded with a defiant laugh. I'm pretty sure I even heard a "fuck you" in there.

The tip of my shovel barely broke the surface. I thought it might have been a fluke, but when I saw my buddy struggling with his shovel, barely making a dent, I realized the ground was impenetrable. We didn't take kindly to being mocked by the earth. We grabbed five blocks of C-4, put it smack-dab in the middle of where the pit was going to be, tamped it with sandbags, and *KAPOW! Take that.* The ground laughed again. When the dust cleared, we got a good look at our handiwork. There was no hole—only a slight depression, like a dusty fingerprint in the earth. Five blocks of C-4 had given us about three inches. We had to order multiple cratering charges and a specific shaped charge designed to penetrate the earth.

So when it came time to build our current hide site, we didn't waste any time with shovels. Instead, we got creative. The only resources we had were the trees growing on the mountain. Luckily, these weren't ordinary trees; they were giant, oversized bushes—trees without trunks. When I offloaded my pack, a brief moment of relief washed over my muscles, but it didn't last. I pulled out my branch cutters, and the others did the same. My team surrounded one of the trees and systematically cut through the lower foliage until there was enough space to crawl in and clear out the center. We lined the space with camo netting, filling any significant gaps in our cover. After about an hour, the hide site was complete, and we were all inside.

We didn't move again until nightfall. Our shooter stayed awake while the rest of us slept. I closed my eyes and drifted off just as the sun began to rise. When I woke, shadows were beginning to gather. Night was approaching, and it would soon be time to move again. The other team leader and I decided to consolidate our teams, sending my shooter and spotter along with his shooter and spotter to conduct a preliminary reconnaissance of the village. We didn't want to approach the village as a group of eight without knowing exactly what we were up against—too conspicuous. They left without a word, and the other team leader and his JTAC joined me and mine in our tree. From there, it was just a waiting game.

We leaned against the trunk of the tree-bush, facing outside. It was my turn to stay awake. At first, my thoughts kept me company, but my mind soon went blank.

Then I heard voices. We were deep in the Afghan wilderness, miles from the nearest village. There was no sign of cultivation, which ruled out the possibility that the voices belonged to farmers. They could be sheepherders, but I didn't hear any sheep. I straightened up, trying to pinpoint the source of the sound and expand my line of vision. No luck. The leaves and camouflage netting obscured my view, and everything looked exactly the same as it had all night. But the voices grew louder, speaking in low, gravelly tones. My field of view was compromised by the dense greenery, making it impossible to see. There were at least six men approaching, maybe more, and they were getting close. *Too close. Fuck.* I raised my weapon, already planning my next move in case of an attack. My best friend, Justin, was no more than a foot away, sound asleep. I needed him awake and ready for the showdown, but I had to rouse him quietly. If he even groaned, we'd be compromised. I smacked him on the leg—hard but silently. *Come on, buddy, wake up.* He didn't budge. He was always a deep sleeper. The voices were growing louder, a mingling of Dari, Pashto, or some hybrid dialect I couldn't quite place. It all sounded the same to me. What was clear was that the group was much larger than I'd initially estimated.

Wake up, you deep-sleeping bastard; we've got a fight on our hands. I smacked Justin again, and this time his eyes snapped open. I jerked my finger to my mouth in the universal shut-the-fuck-up signal. He looked at me, and my eyes locked onto his, conveying everything I couldn't say. I pointed toward the voices, and he nodded, understanding instantly. We could read each other's minds better than an old married couple.

I turned my attention forward again and saw movement. Six heads came into view, followed by six bodies moving fast just twenty yards away. *Shit, they've got guns.* I positioned my weapon to point directly at them but kept it low. Justin and the JTACs did the same. We froze, barely breathing. The voices were almost on top of us. *Ten yards.* I watched for any sign that it was time to act. *Two yards.* A surge of adrenaline hit me, bringing clarity. One of the men glanced our way, but then they walked right past. It took about fifteen minutes for the voices to fade. We didn't say a word; we just lay there, eyes wide open.

A month later, I was called to leave the outstation and go to Kandahar for several days. After eating MREs for more than a month, I had one thing on my mind: *the chow hall.* The base was large and well-developed, a luxury compared to living at an outstation for over thirty days. Everyone seemed relaxed; Kandahar hadn't been hit by a mortar strike in months. A young private walked past, his round face beaming with inexperience. I knew he'd soon be back in his hometown, telling war stories about how tough life in Kandahar was. We were all on the same side, fighting the same war, but none of us experienced it the same way.

As I approached the chow hall, music wrapped around me. It wasn't one of those Arabic songs that sounded like a cow slowly dying; it was full Americano. A makeshift stage near the chow hall came into view. I saw legs first—glossy, sleek, feminine legs. White miniskirts swayed with the beat, revealing glimpses of smooth skin. Tight blue tank tops clung to gentle curves. I recognized these girls—a cheerleading squad or dance troupe I'd seen on television. I stood frozen, overwhelmed. It had been thirty days since I'd seen a female. My senses were overloaded. Hips swayed to the music; smiles beamed on soft pink lips. Curves bounced to the melody. It was hypnotic.

It felt like I was meeting with luscious little beings from another planet—the most beautiful little alien creatures I'd never seen. My world had been filled with nothing but aggressive, hairy creatures and dirt, grime, bullets, blood, and rocks. I'd watched an American soldier die right before my eyes. Now, a deep feeling suddenly washed over me, one I hadn't felt in a long time. I remembered what home felt like. I remembered that life wasn't all suffering and brutality; it couldn't be, not with beautiful creatures like that still roaming the earth. I felt a sense of anticipation rising in me, but it was more than that. It was purpose.

If there was a beauty in this world that would look at me and love me, I knew deep down that everything would be okay.

The memory fades as I lie in bed, staring at the ceiling. I'm still clinging to the hope that there's someone out there who will love me for who I am, that I will experience a great, epic love story at least once in my life. I'm trying to become a man worthy of that kind of woman and that kind of love, but I'm not sure if I ever will.

CHAPTER 20

NO HEROES HERE

VENICE BEACH IS NEARLY EMPTY when I arrive just before 9:00 p.m. Only a handful of people are out at this hour—a couple of teenagers and an old man wearing a cap adorned with an array of strange buttons and paraphernalia safety-pinned onto it. Near the water, a small group of people stands huddled together, and I spot a few familiar faces—the same ones I see at CrossFit nearly every day. I'm in the right place.

I'm not quite sure what to expect tonight. A week ago, my buddy Jack approached me and asked if I'd like to join the group for an endurance challenge event called Go Ruck, led exclusively by Special Forces veterans. I said, "Why not?" and here I am. Endurance races, mud runs, Spartan-this, and tough-that seem to be all the rage these days. You can't open Facebook without seeing a picture of mud-covered middle-aged women in sports bras and shirtless guys flexing, captioned with something like, "Did it for the pizza! #mudrun." I've never participated in a mud run myself, but tonight will change that.

"How's it going?" I pat one of my CrossFit buddies on the shoulder as I approach the group. There are several people I don't recognize, but one man catches my eye. He's standing with his hands behind his back, and I can tell just by looking at him that he'll be leading the event. He nods a welcome to me, and I nod back, then stare out at the ocean. The blue and green hues have disappeared along with the sun. Now, there's nothing but a vast sea of gray.

A short, barrel-chested man with a red beard and a woman with dark brown hair and stout thighs join the group. There are now twelve of us. A tall guy with big biceps starts contorting his body in a series of stretches while we wait for the event to begin. The others nervously chatter and introduce themselves in low whispers, though I'm not sure there's any reason to be quiet. They continue whispering and shooting glances at the man with his hands behind his back, like middle school students trying not to disturb the teacher.

"Alright, gather up, everyone," the man says, stepping forward, and the group instinctively tightens around him. "My name is David, and I am your cadre. What will take place over the next twelve to fifteen hours will not be easy. You will be wearing a rucksack for the entire duration of this challenge. Your mind and body will be pushed to their limits. Some of you will probably quit. Those of you who have what it takes to make it through our little 'welcome party,' which will last for the first two to three hours, will move on to the second part of this challenge, which will last anywhere from ten to twelve hours. Take a good, hard look at your teammates around you. A few of you know each other, but most of you are complete strangers. Over the next few hours, you will become a team, learn to work together, and be forced to rely on one another." When he pauses, no one says anything. "Is everyone ready?"

The group nods eagerly, and the tall contortionist issues a grunt of approval. He definitely doubled up on the pre-workout. Everyone grabs a rucksack and begins strapping it on. I sling mine over my shoulders, and a deep familiarity washes over me as the weight settles in. My hands move quickly to adjust the straps and position the weight evenly. *Ready to go.* I look around at the others as they work to secure their rucksacks, excitement shining in their eyes. I hadn't really considered that for everyone here except me, this was a novel experience.

"Have you been training with it?" the red-bearded man asks, looking from the rucksack to me.

"You could say that," I reply with a smile.

"Me too. My wife and I have been bringing it to the gym and training with it four to five times per week." He nods toward the woman with stout thighs beside him.

"I can't figure out how to…" The woman inspects the straps on her rucksack. I reach over and give the straps a few strong tugs, adjusting them for her. She stands taller and smiles.

"Thanks," she says.

"Follow me!" The cadre orders us down to the beach and onto the sand. "We're going to start with push-ups," he says matter-of-factly. As all twelve of us drop to our knees, he checks his watch.

"Let's go!" he shouts, and the push-ups begin. I lower myself and push back up. I can manage a decent set of push-ups now that I'm training regularly, but my range of motion is still limited due to an injury. After twenty minutes, my muscles are burning, the weight of the rucksack presses down on my lower back, and sharp shards of sand dig into my palms. The cadre directs us to a line of five-gallon jugs filled with water.

"Down and back!" he yells.

I jump up, grab one of the jugs, and position it over my left shoulder. I feel a twinge of discomfort in my right arm but ignore it. It feels good to be out of the push-up position. Alongside the tall guy and another middle-aged man with a runner's build, I jog down the beach. The way down isn't hard, but on the way back up, my thighs start to burn. Running in the sand always makes you feel slow and heavy, and with the five-gallon jugs and rucksacks, we are indeed slow and heavy. The tall contortionist, who had excelled at the push-ups, is now breathing hard and looks like he might puke. Mr. Redbeard is locked in, maintaining a steady pace. It's clear he's been training. I feel a charley horse coming on in my left calf but shake it off and glance at my watch. We've been at it for an hour now. Only thirteen more to go.

"BACK TO PUSH-UPS!" the cadre yells.

Everyone drops back onto the sand. Gasps of heavy breathing mix with the rhythmic sound of waves hitting the beach. My arms ache and my shoulders feel fatigued. The others in the group start encouraging each other. The pain and grunts of effort are becoming more apparent. I know this pain well. I've been baptized in suffering and emerged stronger more times than I can count. I've explored the pain caves and delved into the recesses of my mind as my body cries out for relief. It's a familiar feeling, but now I'm starting to question why I ever agreed to this.

With my face close to the ground, every time I dip into a push-up, I notice a little brown stick in the sand, and it becomes my focal point as I concentrate.

I'm in fucking Venice Beach, California, getting smoked by some young Recon Marine at 10:30 p.m. when I could be sleeping. One part of me is kicking myself for agreeing to this suffering. I'm not going to quit—it's just not in my nature—but my body is definitely not happy with the choice. *Goddammit, Tyler, why?*

The man built like a runner stands up, walks a few steps away from the group, and puts his hands on his knees. I see vomit trickle from his mouth. He wipes it away and approaches the cadre.

"Man, I'm going to have to call it. My shoulders are locked up, and I don't think I'm going to make it twelve more hours." He extends his hand toward the cadre. "Thank you so much. It's a pleasure to meet you."

The cadre smiles and shakes his hand, granting him the dignity of a gracious withdrawal. The rest of us continue our suffering. By the two-hour mark, a quiet-looking young guy, no more than twenty-one or twenty-two, puts his head in the sand and groans. He's not going to make it either. By the time we reach the three-hour mark, only ten of us remain to move on to the second part of the challenge, which will last another eight to ten hours. There's a time requirement to cover the distance of the next leg, and we'll really have to pick up the pace if we don't want to be disqualified.

"Buddy carries!" the cadre shouts as we move away from the beach. Instinctively, I squat down and offer my back to another team member. One of the women from my CrossFit gym catches my eye, and I nod her over. She looks timid and unsure of how to position herself.

"Like this," I say, helping her into a classic buddy-carry position—her torso behind my neck, legs on my right side, arms on my left.

"Loop your arms through my shoulders and hold on, okay? I've got you." She clings to me for dear life.

A big guy in his late twenties with a sweat-soaked bandana secured around his head offers himself to another team member, who hops on in classic piggyback style. Mr. Redbeard slings his wife over his shoulders like a sack of potatoes, holding onto her ankles as her head bobs behind him, close to his heels. We set off at a steady pace, and my ankles and knees alert me to the discomfort of the added weight. I return the woman to the ground after a while and glance behind me. The rest of the team is still back where we started. Three people are trying to get a team member on their back but only manage a few steps at a time. One rider falls off into the sand, another carrier collapses to their knees from the weight, and the others crumble into a sweaty heap.

The cadre skillfully directs the group, fostering a sense of teamwork in everyone—he's an upright guy, I'll give him that. But after at least a dozen failed buddy-carry attempts, it's clear that only Mr. Redbeard, Sweaty Bandana, and I are going to be able to pull this off. *Time to dig in and pull the team through.* Progress is slow, but we don't stop. The atmosphere has shifted now—no one is timid or awkward about touching someone else. There is no more personal space. We are moving like one big machine, arms and legs interlocking like gears, holding onto each other and moving as one. Polite words have been replaced with rough, to-the-point communication that happens when you're teetering on the edge of physical collapse and refusing to give in. Friendly exchanges are replaced with one-word commands and answers, but there's an unmistakable connection and camaraderie.

After the second mile of buddy carries, I'm exhausted and a little irritated that only Mr. Redbeard, Sweaty Bandana, and I are carrying the other ten members. At least half the group seems incapable of functioning as a team. They're not bad people, just hopelessly individualistic—and there's nothing I can do to change that.

Why is no one pulling their weight? The injustice of it bothers me. Frustrated, I look around at the group. That's when I see it: exhaustion, fatigue, and resilience etched on every face. And it hits me: They're giving this everything they've got. I've been an asshole. I'm used to working with teammates whose physical training and performance mirror my own. For everyone else here, this is their first experience. The real injustice is in my judgment, not their performance. I've been coasting at 80 percent, trying to slide under the radar. Everyone else is giving it their all. It's time for me to step up and lead.

As night turns to morning, everyone is dirty, sweaty, and deeply fatigued as we make our way through Venice, Santa Monica, and then Brentwood. A few late-night partiers look at us with confused faces as they stumble down the street, but we're too tired to care. Another hour goes by, then another, filled with new challenges—just as fatiguing and heavy as the ones before.

"The bottom of the canyon is your finish line!" the cadre announces, and we head down the Runyon Canyon trail. With the finish line in sight, he seems to lighten up from the basic training style, and fresh energy spreads through the group. "Two miles to go!"

The pain and fatigue haven't subsided, but after a grueling night, we all know we're going to make it as the sun begins to rise, painting the sky orange and pink. I speed up a little to match the cadre's pace.

"So, what do you have to do to become a cadre?" I ask, keeping pace with him.

"Well, first you have to be a former member of US Special Operations," he replies with a polite smile, staring ahead. It's clear he expects the conversation to end here. He has no idea that I served in the military, and he likely gets asked this question often by enthusiastic participants high on the endorphin rush of victory.

"Alright. And what else?"

He shoots me a sideways glance of surprise, sizes me up, and then nods in respectful acknowledgment.

"Well, if you check off that box, the only other requirement is to personally complete a challenge."

I nod toward the bottom of the trail, just ahead. *Check.*

"And what else?"

He chuckles. "Well, after that, you just call the office, I guess."

"Sweet. Thanks, man."

I file away the information for another day as we cross the finish line together as a team. The morning air is crisp with dew, and the sun bathes us in a soft glow as we remove our heavy rucksacks and revel in our hard-earned victory. I had forgotten the sheer satisfaction of feeling utterly exhausted yet profoundly proud. The simple joy of unburdening ourselves from the weight of our rucksacks and finally taking a seat after a long and challenging trek is overwhelming. The rush of endorphins consumes us like a drug. Amid the chatter, high fives, hugs, and photo-taking, we are no longer strangers—we share a unique bond forged through enduring extreme adversity.

As I take a moment to relax and listen to the group reminisce about the night, discussing the various challenges we conquered and reliving the highs and lows, I notice that everyone emphasizes the significance of teamwork. It suddenly dawns on me that carrying a rucksack wasn't the only new experience for everyone. From their conversations, it's clear that none of them has encountered this level of teamwork before. As they recount the night's events, I see profound emotions in their eyes. That night was transformative for them. It allowed them to experience camaraderie and teamwork in a way they never had before.

Perhaps I've taken for granted the privilege of belonging to a team and experiencing the powerful connection of entrusting your life to another person, relying on them to wholeheartedly support and protect you, while bearing the responsibility to do the same for them. A wave of gratitude washes over me. I guess I've had a pretty extraordinary life. I've been fortunate enough to learn about teamwork, leadership, and resilience in ways that most people never will. I didn't really realize how lucky I was.

Emotions among the group are high, and I study the faces around me. I'm not sure if I'm capable of feeling the kind of emotions I see etched on their faces, but I feel a sort of vicarious satisfaction as I soak in the moment. I like it. I like it a lot.

One year later, I find myself standing in the dark on Venice Beach once again. I'm officially a GoRuck cadre. After completing my first challenge, it didn't take long to meet the requirements to become a cadre. I shadowed a few events, guided by one of GoRuck's seasoned cadres, then led an event while a cadre observed. A bit of paperwork followed, and just like that, I was one of them. It might seem like an easy process, but considering that becoming a cadre starts with being a United States Special Forces operator, the toughest part of the job requirements was already done. I'm still working as a bodyguard in Los Angeles, taking on all the extra work I can get.

Part of being a cadre is having free rein over the design of the challenge, and I've spent days scouting the area and mapping out the course.

As the start time inches closer, today's participants begin to trickle in. I'm hiding behind a lower beam of the pier, watching them gather. I want to capitalize on the element of surprise. My phone dings in my pocket, and I pull it out. It's a text from Vanessa. *Good luck, hope it goes well!* I smile, tap out a short reply, and stuff the phone back in my pocket. Tonight's group is a mixed bag, I can see everyone talking amongst themselves, trying to figure out who is leading the event tonight. There are a man and woman covered in colorful tattoos, a group of guys in their late thirties with a fit-dad vibe, and one very pretty brunette. I count seventeen people, with three more to go. I hear a car door shut, and two guys and a woman approach the group. *Definitely CrossFitters*, I think when I see their silhouettes from afar.

The trio is decked out in Reebok Nano shoes, tall socks, and knee sleeves, with CrossFit support tape jutting out from beneath their shirt sleeves. One of them has taped-up hands, another is wearing a pair of special grip gloves. *CROSSFIT GAMES* is scrolled across the chest of one of the guys.

Bingo. When the start time comes, I walk forward, briefly introduce myself, and immediately direct them toward the pile of rucksacks.

"Alright, we're going to start with a little something I like to call hydro burpees!" The CrossFitters exchange glances. "You're going to stand in the water, up to AT LEAST mid-shin. Then I want to see a full burpee. YOUR CHEST MUST TOUCH THE GROUND. And…GOOOOOO!"

The idea of a hydro burpee popped into my head two days ago, and seeing it in action is better than I'd imagined. There's a look of surprise and horror as everyone emerges from the icy water of the Pacific Ocean for the first time and experiences acute discomfort. No one likes burpees. But burpees in the water, with a rucksack, are a whole different ball game. The CrossFitters come out hot. Their form is strong, and their pace is fast, but I'm doubtful they'll be able to maintain it. At the forty-five-minute mark, everyone looks desperate and exhausted. The female CrossFitter begins to complain about her lower back hurting.

"Come on, babe," one of the men, presumably her husband, barks at her. It's clear he intends to return to his home gym with a victory. But the woman isn't kidding—she's nearly in tears now.

"I'm sorry, I just can't do it." She stands, wipes her eyes, and nods at me. She's done. The rest of the group continues. Thirty minutes later, the two remaining CrossFitters are barely moving. They expended far too much energy in the first forty-five minutes.

"You got this!" The woman offers encouragement from the sidelines, but it falls on deaf ears. Her husband is getting angry now. Another ten minutes go by, and suddenly he jolts upright, shaking his head.

"Look, I'm not doing this." He jerks off his special wrist-wrap hand grips and throws them on the sand next to him. "This is stupid. I don't need to prove myself to anyone!" He storms off, and the other guy follows. I don't chase after them. We lose one more man during the welcome party, but the remaining participants stick it out. I feel a deep sense of satisfaction as I watch the group begin to work together, depend on each other, and sacrifice for each other. I'm intentional with my instructions, working hard to help leadership and teamwork develop within the group. They finish together after fifteen hours of grueling hard work as the sun rises. The high of victory hits, and the group buzzes with conversation and snaps photos, gathering around me with faces shining in appreciation and happiness. I feel a profound sense of satisfaction.

"Hey, man, I just wanted to take a minute to thank you for your service." I look down to see a hand outstretched in my direction. One of the athletes has stepped away from the group to show his respect for me. I appreciate the gesture, but I feel deeply uncomfortable as I shake his hand.

"Can't tell you what an honor it is to be trained by one of our nation's heroes."

I mumble a reply, but his words keep ringing in my ears as I walk back to my car.

"*One of our nation's heroes… One of our nation's heroes… One of our nation's heroes…*"

Back in my car, I pull out my phone before driving home and see there's a text from my buddy: *Got plans tonight?* I smile. Five hours later, my buddy stands outside my front door with two gorgeous women, one on either side—a tall blonde and a curvy brunette. They are both stunning, the kind of beautiful that usually means it's a full-time job.

"I brought a plus-two, hope you don't mind," he winks and strides into the room.

"Welcome, ladies." I open the door a little wider.

"Victoria's Secret models, both of them," he whispers in the hallway.

"Runway?"

"Catalog."

"Fair enough."

The girls follow us into the main room.

"Look what I have," my buddy says with an almost childishly mischievous smile, holding up a tiny plastic bag with a small white ball inside *Cocaine*. "Woohoooo!" the blonde girl exclaims in a high-pitched celebratory shout that makes me wonder if she used to be a cheerleader. Suddenly, everything is happening fast: white powder on the coffee table, credit card, and straw. The brunette does the first line, then the blonde. *Ladies first*. My buddy is next, and then he hands the straw to me. I lean down close to the little white line. Fuck, I'd planned to have a quiet evening tonight, maybe watch a movie, and hit a good workout tomorrow. But who says no to two models and a bag of coke? I inhale. The earthy burn registers in the back of my throat, and a surge of adrenaline follows. When I raise my head, the brunette's eyes are resting on me, and I feel my confidence soar. She wants *ME*.

My mouth is dry and my head hurts when I wake up. I roll over and open my eyes, though they feel crusty. The brunette's body is splayed out at an odd angle, a leg draped over mine. The sight makes me feel uncomfortable, as if I've walked in on a stranger sleeping. The other two must have disappeared into the bedroom at some point during the night—I can't remember. The coffee table is littered with trash and half-filled drinks diluted by melted ice. A hint of sunlight is coming through the window, creating gloomy shadows across the room. The mess, the half-filled drinks, and the gray light make me feel sad. I need water, I need to blow my nose, I need to pee. I don't want to move and close my eyes instead. The man from the GoRuck event flashes through my mind. I can see him standing there, arm outstretched with admiration and respect on his face.

"Can't tell you what an honor it is to be trained by one of our nation's heroes."

I open my eyes again and look around at the mess in front of me. Dried blood is caked on the brunette's left nostril, and I notice a used condom wrapper on the floor beside us. I feel empty and ashamed.

No heroes here…

CHAPTER 21
ROOM 406

MY HEART RACES AS I walk through the dimly lit halls of an old French hotel, searching for room number 406. The excitement surging through me is a sensation I haven't felt since I last saw active combat. Every cell in my body is alert, and my senses are heightened. It's not just the cocaine coursing through my system, though that certainly adds to the intensity. It's the complete uncertainty of what awaits me on the other side of door 406. The thrill of the unknown is intoxicating, and God knows there's nothing else in this world that excites me anymore.

403, 404, 405. Almost there… Only time will reveal what lies beyond the door. It might be the most stunning woman I've ever encountered, waiting for me on the bed—wild and eager to please. Or maybe that's just what I imagine. Maybe there are two men behind the door, ready to ambush me the moment I knock. *406.*

My hand rests on the door now, my heart pounding in my chest. I knock three times and then pause as I hear movement on the other side. The door opens, and there she is: a tall French woman with dark brown hair and eyes to match. She's stunning. I smile, and she returns the smile. I congratulate myself for having the foresight to book three hours instead of two. She's definitely worth it.

I pull a bag of cocaine from my pocket and offer her some. She nods approvingly, her gaze locked with mine as she raises her head and inhales. The approval in her eyes as she takes in my presence is a high in itself. I feel myself climbing higher and higher…

Until it's over.

My body begins to crash as I make my way to the bathroom to rinse off three hours later. The water flows over me, but it does nothing to cleanse me of the guilt and shame I feel. *This isn't me. This isn't me. This isn't me. So why am I doing this?* The mental flogging has begun, and I show myself no mercy as I walk through the hotel halls again, feeling nothing like the superhuman dynamo I was just hours before. By the time I'm back at my own hotel room and preparing to sleep, I'm exhausted, sad, and deeply disappointed in myself. I close my eyes, but sleep eludes me. *Why do I keep doing this?*

Yesterday, I led a GoRuck event on the beaches of Normandy for the seventieth anniversary of the Normandy landing. The entire day was a surreal experience—every movement felt somehow sacred as we remembered the warriors who struggled and fought on those shores. I watched a transformation occur within the participants over those fifteen hours as the intensity of the physical adversity forged bonds of camaraderie and trust where fear and mental barriers once stood. I witnessed catharsis, breakthroughs, and growth unfolding before my very eyes. The significance of where we stood and the weight of the legacy was not lost on a single one of us.

After it was over, they didn't just express gratitude for the experience; they said it had changed their lives. There it was again—their admiration, gratitude, and respect. They looked at me like a real-life hero. For a moment, I could see myself through their eyes. I saw myself patiently instructing each athlete with genuine care and passing on the lessons of courage, leadership, teamwork, and sacrifice that I have accumulated over the years. As I reflected on my life and the years I dedicated in service to the defense of this nation, I knew I had contributed meaningfully. I deeply care about the people I have the opportunity to lead. But that's only one side of the portrait.

For the past two years, I've led countless GoRuck events—sometimes alone, sometimes with another cadre. Initially, it was about earning extra money to pay off my debt. I made it clear to the leadership that I would take any job, anywhere, be it the armpit of Kansas or the freezing butt crack of Alaska. I didn't mind the work, and I needed the money. But it quickly became something much more significant. Joining the GoRuck community page on Facebook, I felt a sense of satisfaction seeing my name in the comments as people shared their experiences with me as their cadre.

For the first time in a long while, I had the chance to use my background and experience to make a positive impact. I wasn't breaching doorways or doing hostage rescues, but I was touching lives for the better. I felt useful, needed, and connected to a community of like-minded individuals. I enjoyed the teamwork of collaborating with other cadres. Eventually, I built a reputation for myself, leading to requests for big GoRuck events in incredible locations like Singapore, Spain, Australia, Sweden, and Germany. It feels rewarding to travel, see new places, and be part of something greater than myself.

Another perk of being a cadre is the increased attention from fit, attractive women who treat me like a bit of a celebrity. Definitely not complaining about that.

But I'm living a double life. Half the time, the Warrior in me is thriving. Maybe it's because GoRuck reminds me of military life: teamwork, leadership, camaraderie, growth through adversity, structure, and discipline. Maybe it's because I feel like I'm making a difference in people's lives. As long as I'm busy, the structure, discipline, and people seem to hold me together. But when the dust settles and I have nothing to do, an ugly darkness rears its head. I feel empty and anxious, and I need to fill that vast void inside me and alleviate the escalating tension accumulating within me. That's when the Destroyer emerges. And then I need porn. I need a beautiful woman on top of me. I need another girl, another drink, another line, another pill. *"Why not enjoy your life? You've been through hell, you're working hard, you deserve to have a little fun,"* he whispers. *"The world is fucked, you're fucked, so might as well just say fuck-it, and have a good time. You're a man, after all. What man wouldn't want to have a good night with beautiful girls, drugs, and sex…lots, and lots of sex?"*

But the more people treat me like a hero, the more I feel like an imposter because my life is governed by the aspirations of the Warrior and the demands of the Destroyer. Most people only see the side of me that I want them to see and believe it's the entirety of who I am. But I know the truth. I'm not the man they think I am, and I don't deserve their admiration and appreciation.

I don't want to be anyone's hero, because I know how disillusioned and disappointed they'd be if they saw the real me. People change the way they look at me when they find out what I used to do for a living, and that look is heavy because I know that I'm no hero. I'm not even sure I'm such a good person.

Nobody wants to see their hero coked up on a toilet. Nobody wants to see their hero alone at night, dick in hand, deep down a porn rabbit hole. Nobody wants to see their hero stuck in a beige office, glued to a computer screen playing stupid games for a year straight. Nobody wants to see their hero blackout drunk. Nobody wants to see their hero waking up next to a strung-out stranger with a used condom still on, feeling ashamed and empty. I can't seem to win this battle of duality inside me, and I'm not sure I ever will. So I keep living a lie—except it's not entirely a lie. I am that warrior, that leader, that hero. I can objectively look at my life and see evidence that I am the man they see me as. But I don't feel like I deserve any of the praise, gratitude, and admiration that people give me. The war inside my mind never ends, and I'm exhausted by it. *I'll be back in town tonight*, I text Vanessa as my plane taxis down the runway in LAX. *Want to get dinner?* Her message comes within seconds. *Sounds great.*

I'm talking to Vanessa a lot more these days. We never really stopped being friends after the breakup, but something is different now. I can't quite put my finger on it or describe what's changed, but I feel it—maybe we both do. We're calling each other more often and talking longer when we do. I find myself collecting little bits and pieces throughout the day—gathering you-won't-believe-what-happened stories, I-knew-you'd-think-this-was-funny moments, and I-just-had-to-tell-you lines. She's laughing like she used to when I first met her.

Truth is I haven't felt a sense of love or connection since Vanessa and I broke up, and I can't help but wonder if, somehow, we'll end up back together again.

"I'll tell you, man, that girl is your kryptonite." The memory of Mike's voice floats into my mind like a warning. I ignore it. After all the storms Vanessa and I have weathered and the toxicity we've been through, doesn't the fact that we keep coming back to each other mean something? How many couples get through a partner having their arm blown off, near financial ruin, an open relationship, a cross-country move, and countless ups and downs, and come out the other side? Maybe our connection is inevitable.

Several hours later, I'm sitting across the table from Vanessa. She's telling me about her week, and I'm sharing mine. We do what we always do when we're together: We laugh, chase conversational rabbits, and form strategies to solve all the world's problems and our own. As the night wears on, the conversation shifts. Neither of us can ignore the elephant in the room anymore—it's just too damn conspicuous these days.

"So, I've been thinking about us a lot lately…" Vanessa says, her gaze fixed on me. She's looking for data from my reaction to inform her next move. I don't say anything, daring her to continue. But she's stubborn, waiting for me to speak first.

"I don't know…maybe we should try this again; maybe we should try *us* again." The words come slowly, but her eyes give me courage. She inches closer.

"After all the shit we've been through," she says, shaking her head and laughing as she reaches for my hand, "I want to, Tyler, I really do. But you know I want to have kids. I've always wanted to be a mother, and it's important to me. I know you don't feel the same way. So I'm all in on this relationship, and I want to give it another try. But in the meantime, I need you to think about whether or not you're open to having kids someday."

I open my mouth to respond, but she holds up a finger.

"Don't give me an answer now. I want you to really think about it. I'm not getting any younger, time is passing, and I don't want to miss out on the chance to have a family. We'll give us another chance, but promise me that you'll think about starting a family in the meantime."

A multitude of conflicting feelings rushes through my mind as I squeeze her hand. I understand where she's coming from. I have no right to demand that she sacrifice her dream of becoming a mother to be with me, but I'm not sure I'm ready to say yes to being a father. I've always known I don't want to have kids. I have absolutely no desire to bring new, innocent little human beings into this chaotic, fucked-up world. I have no desire to spend years changing diapers, worrying about nap times, and attending soccer practices. I admire people who do, but that life is not for me.

But I do want to be with Vanessa, and hell, if we've weathered everything else, maybe we could do the parent thing too. But fuck, I don't know if I'm ready for it. I promise her that I will consider it, and I mean it with all my heart. And just like that, we're back together.

The motivation of having Vanessa back and the idea of a real future together lights a fire inside me, and suddenly I feel like I can take on the world. I make ruthless changes in my life—no more casual sex, no more prostitutes, no more coke. Within a few months, I move back to Las Vegas to get away from the girls and drugs of LA. I have a clear target for my life now, and it changes everything.

◄►

A blast of icy wind hits my face as I walk out of the Portland airport and hail a taxi. It's colder than I'd expected, and I hope the jacket I brought will be enough to keep me warm tonight. With this weather, it's going to be a long night, especially for the twelve people participating in tonight's GoRuck challenge.

I call Vanessa to check in as the taxi heads to my hotel. After we hang up, I scroll through Facebook mindlessly. I see five new friend requests, all from pretty-looking girls. I recognize two of them: One participated in a GoRuck event, and the other is a new member at my CrossFit gym. A message from the CrossFit girl is waiting for me. I don't accept the friend request or reply to the message. Vanessa and I have been together for nearly six months now, and I'm determined not to let anything stand in the way of our connection this time. No open relationship. No lies. I really want to make this work. Thoughts of children pop into my head again.

I gaze out the window, observing the passing cars, lost in thought. The familiar loop plays in my mind as I chase closure on this topic. I want to want to have kids with Vanessa. I want to make her happy. But why would I want to bring children into such a chaotic world? Why would I want to change my entire life to raise new little humans when there are already plenty of them in the world? These are the reasons I've always cited for my aversion to having children, but deep down, I know that's not the whole story.

Suddenly, I'm back on my childhood couch, bathed in the blue light of the television, hearing the sound of my mother screaming as my father's hand connects with the side of her face. I see my father's face, but it's not really him. It's the eyes of a destroyer—bright with anger and capable of anything. And I see myself frozen as my mind races.

"I'm going to be just like him when I grow up. I'm going to be just like him when I grow up. Oh NO, NO NO…I DO NOT WANT TO BE JUST LIKE HIM WHEN I GROW UP."

The truth is, deep down, I'm afraid I'll turn out just like my father. Plain and simple. The Destroyer is still strong in me; the War Within rages constantly. I haven't made any major fuckups in a while, but it's still not a peaceful place. Just the thought of a little kid looking up at me and calling me Dad scares the shit out of me. I'm not sure I can handle it.

But maybe it's time to stop being so afraid of turning out like my father. Who knows, maybe I won't be like him at all. I learned years later that my father was discovered in the bottom drawer of an old wooden dresser, malnourished, and abandoned when he was just a baby. His parents had left him for dead. A concerned neighbor adopted him and raised him as their own. My dad, for all his mistakes, did a hell of a lot better job than his father. Maybe I'll do better than mine. Maybe it's time to stop running from the man I'm afraid to become and just be myself.

I think of Vanessa and our relationship. It was born in the midst of hardship and trauma, but we seem to thrive on chaos. We both know we're imperfect and a little fucked up, but we keep sticking it out together. We are at our best when we're solving challenges and dancing in the eye of the storm. More than anything, I don't want to let her go.

And suddenly, in the back of a taxi, after six months of consideration, I have my answer for Vanessa. I am open to having kids. Maybe not right away, but someday, yes. *Let's get dinner Sunday night*, I text her, already excited to see the look on her face when I tell her. *Can't wait*, she replies within seconds.

I arrive early at the location to scout out the route for tonight's GoRuck challenge. With my experience, I've become adept at improvising challenges on the spot. I've already mapped out a basic course using online maps, so finalizing the route shouldn't take long. I start at the Portland Riverwalk, where we'll kick off tonight's welcome party. As I study the area, something catches my eye: a very large log laying nearby. I estimate it's about 45 feet long by over a yard in diameter. Judging by its size, it's got to be incredibly heavy. Suddenly, a new idea pops into my mind, and I know exactly what challenge awaits the Portland GoRuck participants tonight.

The group arrives early and gathers around as I introduce myself, which takes no longer than five minutes—I always save the small talk for later. Once the rucksacks are strapped on, we begin. Within thirty minutes, I see expressions of pain and discomfort on the participants' faces. The first hour serves as a harsh reality check for them as they come to grips with the intensity of the challenge and the discomfort that will accompany them for the next twelve to fifteen hours.

This moment is crucial as I coach them in discovering a new level of mental resilience and building teamwork. But tonight, I'm distracted by a man standing across the sidewalk, staring at us. He's a big guy in his late twenties, with arms and legs like tree trunks, though his doughy midsection hints at a fondness for beer. He's been drilling us with his eyes for at least fifteen minutes now, without shame. It's typical to get curious glances from people passing by—it's not every day you see a group with rucksacks running around town. But most people look for a moment and then move on. This guy is different. He's bold-faced staring at us for far too long, and now he's walking our way. I watch him carefully as he approaches. He's not exactly swaying, but his gait suggests he's had more than a little alcohol.

"What's going on here?" he asks loudly, too loudly for a conversational distance. His bloodshot eyes confirm my initial assessment—he's definitely drunk.

"It's a military-style challenge called GoRuck," I reply, nodding at him while keeping my focus on the group—a clear signal that it's not the time for a prolonged conversation. He doesn't take the hint.

"Why are you doing this?" he asks again, his volume still about ten notches too high. Several people from the group look up, annoyed by his obnoxious tone. I offer another brief answer and turn my face again. He lingers for a while, mutters something to himself, and then walks away. We're all relieved to see him go.

The welcome party is completed in two and a half hours, without a single person quitting, which surprises me. At first glance, the group didn't strike me as the ultra-athlete type, but what they lack in physical strength, they make up for in heart. But the night is still young.

"See that log over there?" I point to the log that first caught my eye when I arrived. The group looks at the log and then back at me. Fear washes over their cold, exhausted faces.

"We've got several miles ahead of us, and you're going to carry it with you every step of the way."

I watch as my words register. Two guys in the group emerge as natural leaders and immediately take charge. The group gathers around the log, and one of the leaders rolls out a plan for how they will hoist it up and carry it.

"On my count!" the group-appointed leader shouts as everyone takes their positions. "One, two, three, and GOOOOO!" With a powerful grunt, the log begins to move, but progress is agonizingly slow. Doubt and fear flicker across everyone's faces. This challenge is grueling, and even I'm questioning if I've set the bar too high. They struggle, suffer, and push, managing to get the log high enough to carry on their shoulders for a while, which speeds up their progress. However, they can't sustain it for long. Each time they drop the log to rest, their attempts to lift it again result in only a few inches of movement.

But I've got to hand it to the Portland GoRuck group—they just won't quit. After seven hours, we've looped back to the Portland Riverwalk area. I check my watch. It's 02:30, and the group is exhausted. When I look up, I notice Mr. Loudmouth approaching us again, even more drunk than before. Just what we need.

"Why are you doing this?" he asks again, clearly dissatisfied with my previous answers.

"They're doing it to push themselves," I reply, finally meeting his gaze. "They want to prove their capabilities and learn to work together as a team."

He nods, and I see his expression change. "I want to help," he says emphatically.

"No, man, you can't get involved. This is a private event, and these people all had to go through a registration process and sign a liability waiver," I say with a polite smile.

"Please, let me help," he pleads.

"Look, man, I—"

He steps closer, looking me straight in the eyes. "Look, I'm a veteran. I want to help. I really need this." Tears well up in his eyes. "Please, I need this."

When I meet his gaze, I see desperation. Behind the haze of alcohol and obnoxious questions, I see a fellow warrior who feels lonely, irrelevant, and lost—someone who just wants to remember what it felt like to be the man he once was and to belong. That tormented look strikes a chord because I know that feeling all too well. Maybe I'm not the drunken guy harassing strangers, but we're not so different.

"I just...I just...I need this, man," he repeats.

The truth is, I need it too. I need this environment to hold together my broken identity long enough for me to see my own reflection and remember who I once was.

"I'll ask the group. If they allow it, I'll let you join. But only for a few minutes, okay?"

I know it's not the smartest move, but I can't say no. He nods and wipes the tears from his eyes.

"Listen up! We've got a guy here who wants to help, but the choice of whether or not to let him join is up to you. What do you say?"

The group looks up at me through mud- and sweat-streaked faces, and then at the big guy next to me. They know he's the same annoying guy from earlier, but they're too exhausted to care. They just need a fresh pair of hands and feet to help move that damn log.

"Get in there." I give him the green light when the answer is a unanimous yes. His face lights up like a kid on Christmas. He sprints to the log, positions himself under it, and starts heaving with the rest of the group. Within five seconds, the log moves faster than it has in hours. I have my doubts about how long he can keep it up. I give him ten, maybe fifteen minutes at most before he taps out. I'm dead wrong.

Three hours later, he's no longer the drunken guy on the street shouting at strangers. He's a warrior, a man, and a core member of the team. He's sweating, sacrificing, and giving every ounce of strength he has, as if his life depends on it. When the sun begins to rise, he checks his watch and walks over to me.

"I'm sad to say that I have to go now. I've got a flight to catch and can't miss it," he says, squaring his shoulders and meeting my gaze. "Thank you for this. I needed it, man. This is the best I've felt since I got out."

I offer my hand, and he grasps it firmly, pulling me into an embrace. When he releases me, his eyes are misted with emotion. He blinks a few times, then sprints back to the group to express his gratitude and say goodbye. They embrace him in a big hug and wave until he disappears from sight. It's quieter now that he's gone, and a melancholic feeling washes over me as the sun peeks over the horizon. I can't seem to get his face out of my mind. There was something about his eyes that felt like looking in a mirror. I push away the unease and focus on the group finishing the challenge, allowing satisfaction and pride to replace it.

The group erupts in excited chatter when it's all over—euphoric from having accomplished such a tough challenge. I stand on the sidelines, listening and watching, and it feels good. I feel like everything in my life is finally lining up. I'm working out every day, giving back to my community, showing loyalty to the woman I love, and I'm about to give her exactly what she wants from me.

Twenty-four hours later, I'm sitting in a corner booth at one of Vanessa's and my favorite restaurants. I've already scanned the entrance four times, eagerly waiting for a glimpse of Vanessa's shiny blonde hair. I take a sip of water and try to focus on another part of the room, but my eyes keep darting back to the entrance.

Then I see her—gorgeous Vanessa, my Vanessa, and maybe, just maybe, the future mother of my children. Her eyes sweep across the room and then lock onto mine. It feels good to know that this beautiful woman is looking at me. I stand to greet her, and she pauses for a moment, taking me in from head to toe. Her eyes have changed; there's something different tonight. She's not looking at me with the same starry-eyed admiration she had when she handed me her phone number on that street corner in downtown Dallas. Still, she wraps her arms around me gently and holds on for a while. When she finally lets go, a guarded smile appears on her face.

"I'm so happy to see you."

A deep sense of anticipation rises in my belly as I sit down. I can't wait to see the look of joy on her face when I share the news she's been waiting for. I'm excited to see that spark in her eyes, bright with thoughts of our future together.

"So, you know that thing you asked me to think about?" I lean in. She studies me for a moment before answering cautiously, "Yes…"

I start to share all the thoughts that have been swirling in my head for the past six months—about starting a family and grappling with what it all means. And then I get to the punchline: "Maybe not right away, but I'm in. I'm all in. I'm saying yes."

I expected to see her eyes fill with joy, to have her jump up and throw her arms around me, and to start making plans for our future. But she doesn't. Instead, she looks uncomfortable and surprised by the entire conversation. Even before I finish speaking, I feel deflated and disappointed. The words were hard to say, and the journey to be able to say them was even harder. This was supposed to be a big moment for us, but nothing feels right. It's clear that my answer was not what she was expecting, and it's evident in her awkward response. She had already anticipated that I would say no.

I'm confused. It's obvious my answer has taken her by surprise, but why isn't she happy? Isn't this what she wants? A future with me and the possibility of having a family together?

Something feels off, but I can't quite put my finger on it. Embarrassed by the entire conversation, I change the subject, but a deep uneasiness settles over me. I can't shake the feeling that something is wrong.

CHAPTER 22
THE LIST

"ARE YOU AVAILABLE TO TEACH a firearm lesson? Will Smith needs someone to prep him for filming *Suicide Squad*."

I blink twice when I see the text from my buddy Kevin, making sure I read it correctly. Kevin, a former Navy SEAL and CIA contractor, has been working in Hollywood for a while as a consultant, helping to choreograph fight scenes, ensure accuracy with anything military-related, and coordinate action sequences.

"Hell, yeah, I'm available." If Will Smith needs to brush up on his shooting skills before heading off to film *Suicide Squad*, I'll happily step in. Kevin makes the arrangements, and two days later, I'm at the shooting range, waiting for Will Smith to arrive. I showed up a half-hour early to be on the safe side, so I'm not expecting him for a while, but five minutes later a black SUV pulls into the parking lot, and I'm glad I did. I expect to see an entourage or at least a small security detail, but when the driver's side door opens, Will Smith gets out and no one else follows him.

He approaches me with a smile and shakes my hand respectfully. I lead him to the designated area where we'll be working. After a quick rundown of safety precautions and an overview of the firearms we'll be using, it's time to get started. I demonstrate first and then hand over the gun. He's a natural. When I offer a few tips for improvement, he listens intently and nods thoughtfully. The real Will Smith is even better than the movie character—more articulate, insightful, and kind than I had imagined.

As I grab my phone and dial Vanessa while pulling out of the parking lot, I can't wait to tell her all about it. She doesn't answer. Strange.

An hour later, I try again. Still nothing. I try to put it out of my mind, but I find myself checking my phone every few minutes to see if she's called. When my phone rings and I see her name an hour later, I'm relieved. But the relief is short-lived. Her voice sounds strange. When I ask her where she's been and why she wasn't answering her phone, she offers an explanation, but it doesn't make sense. There are several small contradictions in her story, seemingly insignificant but enough to feed the uneasiness inside of me.

At 10:00 p.m., I feel my hands starting to shake. We're home now, and Vanessa is crying—talking, crying, and then talking some more. I shove my hands under my legs to hide the tremors and don't say a word.

"I'm sorry, Tyler, I'm so sorry."

Two minutes ago, I learned that Vanessa never actually broke it off with *him*. She's been seeing him the entire time we've been together these past six months. I feel angry, betrayed, and devastated. I feel like a fool. I can still hear the sound of my voice telling her that I'm "finally ready" to start a family. How naïve I was to think that I was the only one.

There are so many emotions coming at me all at once, and it seems I've lost the ability to regulate them. My hands are still shaking, and I feel cold all over. I want to leave, run, to be anywhere but here, but she's still talking. Telling me that she wants me. Telling me that it's over between her and the other guy. Telling me that she's been in a dark place and is struggling to know how to handle this situation.

Now I feel dizzy and cold, just like I did the first time I learned she'd slept with someone else. I can't stop the shaking, and it's fucking embarrassing. I have cold chills, and my jaw is clacking uncontrollably like I'm freezing, but inside I'm on fire. I feel myself breaking, fracturing, crumbling, and I don't know how to stop it. I need a drink. I need a line. I need a pill. I need to be alone.

When Vanessa runs out of things to say, I pop two Klonopins in my mouth and lie in bed, waiting for my mind to go numb. It takes ten minutes before nothingness wraps itself around me and disconnects me from the torrent of emotion. Sleep comes over me with sweet relief. When I open my eyes again, Vanessa is there—awake and ready to talk.

"Tyler, I want to get out of this situation. My mind is trapped in a fog. I can't think clearly, I don't feel like myself. I know this is toxic; I know I need to break it off for good, but I'm scared, confused, and so overwhelmed." Tears stream down her face, and one falls on my arm.

"I'm sorry I didn't tell you about him. I just didn't know how. I didn't want to hurt you; I wanted to find a way to fix this myself, but I just couldn't."

She buries her face in her lap, and her body shakes as she sobs. Her eyes are pleading, raw with emotion, when she looks up at me again.

"Please help, Tyler. Please help me get out of this situation. Please don't leave me alone. Please be patient with me."

I don't say anything for a while; the thoughts in my head are too loud. I want to scream in rage, resentment, and indignation. I want to break free from this toxic dance. I want to save her and love her. I know what it's like to feel like your mind is trapped in fog. I know what it's like to lose yourself. I know what it's like to feel confused and overwhelmed. She was the only person who braved that vast ocean of darkness to find me when I was lost. She held me together when I was broken. She kept me afloat when I was drowning inside my own mind. Maybe I would still be stuck in that beige office, depressed and alone, had she not pulled me out of there. I needed her, and now she needs me. I owe it to her to brave the darkness of this vast ocean she's lost in and help her find her way. I owe it to her to stay.

I move closer and pull her into my arms. I'm the life raft that she clings to as the storms of chaos rage around us.

◆◇

I wake up in Vanessa's apartment six months later, feeling exhausted. I'd just returned from another weekend of back-to-back GoRuck events and driven straight from the airport to her place. It was good to see her, but she only had three hours to spare before heading to work. I love leading GoRuck events, but I hate leaving her alone. That's when she's vulnerable, that's when *he* tends to call, that's when they always seem to find each other again.

She wants to distance herself from him; she wants me. But it's a complex situation. She can't just walk away easily. *"Just be patient. You need to protect her, you need to fight for her, you need to win,"* the Warrior whispers.

"Be patient?" the Destroyer fights back. *"She's with another man! What the fuck are you doing?"*

"I'm saving her."

Today is my day off, but I can't say I'm looking forward to it. Sure, it's nice to sleep in and be off my feet, but that familiar anxious, restless feeling creeps in whenever my schedule isn't filled to the brim with things to accomplish.

I shower, dress, and prepare to leave the house but pause momentarily when I realize I can't find my keys. I retrace my steps from last night without success. After five minutes of searching in obvious places, I start to check less likely spots.

I slide open the nightstand drawer beside the bed and sift through a pile of papers inside. Suddenly, something catches my eye. Handwritten at the top of a sheet of notebook paper is my name. But it's not alone. *His* name is scrawled boldly beside mine with a line separating the two. Below is a list. At first I struggle to comprehend what I'm reading.

- Sense of humor
- Romantic Sensibility
- Looks
- Financial Status
- Sexual Connection
- Physical Shape
- Fatherhood Potential

Beside each item is a number. And then it hits me: Vanessa made a pros and cons list to help her decide which man she wants to be with. She's rated each of us on a scale of 1 to 10 for each category. My reality spins, and I feel deeply hurt, wounded, and betrayed. All this time, I thought she was afraid of him, thought she wanted to get away from him. I thought I was the clear winner in her mind, no questions asked. But I was wrong. There is a very big question in her mind, such a big question that she had to *write it down on a fucking piece of paper.* The list changes everything.

I spot my keys peeking out from the pocket of the jeans I hastily discarded last night. I grab them, snatch the list, and leave the house.

Vanessa returns home from work looking tired. After showering and changing into her favorite pajamas, she settles beside me on the couch, chatting about her evening. I could confront her. I could tell her about the list and how it changes everything, but I don't. I keep it a secret, letting it fester like an infected wound. The Destroyer begins compiling a list of his own—an account of all her wrongs, offenses, rejections, and betrayals. I once vowed to repay her for all her love, care, and kindness, and I've kept my word. I've been a fucking saint these last six months while she's been going back and forth between him and me. Okay, not a fucking saint. I found ways to strike back at her, and she's always matched my efforts. Blow for blow, wound for wound, we've kept the tally even. But the list—oh, the list changes everything. I'm not ready to let go. I still want to help and protect her. I want to pull her away from him. And I want to *win*.

Vanessa falls asleep beside me, while I lie awake in bed for hours in the quiet room, the static white noise of anxiety raging in my mind.

Is this it? The crazy, epic love story I always dreamed about? I'm consumed by her, I have to have her, and I care about her. But is it love? I know it used to be. These days, I'm not so sure.

CHAPTER 23
HOLLYWOOD ISN'T DEAD

"HELLO?" I ANSWER MY PHONE, wedging it between my ear and shoulder as I finish preparing breakfast the next day. It's Kevin, my buddy who recently connected me with Will Smith. He gets straight to the point.

"Hey, Tyler. I'm flying to Toronto on Sunday to prep for *Suicide Squad*. I want you to come with me as a consultant and be on camera. You'll be brilliant on set, and I need someone I can trust who knows their stuff. We'll be there for at least five months. I know it's a big move, but it's a huge opportunity. Think about it, man."

I always dreamed of working on a big Hollywood movie as a kid, but I never imagined it would come full circle. But my excitement turns to anxiety when I think of Vanessa. *I can't leave her. Not now, not like this.* If I go, we'll never recover. She'll go back to him, and I'll lose her forever. If I stay, we can work things out. I can help her navigate this confusion, as we always have. We'll find our way through. But I'll miss out on a once-in-a-lifetime opportunity, always wondering what might have been. Then I'll resent her for holding me back. I want to save her, protect her—be the knight in shining armor she needs now. I need to win this battle and help her break free. Or maybe it's me that needs to break free. Maybe this is just the wakeup call I needed to get me away from my kryptonite. Maybe it's time for me to finally let go. But can I?

"Tyler, no, please. You can't leave now." The tears come fast, gushing like a fire hydrant as soon as I tell her about the call. "I need you right now."

Everything in me wants to pull her close and assure her that I'll stay, that I'll fight for us, that I'll see this through. But I'm not so sure.

"I want to, I really do. But I don't know, I just feel like I need to do this for me." I search her eyes, hoping she'll understand.

"So all the things you've said about me being important, about fighting for us, that's all just an act? I was loyal to you, stood by you for years while you struggled to find yourself. I loved you even when you were at your worst. I came knocking on that office door when you locked yourself away from the world, and all I wanted was to have YOU. To go out and feel like that girl with butterflies in her stomach on our first date. I was patient with you, I was loyal to you, I gave you everything. And look at you—one offer from Hollywood and you're out the door."

Now my blood is boiling, and anger rises like acid in my throat.

"YOU WANT TO TALK ABOUT LOYALTY?" My voice rises in righteous fury. "You want to play that game with me?" I scoff inwardly as I open the ledger in my mind, the carefully itemized list of evil deeds, offenses, rejections, and betrayals. "YOU FUCKING CHEATED ON ME BEHIND MY BACK—NOT ONCE BUT TWICE! You are such a fucking hypocrite! I was ready to have KIDS WITH YOU, and you were screwing around behind my back that WHOLE FUCKING TIME!"

Now her tears have been replaced with fire.

"Can you not hear yourself?" she says calmly, *lethally*. "You want to call *me* a hypocrite; you want to call me dishonest; you want to sit up on your fucking high horse and judge ME? You never wanted to have kids, and we both know it. You just said that because you wanted to get me back. You were willing to tell me anything, *anything* you thought I wanted to hear so that I'd agree to come back to you. It was the same story with our open relationship the first time! You just sat there and agreed to it, acted like you wanted to bang other people more than I did. You never had the BALLS to be a man, to be HONEST, and to fight for me! You've been giving ME ultimatums for months now, pushing and pushing and pushing me to give you EVERYTHING, and yet the moment YOU get a nice job offer, off you go!"

Her words hit me like knives, plunging into all the tender places she aimed for, and she's relishing my pain. The Destroyer raises his shield and pulls back his spear.

"YOU ARE SUCH A FUCKING BITCH! All I've done these past few months is fight for you, and how do you repay me? You keep going back to *him* every time I turn my back, like a fucking WHORE!"

Now it's my turn to stand in victory as my words pierce the tender places I aimed for.

"And you want to know WHY I go back to him? Huh? Because he satisfies me in ways you never could. And *you*? You will wind up on that Disney park bench, all alone forever." Her face is inches from mine as the blade pierces the armor of the Destroyer and cuts deeply into the Warrior's heart. Now we are silent, staring at the open wounds we've created, watching each other bleed.

How did we get here? We were the perfect love story. We were the unbreakable duo that was supposed to grow old together. How did something so tender, so beautiful, become so toxic and grotesque? I thought she was my partner in crime, the one I could rely on to face this crazy, chaotic world arm in arm. Maybe we were the ones creating the chaos all along. Maybe this fucked-up world squeezed the love right out of us until our innocence died. Or maybe we suffocated it out of each other, clinging to one another like a life raft, white-knuckled and afraid of letting go. One thing I know for certain: If we keep this up, we'll both drown. Maybe it's time for one of us to swim to shore.

◄►

I grab a bottle of Adderall and shake out four 20 mg time-release tablets, popping them into my mouth and swallowing. My suitcase is open on my bed, empty. I snatch a T-shirt from the top of the clean laundry pile and lay it neatly inside. The next time I pick it up, I'll be in Toronto. Vanessa's voice plays over and over in my mind—sobbing, pleading with me to stay, begging me to fight for her, to fight for us. And I want to. I want to stay and fight. But I can't. I need to escape this orbit of toxicity that we're in. I've made my choice. I'm leaving. I'm choosing to fight for my life and my future instead of her. I'm swimming to shore, leaving her to fend for herself in the midst of the storm. And I feel like a fucking asshole.

I'm starting to think that we're not really Bonnie and Fucking Clyde or partners in crime. We're more like partners in chaos, facing challenges together arm in arm. And now I'm leaving her alone, right in the middle of the storm, and she'll have to face it all by herself. I know that the moment my plane leaves the runway, she'll go running back into his arms, and I'll have to live with the fact that I gave up the fight to pull her back into mine. That's the thought that eats at me more than anything. I grab the bottle of Adderall and shake out three more tablets. Fuck it. My plane leaves in twenty-four hours, and the war is raging inside me again. The Warrior is fighting for a better future, fighting to grow, fighting to remove me from what has become a toxic relationship. The Destroyer is filled with jealousy, guilt, self-hate, and a raging desire to disappear into the hazy oblivion of Adderall. I put another T-shirt into my suitcase and wait for the pills to kick in. My phone rings, and I expect to see Vanessa's name on the screen, but it's one of the GoRuck cadres. I guess news has circulated by now that I'm leaving. He's sad to see me go but offers his hearty congratulations for the big opportunity.

"Man, are you just *stoked?*" he asks, his voice carrying far more excitement than I feel. I muster an enthusiastic response, even though I don't feel much at all. But the longer we talk, the more I do feel stoked. My mind feels clear and sharp. The fog is gone, and now I'm one step ahead in the conversation—the words flowing from my mind to my mouth with precision. By the time I hang up the phone, I am flying high. It's working. But I need more.

I waste no time in popping two more 20 mg tablets into my mouth before I finish packing. It's almost 10:00 p.m. now, and my flight doesn't leave until morning. I know I'm not going to be able to sleep because I'm flying high, intergalactically high.

At midnight, I shake out two more tablets. Now there are nine 20 mg Adderall tablets in my system, and there's only one word to describe how I'm feeling: *horny*. My entire body is pulsing with raw appetite, and suddenly I can't think of anything besides sex. It's absolutely consuming.

When I log on to my favorite porn site, I feel like I'm seeing it for the first time. My body reacts to the images, movements, and sounds like never before. Another hour passes, then another and another, but it feels like minutes. I grab the Adderall bottle and take three more tablets. Now I'm glued to the screen and can't look away. Another hour goes by—except this time it's not just an hour, it's three fucking hours—and I really need to get to the airport. I feel dizzy as I stand, and my vision is so spotty that I feel like I'm walking through a tunnel when I enter the airport. But my body is still on fire, and I can think of nothing but opening my iPad again—that portal to the land of pleasure and porn. I feel my face and arms twitching in strange ways, and I'm sure I'm not the only one noticing my odd behavior, but I couldn't care less about anyone or anything around me. I just need to get back to my iPad.

Once my bags are checked and I'm past security, there's still an hour and a half to go before my flight leaves. I head straight for the men's bathroom, hang my backpack on the stall door, and pull out my iPad. *Back in business, baby.*

I pull the lid of the toilet down for a more comfortable place to sit and settle in. The moment the images are in front of me, I'm consumed. My greedy eyes devour them, but it's not enough. I need more and more and more. A knock on the door makes me jump.

"Hey, man, get up! You need to stop and get out of there."

I freeze when I hear a man's voice on the other side of the stall, and by the sound of it, he knows exactly what I'm up to in here. I stand up, zip my pants, and flush the toilet, even though we both know it's a waste of good water to do so, and walk out with my head held high to the waiting area for my plane. Only twenty minutes until boarding.

I take a seat, but my legs are bobbing up and down, and my eyes keep twitching. I know I probably look like a meth addict right now, but I still don't care. I feel disconnected and indifferent about my surroundings, hell, even my life. The only thing I feel connected to is the voracious sexual appetite inside me that can't seem to be satisfied. I notice several people looking at me strangely as I board the plane, but I just look the other way. A man settles into the middle seat next to me and offers a polite nod, but I hardly notice. As soon as the plane lifts off, I grab the airline blanket in front of me and throw it over my entire body, including my face, and secure it on the seatback, creating a nice little tent. When the blue light of my iPad welcomes me down the porn hole once again, I feel relieved. The captain's voice takes me by surprise as it crackles over the loudspeaker, announcing our descent.

I stumble through Toronto Pearson International Airport, still higher than a kite. I tap my feet impatiently beside the baggage claim as I wait to retrieve my luggage. Inside the taxi, I close my eyes and rest my head on the back of the seat, and my mind flashes through a stream of pornographic snapshots that I've saved up over the past twelve hours. I haven't slept in thirty-six hours. I check into my hotel room, park my suitcase in the corner, take out my iPad, and settle into bed.

But now I'm not feeling like I did on the plane. A mixture of sadness and dread suddenly invades my world of euphoria like an alien presence. I've gone as high as I'm going to go, and now the crash is coming. I take four Klonopins and wait for the little benzos to kick in. I can feel it. I fall asleep with my iPad on my chest.

When I wake up fourteen hours later, sunlight is peeking around the corners of the hotel's blackout curtains. Every nerve in my body feels like it spent eighteen hours propelling me toward that intergalactic high, only to crash and burn. Now I'm just a pile of ash, a burned-out nervous system, lying on the bed, unable to move. This also provides the perfect opportunity to replay the last thirty-six hours in high definition. I'm captive at the premier showing of *Tyler Grey's Most Shameful Moments*. I watch the man with the iPad in the men's bathroom stall and the twitching, drugged-out loser with a blanket over his head, looking at porn on a plane. It's not me. It can't be me.

I roll over on my stomach and close my eyes as shame twists around me, suffocating me until I want to disappear. Regret, guilt, and emptiness throw open the doors, and that vast black void is back.

"*Come on, cut yourself some slack,*" the Destroyer whispers. "*Your girlfriend just cheated on you. She's the one to blame here. You're taking a big chance on your career, and you're under a lot of stress. So you took a few too many pills and looked at some porn. So what? You're a man. You're just blowing off steam."*

I try to make a compelling case for the defendant in the courtroom of my mind, hoping to reduce the harshness of my initial judgment. For a moment, I feel relieved. But it doesn't last long.

Because I know this isn't just stress, this isn't "just what men do," and this isn't a funny story I'll tell my buddies for a few laughs. It's not funny at all. It's downright scary. The last eighteen hours are another piece of evidence that I'm losing control. And it's that—the element of uncontrollable compulsion—that makes me deeply uncomfortable. I feel like something else invaded my mind, grabbed the controls, and used me like a puppet for the night. It's me, I know it's me, but it doesn't feel like me at all. And the worst part is knowing that if I say this out loud, people will assume I'm just making excuses. *"Oh, it's not me! I couldn't have possibly done all those things!"* I wish it were a weak-ass excuse, but it's not, and that scares the shit out of me.

I've always been able to control my actions and responses—I built my career on the ability to regulate my reactions, even in high-stress scenarios. But this is different. The Destroyer is taking hold of me from the inside out, and I'm beginning to fear that it's beyond my control.

My mind offers temporary relief with an alternative line of thought: the fact that I left Vanessa, and now he's comforting her, pulling her closer than ever. I have a front-row seat to another film: *I Wonder What She's Doing With HIM*—but this isn't a premiere; it's a rerun. I've watched it a hundred times over the last few days. My mind is now more exhausted than my body. I'm alone. Totally and completely alone. But I've had enough of my own pity party. Fuck this, enough is enough. I'm in Toronto, ready to shoot *Suicide Squad*. How proud lanky nineteen-year-old Tyler would be if he could see me now. I take a shower, order room service, and try to shake off the lethargy that's settled over me. I need to be fresh for tomorrow morning. *New day. New chapter. New beginning.*

CHAPTER 24

SUICIDE SQUAD

WORK BEGINS ON MONDAY MORNING, and from the moment I arrive on location, I'm swept up in the electrifying current of a production of godlike proportions. The momentum is exhilarating. Making a movie is pure chaos, *just how I like it.*

"You ready for this?" Kevin, my buddy and the lead military adviser, asks when I enter his office. He extends a thick palm for a friendly handshake.

"Hell yeah."

"Look, we've got six weeks until we start shooting and a shitload to do before then. Get ready for some long days—we're going to be working around the clock."

I couldn't be happier to hear that. I thrive on being busy; I need it. Structure, productivity, and good old-fashioned hard work are exactly what I need right now.

Kevin shows me around the offices and then leads me down a hallway to another area.

"And here's the concept art room," he grins, holding the door open for me.

When I step inside, I feel like I've entered another world. The walls are covered in sketches and drawings from floor to ceiling. The imagination, detail, and emotion in each piece are nothing short of extraordinary. One illustration shows a city street with the Joker's car. Another depicts Harley Quinn standing in front of a skyscraper. Yet another shows the Joker inside a helicopter, grinning from ear to ear. With just one glance, I can see it, smell it, and feel it. I look from one drawing to the next, awestruck by the time, effort, and dedication invested in bringing this world to life.

"Holy shit!" is all I can manage to say, though it pales in comparison to what I'm feeling.

"Come meet David." Kevin waves me out of the concept room and down another hall. Within minutes, I'm standing in front of David Ayer, writer and producer of *Suicide Squad*. He stands, shakes my hand, and welcomes me to the team. As we chat, my eyes drift to his desk, where a stack of *Suicide Squad* and *Harley Quinn* comic books is neatly piled. David is the real deal. When his phone rings, he smiles apologetically and Kevin and I show ourselves out.

"Alright, first things first. You need to get to the script room and read the script so you know what we're doing here. Show him, will ya?" Kevin nods to a young female assistant wearing wire-rimmed glasses and a black graphic T-shirt. I'm not exactly sure what the script room is, but it doesn't take long to find out.

As an operator, I had top security clearance to review sensitive information, state secrets, and more. But nothing compares to the security for the *Suicide Squad* script.

"They'll need your phone before you can go inside," the assistant says.

A burly man with a mustache takes my phone, and I'm led into a small, bare room with a table and four chairs. A thick binder sits in the middle of the table.

"You can have your phone when you're done." The burly man nods, then shuts the door behind him.

The room is silent. It's just me and the script. I feel like I'm actually in a movie instead of helping to make one. For the next several hours, I dive into the script, absorbing every detail. It quickly becomes clear that there's a strong military theme throughout and a ton of fight scenes and action sequences. We've got a lot of work ahead to be ready for production.

As I turn the pages of the binder, reality begins to sink in—where I am and what I'm doing. I was so focused on leaving Vanessa, so preoccupied with the war inside my mind, and so numbed and high that

I hadn't stepped back to see the big picture. *Holy fuck! I'm on the set of a movie that takes place in the DC Comic Book Universe!*

Over the next six weeks, the entire crew works around the clock, just as Kevin had forecast. There's an endless list of tasks: testing camouflage patterns with the director, designing each fight scene with the fight coordinators, and advising on gunplay. We're also in charge of coordinating the action sequences with the stunt players. The Canadian stunt crew, fresh off filming *Mad Max: Fury Road*, is on fire. Within an hour of working with them, I'm blown away by their talent. From sunup to sundown, I stay busy and happy. As long as my body is moving and my mind is engaged, I'm okay. I volunteer for every task, wanting to be utterly exhausted by the time I return to my room at night.

Still, in the quiet moments just before sleep, thoughts of Vanessa invade my mind and consume me. Anxiety, guilt, anger, and sadness mix into a cocktail of emotions that eats at me like a parasite.

But all that fades as I walk down the hallway of my hotel in downtown Toronto a few nights later. Every cell of my body is alive, and my senses are on high alert. It's not just the cocaine in my system, though that certainly adds to the thrill; it's the fact that I have no idea what awaits me behind door 808. *Here we go again*. The door opens, and there she is.

"Hi, I'm Mila," she says, her eyes sweeping over me with approval. I return the gesture. Oh Mila, we're going to get along just fine.

As days turn into weeks, the set begins to take shape, and we're all in awe. The Arkham Asylum set is not only massive but intricately detailed. The sheer scale is breathtaking, like stepping into another world. It becomes clear why it costs $175 million to make a movie like this. The sense of collaboration and excitement multiplies when the main cast arrives. At first, it's surreal to see Margot Robbie's smile one minute and Will Smith walking past the next. I've heard stories about movie stars being aloof, but this experience refutes those tales. I'm pleasantly surprised by how friendly Jay Hernandez and Joel Kinnaman are as they work with our team. Everyone is down-to-earth and grateful for the chance to bring this iconic story to life. The camaraderie and teamwork exceed my expectations.

"The new gym is opening tomorrow. Want to come?" one of the stunt coordinators asks one night before I head back to my room. Will Smith has decided to build an on-site gym for the cast and crew, and we've all been eagerly awaiting its completion.

"Of course!"

I show up in my gym clothes at 7:30 a.m., but I'm already late—it seems the entire cast and crew are ahead of me. Margot is in one corner with headphones on, doing Pilates, and Will is with his trainer in another, lifting weights. I join a group of crew members warming up with the Gym Jones Method training program. I glance at the whiteboard where today's workout is listed. *Jesus, it makes CrossFit look like a warm-up!* Within minutes, the workout is in full swing, and I'm pouring sweat along with everyone else. Ten minutes in, I feel discomfort in my right arm. I should lighten the weight on my barbell and slow down, but I don't want to. The gym is full of bulging muscles and perfectly defined bodies, and I'm not about to be shown up, not here, not now. Mind over body, I push past the pain. By the end of the session, I feel worse than when I started. But after a quick shower, I'm ready to go.

"How's it going, man?" Kevin greets me with a smile when I arrive at the work area.

"Pretty good, thanks," I reply, setting down my backpack and pulling out a bottle of Norco, a combination of hydrocodone and acetaminophen, that I brought from California. I'm already in a lot of pain, and the day is just beginning. I want to double the dosage but know too much acetaminophen can cause liver damage. I'm already taking more than the maximum recommended dose—three 10 mg tablets a day. As I pop the pills and wash them down with a gulp of water, Kevin's eyes narrow.

"Dude, what the hell? You're going to be knocked out if you take all that. You'll barely be able to work."

He's not the first to say this. Everyone says Norco is supposed to make you sleepy, but it has the opposite effect on me. I feel wired and pleasantly numb, just how I like it.

"Nah, I'll be alright." I glance at the dwindling supply and make a mental note to find out how to get a refill in Toronto. Kevin doesn't press the issue, and we get started. The work is grueling, but I love it.

I'm utilizing skills I haven't tapped into for years, working with the team to choreograph fight scenes, teach firearm techniques, and collaborate with the stunt crew. Corners of my mind that I thought were dormant are awake again, and it feels amazing.

When I check my watch and realize it's been four hours since I've had anything to eat or drink, I grab a bottle of water. As I take a few big gulps, I notice Kevin staring at me.

"Dude, I can't even tell you took anything this morning. You're out there fucking killing it with three Norco in you. It's insane."

I guess I've become so accustomed to taking pills that I don't think about it anymore. Kevin, a former operator and Navy SEAL, is also a medic, so I know better than to dismiss his opinion. Maybe it is crazy, but it's working. I'm performing well, so what's the harm?

It shouldn't be hard to get a refill; all I need is to pull up my right shirt sleeve. Every doctor I've seen knows I live with chronic pain, and no one has refused to give me relief. It turns out Canadian doctors are no different.

A few days later, I get a new prescription—not exactly Norco, but straight hydrocodone, the opioid pain reliever, without any acetaminophen. This is perfect for me. Without the concern of liver damage, I can double the dosage without hesitation. The Gym Jones workouts are brutal, and the long hours on set are no joke. I need all the help I can get to perform at my best.

But if I'm honest, the pain I'm trying to alleviate isn't just from workouts or work. It's the pain of feeling alone, worthless, and empty. It's the struggle to contain the chaos in my mind. When I'm quiet and alone, it's almost unbearable.

"But the workouts are tough, especially with your injury..." The lawyer for the defense rises again to make a compelling argument. I push these thoughts away, pick up my phone, and text Mila. We've seen each other every week since our first night together, and she never disappoints.

"Don't do it," the Warrior whispers. "This isn't you."

"What's the harm?" the Destroyer counters. "It's legal here. You're a man with needs, and you're not in a position for a relationship right now. Vanessa hurt you, tore your heart out and beat it with a baseball bat. It's her fault you're damaged goods. Any woman you get involved with will only end up hurt. You're doing everyone a favor."

The high returns as I walk down the hotel halls, even though I know what awaits me on the other side of the door. I knock, Mila opens it, and excitement surges through me. But three hours later, as I walk back through the hotel, it's all gone. The guilt, shame, emptiness, and self-hatred are back. *This isn't me. This isn't me. This isn't me.*

At 6:00 p.m. the next day, we arrive on set in downtown Toronto. Filming begins today, and as I open the side door of the van and step out, my mouth falls open. I've entered a postapocalyptic world of gargantuan proportions. The streets are roped off and deserted, like Times Square without a soul. In the middle of the street is the tail section of a 737, as if a plane crash happened moments ago. Nearby, a Humvee looks like it's been torn apart by the Hulk. A parachute and an ejected airplane seat lie on the ground, discarded like afterthoughts. I can hardly believe my eyes, and I'm not alone in my awe. We're all feeling fortunate to be part of this.

Once filming starts, the cast and crew fall into a rhythm—sleeping during the day and shooting at night. My role has evolved beyond planning, consulting, and assisting. I'm now part of the film itself. While I expect only a brief glimpse of my uniform in the final cut, the experience is incredibly rewarding. Every time I'm on camera, I give it everything I've got. I wear a full combat uniform with armored plates and perform every action sequence as if it were real life. It's the only way I know to perform. This is my team now, and I'm ready to make any sacrifice necessary for it.

Fuck.

Panic spreads through my chest as I stare at the one remaining hydrocodone pill in my prescription bottle. After five months on the set of *Suicide Squad*, which is now winding down its final month of filming, I got an unexpected invitation for a weekend getaway from good ol' Med Shed Dan in North Carolina. It's the first weekend off I've had in five months—this will be a chance to decompress and have some fun. But now I've got a problem. A serious problem. I planned to pick up a fresh supply of Norco when I landed, but I've been to three pharmacies since I woke up this morning and all of them say I need a new prescription from a doctor before they can fill it. Getting pain meds has become a hell of a lot more difficult since they started cracking down on the opioid crisis. I've called every doctor I can find, and no one has an appointment available today. I pop the last pill into my mouth and swallow, knowing full well that one pill isn't going to do shit when my body is used to taking twelve to fifteen of them. I already feel the withdrawal coming. My muscles are aching, my head hurts, and a thick fog has descended over my mind.

A few miles away from where I'm standing now is the little beige apartment where I used to live. The same place where I stood over the toilet and flushed away all my medication just weeks after being released from the hospital.

I had no fucking idea what was happening then. The doctors sent me home with all kinds of instruction forms and directions on how to take care of my arm but forgot to tell me that my body was now dependent on drugs.

In those days, I didn't understand what I was up against. I thought I'd already faced the darkness and come out the other side. I thought I was going to be back in the field, that I'd have the injury beat in no time. I just had no fucking idea, so I flushed all my medication down the toilet. I remember how surprised I was when my doctor told me to ask my neighbors to drive me to the hospital, and even more shocked to learn that my body was now dependent on all those tiny little pills swimming in the turd soup of the sewage line. Now I know better. Now I know exactly what will happen if I don't find a way to get my hands on those pills soon. I also know that I'm not just taking them for pain in my arm anymore. Yeah, sure, it still hurts. But after I started doing CrossFit every day, I managed to keep my dosage to a minimum for years. The evidence for motive is clear: I took three Adderalls the moment I found out that Vanessa had cheated on me and started taking high dosages of hydrocodone ever since. I did it when I felt worthless, alone, nothing. I did it to take control, to hide that shameful, weak, worthless man seeking love and approval in a whirlwind of chaos. Pills, porn, sex, grueling work, a toxic relationship—any and every form of chaos I could find. And I need it. I thrive on it. Give me a challenge, give me pain, give me discomfort, give me a dangerously sky-high feeling any day over facing the darkness inside me and the fear of what I'll find in the shadows. *Give me anything or anyone to fight so I can stop fighting myself.*

It's the quiet moments, when everything is good and my environment is calm, that I hate the most. Give me noise, give me a mission to accomplish, give me something to do, give me anything other than the fog of this War Within.

But the more I stare at the empty bottle, the more I feel ashamed. I've come all this way to see my buddy, to have a nice weekend, and I can't because I've run out of drugs. Once again, I feel like I'm living someone else's life.

An hour later, I'm standing in front of Womack Army Medical Center—the same place where I spent months recovering after my injury and where I checked in after flushing all my medication down the toilet. I remember how confident I was in my righteous stance and the disdain I felt for those "weak people" who relied on booze and pills to get through the day. That day when I flushed my medication, I was brimming with self-assurance. I hadn't touched so much as a baby Aspirin before my injury; I'd always managed on my own. *Look at me now. This isn't me. This isn't me. This isn't me.*

It's been roughly a decade since I stepped foot inside this building, and I still remember standing in this very doorway with my casted arm on the day they released me. How naïve I was to think that the hard part was over. I really did think I'd beaten the worst of it. Suddenly, I think of the years that have passed since that day. I've done a lot that I'm proud of. I've learned a lot; I've built a lot. But I'm here again. They successfully reconstructed my arm and found a way to hold the fractured bone and flesh together. Turns out that wasn't the hard part. The hard part is trying to find a way to hold together the fragments of my fractured identity—*that* is the battle. And right now, I really need hydrocodone to help me fight that battle. I'm about to walk through the doors here at Womack with the express purpose of getting drugs—and I hate myself for it. I'm embarrassed and ashamed. This time, there's no defense, no excuses to offer the judge and jury in my mind. I'm well aware of who I am now and what I'm doing. And I don't hide this from the nurses and doctors either.

"I'm not going to lie to you." I look the nurse straight in the eyes because I will no longer lie to myself. "I'm seeking drugs. If I'm exhibiting drug-seeking behavior right now, it's because I am, in fact, seeking drugs."

They look at my arm and my medical history. They're kind and understanding—they always were. They give me a shot that provides immediate relief and a prescription that will tide me over until I make it back to Toronto. I am grateful but I am ashamed.

My head rests on the hospital bed, and I close my eyes even though I'm not tired. Too many thoughts and questions are swirling around in my mind. *How did I end up back here again? Why do I feel like I'm going around and around in the same loop, falling into the same patterns over and over again? Why...?*

I wasn't like this before. I never drank, never did drugs, never hired prostitutes. I was disciplined, full of purpose, and dedicated to a mission. I'm still a hard worker, I'm still disciplined, and I've still got aspirations, but something about me is different than it was before. Will I ever be at peace, or will I spend a lifetime fighting this war inside my mind?

Will I ever feel healed and whole, or will I spend my life just trying to find something to numb the pain and hold the brokenness together? I wish I knew.

That's the part that bothers me the most, I don't really know why. I don't know why I keep doing things I don't want to do. I don't know why I feel like my identity has been fractured into two sides of myself that are now at war. I don't know why I feel a deep sense of grief and loss. Why I chase the highs and create chaos. Why I avoid stillness and destroy peace. Why I feel so worthless all the time. I wish I knew how to find myself again. If someone would just show me how to conquer this battle, I'd fight to the death. But I've asked. I've talked to therapists and counselors. I've looked for answers, read and studied everything I can get my hands on. I've done all the things I know to do. And yet I'm here again. Trying to heal an invisible wound—not just invisible to other people but invisible even to myself. I'm trying to fight a battle against an unknown enemy. *Who and what is it?*

I'd do anything to find peace. I'd do anything to feel like myself again. I'd do anything to win this war. When I exit Womack, I feel physically better, but the shame, guilt, and self-loathing are still there. I've spent half of my weekend getaway getting drugs just so I can function. I try to enjoy the rest of the trip, but I can't shake the disgust I feel for myself. When I enter the airport for my return flight to Toronto, I'm relieved to be returning. I'll feel better when I'm busy again. I'll feel better when... I pull out my phone and text Mila. *Are you available tomorrow night?* I wait for a reply, which comes within minutes. *For you, of course. What time?*

◂▸

"Holy shit, look!" One of the crew members jabs his elbow into my ribcage, and I follow the direction of his pointing finger. *Holy shit is right.*

A giant crane is swinging a helicopter through the air. We're on top of a building in downtown Toronto, so far away that it's hard to see the details of what's happening. Maybe this is just a test run, but damn, it's incredible to watch! Our eyes are glued to the scene. Suddenly, the helicopter makes a sharp turn, and through the open doors, I catch a glimpse of the Joker, decked out in all his glory, holding a golden AK-47. He tilts his head back and bursts into a maniacal laugh. For a moment, it feels like we're not just shooting a movie, we're actually part of it, and it's amazing.

When the helicopter vanishes from view, a wave of gratitude washes over me. My life isn't perfect. It's crazy, fucked up at times, hard as hell, and painful too. But damn, I've had the chance to do some incredible things, and tonight will be one of those good memories I'll cherish. Maybe it's the view, or the electric atmosphere tonight, but I feel like this whole experience is going to change my life. I can't see exactly what's ahead, but I sense that my life is shifting in ways I can't quite explain. I've made a lot of great connections here and worked my ass off to prove my worth to the team. That hasn't gone unnoticed. It was fucking hard to get here, and I still feel guilty most nights about everything I left behind, but I know it was the right decision. Tonight feels like a turning point. I'm going to wean myself off these pain meds and all the toxic behaviors that no longer serve me. I just need to get back to the old me.

CHAPTER 25
NEW ORLEANS BY FRIDAY

"CAN YOU BE IN NEW Orleans by Friday?" The question hangs in the air for a moment before I respond. It's been two years since I wrapped up my work on *Suicide Squad*. Though I've taken on various Hollywood projects since then, my main role has been as the security team leader for a Fortune 100 chairman of the board in California.

A lot has changed in a year. I've successfully weaned myself off both pain meds and only take Adderall occasionally. The moment of clarity came after wrapping up *Suicide Squad* and confronting my addiction head-on when I ended up back at Womack Army Medical Center. When I returned home, I scheduled an appointment with my doctor, and together we devised a three-month plan to reduce my dependency gradually. By the final week of the plan, I decided to leave the country with only two tablets left, fully aware they'd be gone in a couple of days and I'd have no means to get more. All willpower, no rehab. And it worked. My body feels better and my mind is clearer. You don't even realize you're walking around with that constant, nagging feeling until it's gone. The only drawback was insomnia, a common side effect when weaning off opioids, but it's been a nightmare. My doctor prescribed Klonopin, which works like a charm. As soon as it kicks in, you're not just sleepy; you don't give a flying fuck about anything. And for someone with night anxiety and a racing mind, that's a gift.

Getting clean isn't the only change. I also have a beautiful girl named Sarah in my life. In many ways, she's like a female version of me. She's a Marine combat veteran and served as an RTO for a Marine engineering unit. We worked together as a male-female bodyguarding team, and what do you know, we fell for each other in the process—a real live Mr. and Mrs. Smith.

We share many similarities and get along really well. Things are pretty good these days. But now, life has thrown me another big curveball. *New Orleans by Friday.*

My buddy Matt is on the other end of the phone. He's about to shoot a pilot episode for a new TV series about the life of Navy SEALs, and he wants me to provide military technology advice for the show. As a Navy SEAL himself, he would normally handle this, but he's swamped with responsibilities as the executive producer. With that one phone call, everything shifts, giving me a crucial decision to make.

Today is Wednesday. I could continue my day as if I never got the call, or I could take a leap, quit my job, and figure out how to be in New Orleans by Friday afternoon. It's a gamble—this pilot could either become the next big hit, or it might never see the light of day. Only one in a hundred pilots gets picked up and turned into a show. And even then, most shows don't make past one season.

When Friday afternoon arrives, I'm taxiing toward the gate at Louis Armstrong New Orleans International Airport, ready for whatever comes next. The work starts immediately.

After connecting with Matt, I meet with the production team to gain a deeper understanding of the project. Beyond my buddy's brief overview, I know very little about it. They hand me a copy of the script, and I spend the rest of the day diving into it. The script is good. Really good. I knew it would be action-packed, filled with heart-pounding combat scenes and covert missions, but I didn't anticipate its honesty about the struggles and challenges of the job. If we execute this right, it could genuinely resonate with a lot of people.

With a tight schedule of six weeks to nail the pilot, Monday rolls around, and I meet with all the department heads. We start planning, designing, and coordinating the technical elements involved in the show, from weapons and gear to uniforms. While the obvious considerations include standard uniforms and types of firearms a typical SEAL would use, there are far more nuanced technical details that need our attention. The script is packed with combat and action scenes set in various locations around the world, each presenting unique environments that influence the weapons and gear needed.

Depending on the episode's setting, I have to assist the special effects department in determining the specific types of charges used to breach doorways. The stunt team also needs guidance on the strategic movements that would be accurate for each location and situation. Every detail matters if we want to create an authentic, compelling experience for the audience. It takes about two weeks to get the gear set and ready, and we move on to coordinating the action scenes. But there's still one major issue I keep running into.

"You've got one big problem," I tell the executive producers one night at their downtown hotel. "You don't have enough people on this team."

They shoot me a quick look. "What do you mean, not enough people?" Making an addition to the cast this late in the game is no minor change.

"Look, you've got conversations happening between your main characters in the middle of a raid, but meanwhile, you've got injured people left alone in another room so your guys can have a talk. There's another scene where you're clearing a room and come across two kids, which means someone needs to stay with them while the others move on. If you want to create an authentic show, you've got to follow basic protocol. And when you do that, you'll quickly see that you run out of people to keep the scenes realistic. Most of the dialogue and sequences hinge on the main cast being able to be together in these kinds of critical situations."

I can see they're considering what I'm saying.

"How about you?" one of the producers asks, staring at me without a smile. I realize he's not kidding. I've never had formal acting lessons and my on-camera experience is limited to a little background work. This would be a big leap forward, but I'm game. Not only will they have an extra person, but I'll also be able to perform some of the more complex movements that would be hard to teach the main cast and stunt crew on such short notice.

"I'm up for it," I say, giving him a nod. And just like that, I'm part of the cast.

It takes three solid weeks to coordinate and prepare, but we're ready by the time the main cast arrives to begin the six-week shoot for the pilot of the show, which is to be called *SEAL Team*. I like all the guys immediately. A. J. Buckley arrives on set full of energy and ready to get to work. I appreciate his laid-back demeanor and strong work ethic as he trains with the gear and firearms we've selected. Max Thieriot is one of the coolest guys I've ever met, and Neil Brown Jr. and I could exchange movie quotes all day long.

But when David Boreanaz shows up and we start rolling, I can't shake the gut feeling that this pilot is destined for success. Of course, everyone says that don't they? Turns out I'm right. The pilot gets picked up, and we begin shooting season one. It's an intense process, but the response is incredible. I find myself in an environment that feels both new and familiar. Being on set is a unique blend of structured chaos, reminiscent of my previous military experience but with a Hollywood twist. In many ways, being on set feels like being in training again—playing Army and doing all the cool stuff, just with much lower stakes and much higher pay. I'm fast-roping from helicopters, handling advanced military gear, and navigating tactical scenarios without the fear of catching an IED or sniper round. To some degree there's something therapeutic about it as well. Maybe it's closure for a chapter of my life that ended abruptly and not by my own choosing.

I never chose to retire, never chose to suddenly stop doing all the things I trained over a decade to do. And while shooting a TV show isn't exactly active combat, it reminds me a lot of the life I used to have. Every day, I wake up and put on my full gear: uniform, armored vest, helmet, and NODs. There's no chance I'm taking the easy road or cheating. I don't care how tiring it is, my team deserves the best, and I'm going to give it to them.

My body repeats movements I trained for a thousand times over. I have a team of guys I'd do anything for. There's a sense of satisfaction and closure in stepping back into that character, performing the same movements and sharing the same camaraderie, but in a much safer environment. I'm utilizing parts of my brain that I haven't activated since the night my right arm was turned to hamburger meat, and it feels damn good. This part feels familiar—like riding a bike.

But learning to perform in front of a camera and oversee all the thousands of details involved in creating a show like this—that's new. I'm constantly learning and improving, working double time to make sure my team is set up for success. Being in the spotlight is also new for me. Random people are following me on social media, and suddenly, girls are coming out of the woodwork. I knew that women liked guys involved in TV and movies, but I didn't realize just how much.

I'm no movie star, yet I'm getting more female attention than I ever have in my life. Almost daily, I get messages from girls I've known for years—girls who never gave me the time of day before seeing me on screen. Women who turned me down cold are now coming in hot. Part of me wants to say, "Fuck you, you superficial bitch," but I keep that to myself. I'm still the same guy now that I was before, which makes it clear that it's not exactly me they're interested in.

But it's not all superficial. Some of these girls are genuinely nice and drop-dead gorgeous. And that's where the trouble comes in. I'm with Sarah, and I want to be with Sarah. She's amazing—tough as nails, sweet, and the woman I see a long-term future with. None of the other women compare to her, but there's an irresistible allure about being the center of desire.

It's not just about *me* wanting *them*, although that's part of it. It's the fact that *they* want *me*. The truth is I've lived most of my life feeling worthless. Sure, I'm confident about my abilities and aware that I have a highly specialized skill set.

But at my core, I've never felt any intrinsic sense of value in who I am. I'm not even sure I really know who I am apart from that character, apart from what I do. But there are moments when I find irrefutable evidence that I have something worth loving, something worth desiring, something valuable. And there's no better proof of that than the attention of a beautiful woman. It makes me feel alive—valuable, wanted, worthy.

When I lost Vanessa, I lost the last remaining piece of evidence that I held onto after my injury—that I wasn't a totally worthless waste of space. She was the proof I needed, the mirror that reflected a version of myself that I aspired to be but wasn't really sure I was. A man worthy of a beautiful woman like her. Now I have Sarah, and that feels amazing. I'd do anything for her. Sarah loves me for who I am, not just for my newfound recognition. But then again, I find sexy little mirrors popping up all over the place these days, and sometimes I just want to take a peek and see my reflection in their eyes, see if I have what it takes to be with a woman like her. I've slipped up a time or two. I've given in to temptation, taken that peek. And Sarah, God love her, forgave me and stuck by me. Her loyalty, even in the face of my fuckups and mistakes, has made me love and care for her even more. I'd do anything for that woman.

But it's new—this environment, this attention, this spotlight. It's a heady mix of validation and temptation that can be overwhelming. Navigating this world is a constant challenge, and it's easy to forget who you are when you find yourself suddenly bombarded with the very thing you've chased after all your life.

"Can you be in New Orleans by Friday?" I never could have foreseen the impact those words would have on my life. The journey has been exhilarating and fulfilling, but the workload is undeniably intense. As the only member of the main cast with real combat experience, I have to rise to the occasion when it's time to execute intricate movements and certain stunts. In addition to my on-screen role, I'm also a consultant and producer, which just piles more on my plate. But this team has become my family, and I'm dedicated to ensuring our mission is a success, no matter what it takes. But I don't want to admit just how taxing it is. Spending twelve-hour days in full gear, constantly moving on set, is physically and mentally draining. As the stress mounts and pressure increases, I find myself seeking out ways to counterbalance the strain.

It's 4:00 a.m. when I toss my backpack into the passenger seat of the car and slide behind the wheel. We've been shooting all night and I'm exhausted, but I still have a four-hour drive from LA to Las Vegas to see Sarah. My mind wanders as the miles pass by. I see the same roads and the same sights I've seen every weekend for two years. I think about the show and make a mental note of all the things I need to do on Monday. I think of Sarah too. She was angry last week when she caught me watching porn again, and I know I need to do something extra nice for her this weekend to make her feel better.

Sometimes I wish I could give her a window into the male mind—or at least into my mind—and help her see that my affinity for looking at porn doesn't have anything to do with my feelings for her. Yeah, I like to look at other naked women, and so does every guy. That doesn't mean I don't love Sarah and care about her. It doesn't mean I'm not attracted to her. Porn is meaningless, categorically and fundamentally different from my feelings toward her. But she doesn't see it that way. I promised her I would stop and made a mental note to do a better job of making sure she doesn't notice. I hate seeing her hurt and want to make her feel loved. She's one of my biggest motivations for working hard like I do. I enjoy being the kind of man who can afford to buy his girl nice things and treat her like a queen. I do my best to make sure she feels well cared for—getting things done, helping out, and supporting her by completing as many little tasks as I can. I can't blame her for not understanding the male mind, but I need to do a better job of making sure my choices aren't hurting her.

For a while, I try to think of something nice I could do for Sarah this weekend. But my brainpower is spent. I feel like I'm always on right now. I need to instruct, consult, decide, and perform every waking minute of every day, and while I love it, it's exhausting. The glare of headlights on the pavement gives way to the morning sunlight as I near home.

"Hey," Sarah closes the gap between us the moment I'm inside the house and wraps her arms around me. She asks how I am, and I can tell she's missed me and wants to talk, but all I can think about is falling into bed. "I'm gonna crash for a few hours. Let's talk when I wake up." She nods understandingly as I disappear.

Five hours later, I blink my eyes open. The moment consciousness stirs, I am wide awake. My body seems to remember my weekend plans before my mind does. I'm alert with anticipation, and a knot of delicious adrenaline forms in my stomach. Within half an hour, I'm shaking out a pile of white dust onto a dinner plate. The back of my throat tightens as I move the credit card back and forth to make a neat white line of powder. Nose down, I inhale. When I rise again, I feel a buzzing sense of euphoria.

This is the moment I've been looking forward to all week. It's the same moment I look forward to every week. I've got two grams and nothing to do all night and all day tomorrow. It's the last sliver of personal time I've managed to keep for myself, and I intend to enjoy it. Work hard, play hard—isn't that what they say? For a while, I'm talkative, ready to chat with Sarah, ready to tell her everything I've collected this week while being away. As the night wears on, a euphoric haze settles over me. Talkative turns to horny. Night turns to day. As Sunday morning sunlight streams into the windows, I don't move. The world is spinning, and I'm spinning with it. All the stress that has accumulated throughout the week seems far away now. But then morning turns to afternoon, and time seems to pass too fast.

As I scrape together the last remnants of the white dust and lean my right nostril close to it, I feel a wave of emptiness wash over me. It will be a whole week before I'm back here again. When I raise my face, I feel tired and numb. I wipe my finger over the empty space to collect what's left of the line and smear it over my gums. I am perfectly, happily numb. It's 8:00 p.m., and I know I need to get up in six hours to make the four-hour drive back to LA before we begin shooting on Monday morning. Sarah is already asleep when I fall into bed beside her.

I close my eyes and suddenly, I'm climbing a never-ending staircase. With every step, I expect to reach the top, but it keeps stretching on. Anxiety tightens my chest—I need to find *her*. I pick up speed, breaking into a jog. Finally, a doorway appears ahead. I reach it, grasp the doorknob, and twist. As the door swings open, I see Vanessa's shiny blonde hair. She's turned away from me, face tilted up, kissing *him*. He breaks away from her lips and looks at me with a taunting smirk. Then she turns to face me. Her eyes are apologetic, but there's a cold, cruel glint in them. As if she's reveling in my pain, as if she planned for me to find her. As if she wants me to watch. She turns back to him, lifts her face, and kisses him again. Her choice is clear and now I'm paralyzed. I want to shout, but no sound comes out. I want to intervene, to fight to win her back, but my feet are glued to the floor. A blaring noise fills the room, growing louder and louder. I try to cover my ears, but it drowns everything out. I blink open my eyes to the sound of my alarm.

BEEP, BEEP, BEEP—the alarm blares through the room. I open my eyes. *Fuck you, Vanessa. After five years and you're still haunting my dreams.* Gritting my teeth, I roll over with a heavy sigh and glance at the clock—02:10. Damn it, it's time to get up.

I slip out of bed as quietly as I can, but Sarah stirs and sits up.

"Drive safe, babe," she says, leaning in for a goodbye kiss. I reciprocate with a quick peck and a nod, knowing I need to hit the road without delay. My thoughts are muddled, and my body feels off-kilter and uneasy as I settle into the driver's seat. My mind drifts as the miles slip by, the familiar scenery flashing past—the same landscape I've grown used to over the past two years. The transition from the glare of headlights to the early morning sunlight marks a shift in my state of mind, as clarity slowly begins to settle in, pushing aside the fog of fatigue. As my head clears, I'm left with a sense of acute emptiness.

"I just wish we could spend more time together." Sarah's words drift back into my mind. I don't remember exactly when she said it—the days all seem to blur together now. I know I'm busy and we haven't seen each other as much as I'd like, but there's not a day that goes by without me working hard for us and doing my best to take care of her.

"Just three more months," I whispered to her in the dark. "We'll finish shooting in three more months."

She didn't seem satisfied with that answer. It feels like there's something more she wants from me than just time, as if she's trying to reach a part of me that no longer exists. I guess that part of me died along with the innocent love Vanessa and I once shared. Either way, it's not there. By the time the signs for Studio City come into view, my mind is racing through a list of things that need to get done today. *Here we go again.*

And I go on, drive after drive, line after line, episode after episode, week after week, year after year, until one Thursday when we are informed that the world is going to end. We've been hearing reports, rumors, and whispers about the COVID-19 situation and the possibility of stopping filming, but I never really thought the day would come.

"Looks like we've got to shut everything down," the executive producer says. "The network says that we can't continue."

We're all stunned. We knew it was bad, but we didn't know it was this bad.

"So, no work on Monday?" I assume that we'll at least finish the episode we're working on since we're so close to having it done.

"Nope. They're sending us home now."

There's a strange energy in the air as we shut down our work for the day and say goodbye—like the beginning of an apocalyptic movie where 95 percent of the characters die. I've got my own opinions about the whole situation, but I try to keep my mouth shut. Everyone is touchy about it these days. After saying goodbye, I drive straight to meet my dealer and head home. I walk through the doors of the house with an eight-ball of cocaine and a big smile on my face. Hell, if the world is going to end, I might as well throw a party.

But the world doesn't end. Season — goes on hold, and life slows down. Way down. My days are no longer filled with constant physical exertion and high stress. I have a lot more time to think. I also have more time with Sarah. I spend more time listening to her and reflecting on what she's saying. She has a hard time with my drug use. More specifically, she has a hard time with the way drugs always open up the floodgate of sexual appetite that leads me down the ol' porn rabbit hole. I hear what she's saying and, in some ways she has a point. I don't think it's necessarily as bad as she makes it out to be. Regardless, I'm going to stop. The cocaine at least. The porn—well, I don't think I'll stop altogether. I'm a man after all. But I'll cut back and I'll make sure that she doesn't have to encounter it since it hurts her so much. *Time to reset. Time to get back to basics.* God, how many times have I said that? Let's hope it sticks this time.

CHAPTER 26
CRASH

MY RIGHT SHIN SMASHES AGAINST the bike's handlebars as I catapult through the air. The world swirls around me as my body completes an entire somersault in midair. The ground rushes toward me rapidly, and my mind races, desperately trying to protect my right side. Years of effort have gone into constructing the cluster of metal pins and tacked-on nerves that make up my right arm, and the thought of crushing it fills me with dread. If this were Haifa Street and I found myself airborne due to an IED orchestrated by a cunning adversary, at least I'd have a good story to recount. But being hit on Lankershim Boulevard because some idiot decided to do an illegal U-turn from the far-right lane—*what a fucking waste.* The dumbass didn't even look left. My body instinctively reacts from years of training. I tuck my head and brace for impact, ready to roll. The left side of my head connects with the ground first, followed by my shoulder. I roll onto my back and continue rolling until I reach a standing position. I'm okay. I'm alive. I'm in FUCKING PAIN! My left shoulder is screaming. This isn't just scrapes and bruises, this is bad.

"FUCKKK!"

I'm not just in pain; I'm furious. I left the gym for five minutes to grab cash from an ATM around the corner and happened to come face-to-face with possibly the stupidest driver in all of LA. Not only that, it was the one fucking time I decided to leave my protective jacket behind and ride with nothing but a T-shirt and jeans. I glance down at my shin and then up at the driver, who is now out of his vehicle and walking around, surveying the damage. I need to walk away. If I stay, I'm going to do something to that fucking moron that I'll regret. My shoulder is a ball of fire, and now that I'm walking off the adrenaline, so is my right shin.

The has his hands in the air as if to say, "I have no idea what just happened." *Idiot.* We both know exactly what happened: You just earned first place in the dumbest-driver competition because you were too distracted by your phone or contemplating whether you wanted a side of onion rings with your drive-thru burger to pay attention and avoid killing someone.

I turn away from the driver and try to breathe through the pain. When I look back, he's pacing around the crash site slowly, like some sort of crime scene investigator. When he sees me looking, he shakes his head in confirmation. "Yep, we crashed, alright." *No shit, Sherlock.*

His stupid face matches his stupid driving.

I turn my back and put more distance between us. I'll end up in jail if I get any closer to him. I'm not sure how long it takes for the ambulance to arrive. I know I need get to a hospital, but I'm not about to leave the scene until I talk to the police and show them exactly what happened. I have no idea what Mr. CSI Dumbass is going to tell them, and I can't leave it to chance.

"Sir, the police will visit you in the hospital, and you can explain everything there. The most important thing right now is to make sure you're okay."

The EMT tries to reason with me, and I know they have a point, but I'm not moving.

"I don't care. I'm staying until I can show them the terrain and exactly what happened and how it happened."

I need to ensure that justice is served by verifying that the facts are accurately recorded, and to guarantee this, I need to remain here and demonstrate what happened myself. So I stay, and the ambulance leaves. It takes an hour and a half of utter misery before a police officer who's an accident specialist arrives on scene. I'm starting to feel nauseous from the pain now. My shin is already turning colors and swelling up like a balloon, and it takes all my concentration to get through the police report.

"Can you give me a ride to the hospital?" I ask the officer after they've finished taking my statement.

"Sorry, we can't do that," he says with a pat on my shoulder. "You'll have to call an ambulance or get someone to come get you." I need to get to the hospital quickly, but I don't want to bother calling another ambulance, so I grab my phone and call my buddy Justin, who just happens to be in town visiting me. At least my cell phone is still in one piece. Twenty minutes later, I'm on my way to the hospital. The pain is getting worse by the minute. I limp into the ER alone and slowly make my way to the front desk. The world is returning to normal after COVID-19, but some protocols remain—they still won't allow anyone to accompany you into the emergency room.

"Yes, sir, how can we help you?" The woman behind the counter looks exhausted. Brief moments of eye contact are all she offers as I detail my condition, and she instructs me to take a seat and wait to be seen. After half an hour, the pain is so bad I think I'm going to vomit. When I limp back to the counter and ask about the wait, I'm met with irritation. Another hour goes by, and then another. I curl up in a chair in the corner, trying to find my happy place, trying to stay on top of the pain. But I can hardly choke back the acid rising in my throat as it intensifies. When I limp back to the front desk after three hours and ask about the wait, she rolls her eyes. Another hour goes by. Another eye roll. *Fuck, I can't do this. Happy place…Disneyland…We're a real family.*

"Tyler Grey?"

Four and a half hours have passed since my arrival when I hear my name called.

I feel dizzy when I stand. I limp to the front desk, grateful to be one step closer to help and relief. But relief isn't exactly what I get. A nurse takes my vitals in a robotic manner, and then the ER charge nurse arrives.

"Hello, Mr. Grey, what can we do for you today?" the charge nurse asks.

I start explaining the accident. Just as I reach the part about landing on my head, the nurse suddenly goes ballistic.

"Your *head*?"

"Yes."

"Give him a neck brace—right now!"

After being in the waiting room for four hours, their sudden urgency to save my life with a neck collar feels laughable. Within minutes, a nurse is strapping a neck brace around me, and if my neck wasn't hurting before, *it certainly is now*.

I'm sent back to the waiting room to be called for an X-ray and MRI. I close my eyes, not hoping for sleep but hoping the darkness might help me cope with the pain. I open my eyes when I hear my name called again.

I limp back to the front desk and then return to the examination room.

"Looks like you're okay," the doctor says when he enters. "Nothing showed up on the X-ray. We're going to let you go home to get some rest."

I'm shocked when I hear what the doctor is saying. I know my body. I know pain. This is not "nothing." I persist. I ask questions. But the doctor isn't budging. They aren't interested in discussion, and they aren't going to give me so much an 800 mg Motrin for the pain. I leave in intense pain—exhausted and angry. Back at home, I take a few Klonopins and lie in bed until they knock me out. My entire body hurts when I wake up.

I can hardly believe my eyes when I swing my right leg over the side of the bed. My leg has swollen up like a black-and-blue balloon and it hurts like hell. I hop on one leg to the toilet and sit, extending the moldy-looking monstrosity in front of me. The pain emanating from my shoulder is still excruciating and I don't want to move. I *can't* move. I just want to be swallowed up or flushed down the toilet into nothingness. I want to escape this exhausted, fucked-up, swollen body I'm in. I just want to crawl into bed, pull the covers over my head, and disappear. But that's not an option. We're in the middle of shooting the fourth season of *SEAL Team*, and there's no one who can take my place. I've got a whole team of people who are counting on me right now and I can't desert my teammates. A switch flips in my mind. *Fuck pain. Fuck discomfort. Fuck swelling and gashes and fractures.* I will not let my team down. I have to show up and finish shooting this season.

On Monday morning, I roll into the studio in a wheelchair. I feel like a fucking idiot, but I can't physically stand on my right shin. The pain in my shoulder is still nearly unbearable, but I'm determined to push through it. An hour into the day, my body laughs at my little mind-over-matter attitude. This isn't the kind of pain you can just mantra-happy-mindset your way out of. By the time the day is over, I've taken eight Norcos. It's been nearly five years since I've taken Norco—I weaned off of it after *Suicide Squad* and never looked back. Instantly, the medication makes me feel lethargic and heavy. Every hour is like trudging uphill through thick mental clay. I make it through the end of the day, but I know that I can't keep this up. I can't function under such intense pain, and I can't function with that many painkillers in my system. There's a reason they tell you not to drive or operate heavy machinery when you're on the stuff. I'm so drowsy I can hardly think. But I do know a way to fix this: *Adderall.*

When I wake up the next morning, I pop a Norco along with an Adderall and head to our shooting location. And it works. I'm still miserable, but at least I'm functional. And that's all I need: enough functionality to keep my body going until May, when we finish shooting for the season. And so it begins. It takes five to eight Norco, four to five Adderalls, and two to three benzos at night to keep me going. But at least I'm going. Six weeks later, I'm sitting in another doctor's office.

"Your shoulder is separated at the AC." The orthopedist doesn't waste time with small talk as he enters the room and offers a diagnosis even before the door closes behind him. "I can see it just by looking from here."

An overwhelming sense of relief washes over me, mingled with a fierce sense of validation, as the specialist declares a definitive diagnosis. The X-ray, taken just thirty minutes later, cements the truth. It brings into sharp focus the oversight of the Emergency Room doctors—a misstep that has prolonged my pain for six agonizing weeks, a thought that stokes the fires of my frustration.

"Ultimately, surgery will be on the horizon," the specialist informs me, drawing a map of my journey to recovery. "But for now, our goal is to alleviate your discomfort as quickly as possible." He lays out a strategic treatment plan for me, one that I adopt without hesitation, supplemented by my own regimented intake of Norco and Adderall. I briefly consider asking him about the side effects of my little "work cocktail," but with the doctor, as with my body, I decide it's better to ask for forgiveness than permission."

"I don't like it. You're different, Tyler. Maybe you don't see it, but I do. You're not yourself these days." Sarah stares out the window at the passing cars and doesn't meet my eyes when she tells me what's on her mind a few weeks later. This isn't the first time she's said it. For weeks now, she's made it abundantly clear that she's bothered by the reemergence of drugs in my life and wants me to get off of them completely.

"You think *you* don't like it, imagine how *I* feel." I'm irritated by her lack of sympathy. "I don't want to take this fucking stuff either. But I had my fucking shoulder separated at the AC. I was in a fucking motorcycle crash. Most people wouldn't have even made it out of bed for weeks, but I did what I had to do for the team and for the show. I'm supporting *us*. I literally have no choice."

Her mouth is set in a straight line and her eyes keep staring straight ahead.

"Yeah, but it's been months since the accident and you're still taking as much as you were back when it first happened. You've improved a lot since then. You can cut back."

I let out a chuckle.

"Then you've clearly never tried getting off medication before. I know I need to get off the stuff and I will, just like I did before. But I know exactly what that process feels like. It feels like you're dying, like you have the flu, like someone has injected you with fucking horse tranquilizer. I can get through it, but I'll need a week to sleep it off. And right now, I don't have a fucking week. I need to be on set five days a week and I need to bring my A game, or else the show and the entire team will suffer. I'm surviving the very best I can, and I'm sorry if you don't like it, but I don't have much of a choice."

Her expression softens, but she still looks distant. I keep going.

"Look, I'll tell you what. Just let me get to the end of the show and I promise you that the day it's over, I'll get off."

Sarah nods and smiles at me, but I feel a wall between us, some invisible barrier that I can't seem to penetrate. Just a couple more months, and then I'll be better, more present, and the man she deserves. Just one more month.

Two months pass. Filming for season four of *SEAL Team* ends. And I keep my word. I begin weaning off my pain meds the same day we finish filming. The first few days are tough. I sleep like a hibernating bear. On the fifth day, I wake up feeling groggy and drained. I check the time, and a jolt of panic hits me when I see it's already 10:30 p.m. Sarah should be home by now. I dial her number, hoping for an answer, but she doesn't pick up.

Fuck, where is she?

I try calling her again, but she doesn't answer. I know she was supposed to hit the gym tonight, and it's in a shady part of LA. It's late and worry claws at my insides. I call again fifteen minutes later. No answer. My gut churns. Something's off. I pull up the vehicle tracking app on my phone and jump into my truck, my mind racing through a thousand dark scenarios. I can feel it in my bones—something bad has happened. I curse myself for sleeping so damn late when she clearly needed me. I slam my foot on the gas pedal and head for her location with a sense of urgency. Every second feels like a lifetime. I'm bracing myself, preparing for whatever I might find, ready to leap into action and rescue her from whatever danger she's in.

When the tracker directs me to a dimly lit parking lot behind the gym, my blood starts to boil. The pit in my stomach deepens. Someone has her. I have to get to her before it's too late.

As I pull into the lot, my eyes scan the area, searching for any sign of her, any clue about what's going on. Then, through the windshield of her truck, I see it: *Sarah in the front seat, kissing another man.*

CHAPTER 27
PURGATORY

"GET THE FUCK OUT OF MY HOUSE NOWWW! JUST GET OUT!!"

Sarah's face turns white. Even I'm surprised by the volume of my voice as rage rises in my throat and erupts like hot lava. Sarah sped away last night when she saw me staring at her, kissing that man in the parking lot. She raced home before I had a chance to confront her, and when I called her, she tried to lie and act like the whole thing never happened. That didn't last for long. When she finally admitted it, the floodgates opened—only it wasn't me doing the confronting; it was her. Somehow, I was the bad guy in the whole ordeal. After an hour of her airing out months of saved-up anger, hurt, and offense, I'd had enough. I was too exhausted to think anymore, let alone listen. I marched upstairs, took two Klonopins and went to sleep.

But when morning comes, so does the rage. The moment I see her face, the image of him kissing her flashes before my eyes. Rage blasts up my throat and spews out.

"GET THE FUCK OUT OF MY PLACE NOWWW!! JUST GET OUT!!"

Sarah stands frozen, paralyzed by the sound of my voice. Then she recoils, moving away from me.

"You're scaring me, Tyler, you're scaring me!" she says. I'm shocked by her words. Not only shocked but hurt.

How can she think I would ever hurt her after all these years together? I've loved her tenderly and protected her fiercely. I've never laid an angry hand on her or any other woman in my life. She's unleashed emotions on me in countless ways, and I never backed away. And now when I'm angry, FOR GOOD REASON, *I'm* scaring *her*? It feels so unfair, and it only makes me angrier. I would never hit her…I'm not anything like my father.

She grabs her purse and heads for the door. But just before she leaves, she turns her head to face me one last time. Her gaze is one of confusion and disbelief, as if I'm a stranger, as if she doesn't recognize me anymore.

And then it comes back to me—the pattern of the couch fabric, the blue light of the television, and the sound of my mother screaming as she looked at my father like he was a stranger, like she didn't even recognize him anymore.

"I'm going to be just like him when I grow up. I'm going to be just like him when I grow up. Oh NO, NO, NO…I DO NOT WANT TO BE JUST LIKE HIM WHEN I GROW UP!"

Sarah is looking at me like I'm the monster. Like it's not *her* who cheated on *me*. As if I'm not the one who used to pull her close in the kitchen while she cooked, who knows all our inside jokes that only we find funny, who feels like his heart has been stabbed and his soul gutted.

Did I grow up to be just like my father?

Back inside the house, I reach for the bottle of Adderall and shake out three tablets. Screw getting clean this week; I'm not about to tough it out through this situation. Within an hour, my mind clears and then begins to race with anxiety. I feel better and worse all at the same time.

The anger is still there, but the Adderall has turned down the volume of my raging emotions.

On one hand, I'm pissed beyond belief that Sarah cheated on me. On the other hand, I cheated on her multiple times our first year together, lost my self-control when sexy temptations kept appearing. She forgave me—okay, maybe not forgave me, but she stayed with me and kept loving me. Now, as I weigh our mistakes and screw-ups, Sarah comes out far ahead. She's offered me more forgiveness than a Catholic priest on confession duty. It seems only fair that I return the favor. Besides, I don't want to lose her.

The day passes, and I lose count of how many pills I'm putting in my body. I float through the next three days in a haze of alcohol and medication, swinging between anger, sadness, and pure numbness. I bounce from one self-destructive behavior to another, indulging in rage and self-pity. How the hell did this happen to me again? Why do I keep facing rejection and betrayal? What is it about me that drives people away? Suddenly, every awful thought I've ever had about myself feels validated. Every ounce of self-respect I thought I possessed crumbles away as I wash down pills like Skittles from an MRE.

By day four, it's time to make a plan. My goal is clear: get back together with Sarah. Achieving this will require strategy. Somewhere along the way—though I'm not sure where—the balance of power shifted. She now expects an apology from me. I should be the one in control here. She ought to be apologizing, begging, making grand promises to make all this right. I should receive weeks of royal treatment from her, while I offer small tokens of forgiveness and affection in return. She should be the one fighting to win me back. I make a list with two columns—me on one side and Sarah on the other. She comes out far ahead in screw-ups. But she has a ledger of her own. That became painfully clear when everything exploded. Her list is filled with far more complicated items than mine: emotionally unavailable, addicted to porn, workaholic, bad communicator, angry, out of control, hooked on pills—the list goes on and on.

I'm irritated that she's somehow managed to position herself on top of this whole ordeal when she's the one who messed up. But if I don't let go of this sense of injustice, I'll never win her back.

◂▸

"I'm going to rehab tomorrow."

When I choke out the words, a rush of fresh, hot, salty tears pours out. The sympathetic smile of the nurse in front of me blurs as fluid fills my eyes. Today I had shoulder surgery; tomorrow I will check into rehab; and tonight the shift nurse in charge of my aftercare has the great misfortune of being the sole witness to my sob session. I've already given her a blow-by-blow account of finding my girlfriend of five years having an affair. I've replayed the scene a thousand times in my mind, but this is the first time I've actually said the words out loud. I hate the taste on my lips. I hate that I'm pouring my heart out to a perfect stranger. But I don't have anyone else to talk to.

As I speak, I feel as if I'm hearing the news for the first time myself. I leave out a few parts of the story as I recount it to the nurse. I don't tell her how Sarah forgave me multiple times when I cheated on her early in our relationship. I also don't mention that the volcano of my rage didn't erupt in front of Sarah in the hours that followed my discovery, or that it later spewed out like red-hot, raging lava, incinerating everything in its path. Sarah made it clear in no uncertain terms that she would never talk to me again unless I checked into rehab, and so rehab it was. Sarah immediately took the initiative and reached out to a close friend, arranging for me to go to a place called Warriors Heart, a privately funded treatment center in San Antonio, Texas. I'd heard of it before. A handful of my good friends went there, and it helped them a lot. Warriors Heart only treats active military, veterans, firefighters, police, EMTs, and active members of organizations across the nation that protect and serve the citizens of the United States. More specifically, they work with people who suffer from substance abuse, chemical dependency, and various psychological conditions.

But I'm not flying to San Antonio tomorrow. Warriors Heart doesn't have an open spot available for another two weeks. Instead, I'm headed to a rehab center in Hollywood to detox while I wait for a spot to open up. In the meantime, I got off Adderall a week ago. I'm not going to rehab because I can't get off the drugs by myself—I've done it before and I'm confident I can do it again. I'm going because I don't want to lose Sarah. I want to prove to her that I have what it takes to be a better man. I want to show her how much I care about her. I want her to believe that I am really going to change this time. To ensure that I earned full points for this big gesture, I asked Sarah to meet me in person. I walked up to her without a word, reached out, and set my bottle of Adderall in her hand.

It was admittedly one of the more childish things I've done in my adult life, giving over my drugs like a kid with a bag of candy. But I needed to see her before I left for rehab, and I figured I might as well go out with a big, symbolic gesture.

She didn't say anything, just took the bottle and left—not even a hint of emotion in her eyes, only indifference. And then it hit me. *She fucking hates me. How did I not see this?*

Now, the nurse stares at me kindly as I wipe tears from my swollen eyes, and I'm suddenly transported back to that hospital bed at Fort Bragg—me just lying there uselessly with raw meat for a right arm, propped up by metal, stomach bloated and painful from stored-up shit, and Sergeant Major Baldy in front of me as my mental barriers crumbled without protection.

I just want to go back. I want to press rewind and start over. I want all of this to have never happened. I want to wake up from this bad dream and be myself again. I just want to be who I was, not who I'm becoming, not this shrimp-scented waste of space that can't even shit by himself.

It's like it's happening all over again, only I don't smell like shrimp right now, and thank God I can still shit by myself. But I feel the same way now that I did then. Every shred of self-esteem I thought I had is gone, and I'm broken and fractured once again. The nurse offers a few anecdotal pieces of advice, and I nod and thank her. When she leaves, I close my eyes. I don't want to stay here. I don't want to go to rehab. I don't want any of this.

But I have no choice.

My buddy Jack Osborn is waiting for me in his truck when I check out the next morning. He drives me straight to the rehab center in Hollywood where I've agreed to spend the next two weeks until a spot at Warriors Heart opens up. The ride is miserable. I'm still in pain from the surgery and well aware that I won't be finding relief anytime soon. The rehabilitation center is situated inside a renovated house just a stone's throw from the Netflix headquarters. The facility is known for "hosting" all kinds of celebrities who find themselves in need of a good detox.

Ironically, the streets around the center are filled with drug dealers. It's a good business plan, I suppose—setting up shop in a prime location to support the disgruntled clients who opt to check out of rehab early. Smart bastards. But I'll tell you one thing: No one is more accepting, all-inclusive, and nonjudgmental than a good dealer. They don't give a fuck if you identify as Kermit the Frog or if your hair smells like McDonald's frying oil; it's equal service for all paying customers.

Jack parks the car, and I slide out of the passenger seat, trying not to wince in pain. When I enter the house, a man at the front desk welcomes me gently and warmly, as if he's been waiting all morning for me to arrive. His smile is too big, his voice is too polite, and he maintains eye contact for just a few beats too long. I'm immediately irritated. I can already tell by the look on his face what kind of place this is, and I'm not happy about it. They're going to tell me that this is a "safe space" and encourage me to "open up." If a spa, hotel, hospital, and therapist's office had a big gang-bang love child, it would be this place. In exactly sixty seconds, I have come to the objective, logical conclusion that I fucking hate everything about rehab, and I don't want to be here.

"So, here's a little paperwork for you to fill out for me, if you don't mind," Mr. Eye Contact is back with his polite voice and unwavering gaze. He frames the instruction as if he's asking me to do him a personal favor, like I won't notice that he's handed me the paperwork equivalent of a colonoscopy.

Keep it together; do it for Sarah.

When I finish filling out the thick stack of forms and hand it back to him, he accepts it with a winning smile, as if I deserve a gold star for the "big step" I'm taking in my life. *Whooptyfuckdo.*

"So, our center is divided into two main areas," Mr. Eye Contact explains with too much gusto. "We have the detox area where you'll spend the first three days. We'll keep close tabs on your vitals throughout the entire detox process, and then you'll be moved to our main area where you'll have your own room. There, you'll have the opportunity to participate in our classes and daily activities and eat with the other residents."

I bob my head in a show of understanding, but I honestly don't give a shit what their process is. I just want to get this over with, get to Warriors Heart, and get back so I can reconnect with Sarah.

"We require you to hand over all electronic devices, including your cell phone, at this point. We will keep them safely stored until you are ready to check out."

My eyes flick up to meet his. Now I'm paying attention, very close attention. Mr. Eye Contact thinks he can just slip in that little detail without me noticing. *Oh wow! I mean, if you're going to "safely store it," instead of running it to the nearest pawn shop around the corner, then by all means, take it. Geez. What a human turd.*

"Yeah, I don't think I'm comfortable with that. I need to keep my phone with me." I offer a firm nod so that he knows this is non-negotiable. This whole rehab thing is one big gesture to win back Sarah. And the only way this strategy is going to work is if I stay in contact with her, ask her how she's doing, keep her up to date on my breakthroughs, and tell her how well the "recovery process" is going. I need to keep myself in the game if I'm going to win her back from *him*, and going off-grid puts me at a huge disadvantage. Dialogue is my thing; talking is my specialty. If I go all silent, I'm sure Mr. Parking Lot Kissing Buddy will be more than happy to comfort her while her "big scary veteran boyfriend" is away at rehab. *Think again, Jody.*

"Unfortunately, it's our policy, and there are no exceptions," Mr. Eye Contact works up a big, fake, sympathetic smile.

Oh, you don't know who you're dealing with, mister. You think you've seen the problematic guy at the drug rehab front desk who wants to speak to your manager, but he's got nothing on the problematic guy at the drug rehab front desk who just had major surgery and is raw-dogging the pain and checking into rehab just to win back his girl who cheated on him a week ago. No sirree. This is not the day to mess with ol' Tyler Grey.

I don't like people telling me what I can and can't do. And the way I figure, if I'm already losing control of everything, I might as well lose my shit too. The manager comes, but he doesn't budge on the rule. He goes straight for an ultimatum: It's either hand over the phone or leave.

I dial Jack. "You gotta get me out of here, man." I'm begging him. "No one told me shit about not being able to have a phone. I'm not doing this."

I expect Jack to join me in righteous indignation over this shocking display of privacy invasion and poor customer service. I'm no constitutional scholar, but I'm pretty sure this qualifies as a severe infringement on freedom of speech. I could take it all the way to the highest court in the land, and I'm just the kind of person who would do that purely on principle.

Instead, he encourages me to stay. Tells me I'll be fine without my phone for a few days. I hang up and let out a big, audible, disgruntled sigh. Mr. Eye Contact and Mr. Bigshot Manager both look at me with irrational levels of compassion, as if I'm just one of the crazy junkies they see every day. Everything in me wants to explain to them that I don't belong here, I don't want to be here, and I don't even think I NEED to be here. I've successfully weaned myself off meds multiple times, and the best "safe space" to do it is in my fucking house!

This is for Sarah. It's either stay or never talk to her again.

I hate myself when I hand over my phone half an hour later, a hatred that's rather disproportionate given the situation. I despise caving to any system.

But I don't have a choice. If I leave now, I will never talk to Sarah again, and I can't stay unless I give up my phone. A woman leads me to the detox area, which is nothing more than a small bedroom with a television and bathroom access. One of the staff members takes my vitals and offers me medication to help with the pain from my surgery. I find that almost laughable. *You want to put me on just to take me off again? I'm in rehab, for God's sake. If I'm going to do this, I might as well do it right.* She smiles and leaves the room. I look around at the walls, listen to the drone of voices on the television, and replay the same cinematic feature film that's been in reruns in my mind for more than a week: Sarah kissing *him*.

The worst part is that I saw it with my own eyes. The images that replay around the clock aren't figments of my imagination; they are memories, seared and burned into my mind, ones I will never forget.

Three hours in, an insidious unease begins to slither over my skin. Mental torture. That's what this is. I'll be lying in bed for three days with nothing to do but watch Netflix, which is ironic because I can see their sign right outside my window. I can't stand this. All I think about, literally every fucking second, is what I saw: my girl kissing another man. And now I know I probably arrived only fifteen minutes after they were doing a lot more than kissing. The thought feels like mental acid burning every neuron. The more I try to distract myself, the more my brain forces me to wallow in thoughts of betrayal that echo in my subconscious with the harsh reality of what it means. *I'm just not good enough—if I were, she would have chosen me.*

Weariness engulfs me, every fiber of my being aches. As darkness blankets the world outside, the respite of sleep eludes me. I glance at the clock, and it reads 11:40. I'm alone now—it's just me and my thoughts. But my mind is a vicious and unforgiving place to be. I'm alone in this purgatory, and I lie awake staring at the ceiling, burning inside my self-inflicted mental inferno. After what seems like hours pass, I check the clock again. It's only 11:54, which means that only fourteen minutes—fourteen goddamned minutes!—have passed in this hellhole of suffering. I'm not going to make it. No way I'm going to stay in here for three whole fucking days. *This isn't me. I shouldn't even be here.*

As I drift in and out of a restless sleep, the line between my vivid imagination and my dreams becomes blurred. Both are filled with the scene I've watched a thousand times: Sarah kissing him. I can't stop this loop of insanity, but there's no relief for my body or my mind; there's no distraction. I'm a prisoner without an escape. When morning finally comes, a woman with a perky smile enters the room. Her chipper spirit is like a cheese grater to an eyeball. I do not return her smile. She looks down at my feet and then pipes up with a helpful suggestion, "Don't you want to put your other sock on?"

Her question seems odd, so I look down and realize I'm wearing only one sock, on my left foot. I hadn't even noticed. But I feel no incentive to change that fact, no desire to care for this worthless, aching body of mine. No motivation to move from this position, even an inch, to comply with her request. So I just stare at her, and she stares at me. I'm not moving a fucking inch, and there's not a damn thing she can do about it.

I'm fully aware that I'm an insufferable, stubborn asshole, but if anyone deserves to be grumpy and miserable, it's me. And so I trudge through hell with one sock on, painfully and slowly, until three grueling days pass. When the doors of the detox room are opened and I'm released from my purgatory, I feel relieved. The interaction with other residents and the daily classes are a welcome change after staring at the same four walls for three days.

When the second episode of season four of *SEAL Team* airs, I sit with the rest of the rehab group to watch it. It feels like I'm in a bizarre dream. I'm watching the episode I directed…from a rehab center. My CBS press junket is taking place in the rehab therapist's office. The woman I thought I would marry cheated on me, and now I'm sitting in a roomful of addicts, trying to win her back. I just want to wake up, press rewind, and get out of this mess.

The next day, I participate in the mandatory therapy session, but it's agony. It's clear that my reputation for being an arrogant, know-it-all, stubborn, one-socked asshole has circulated throughout the staff, and they've made it their mission to cut me down to size.

"Look, you're the one in rehab, not me." The therapist finally plays the trump card when I decide, yet again, to challenge the logic of one of her statements.

"Yeah, and I'll get out of here in a week. You WORK HERE. You're spending your entire life listening to other people's problems and giving canned, obvious advice so you can feel better about your own. What kind of life is that?" Every work is a dagger, every sentence wrapped in barbed wire. I want her to bleed like me. She redirects the conversation, and I count down the minutes until I can get out of this damn place and back to *her*.

CHAPTER 28
WARRIORS HEART

JOURNAL ENTRY #8

I feel like I'm searching, swimming in a vast ocean, looking for something I can't even name.

Which begs the question: Have I already found it? Was it right in front of me all along and I just didn't see it? This is among my greatest fears and the subject of most of my nightmares. I wake up in a cold sweat, still wet from the water, as the intangible, shapeless creature disappears. If only I knew what I was looking for...

I've seen "experts." What I learned from them can be summarized by the quotation marks around that term. I've been given labels starting with A's, O's, and P's. Diagnosed, medicated, and nearly confined to a white room with a matching jacket that's poorly designed and very hard to take off. I've read their hypotheses, books, and theories. I've tried all their techniques, taken all their drugs, and even prescribed some of my own. I've traveled the world, fought in two wars, and knocked on death's door several times.

In the end, what did I learn? Mainly that we know nothing, and what we do know will be disproved and then re-proved continuously. I've also learned that you can't expect the human masses to understand the aliens among us. In the past, such individuals were killed for who they were. I can't help but think how much further mankind would be if we hadn't, throughout history, exterminated those who were so exceptional they were regarded as heretics.

"Exceptional" isn't a label you can assign to yourself, but one thing I do know is that I am a heretic. What I believe is considered lunacy, yet to me, it is so truthful and obvious that I must hide about 99 percent of my beliefs for fear of being figuratively burned at the stake. The masses seem to punish

both those below and above them; it's homeostasis in its purest form. I must hide in plain sight.

The average masses like to identify themselves and their beliefs with names and groups, which isn't ironic considering the entire group is, by definition, made up of these people. Sometimes I want to belong to those groups, if for nothing else than to explain myself and what I believe in one or two words. I think about how interesting and foreign it would be to attend a function of one of these groups and talk to people who share my views, with whom I have at least something significant in common. Religion, politics, general philosophies, even morals and ethics are subjects I must stay far away from lest I be discovered. It's not like I haven't tried. I've hidden who I was, been ashamed of being different, lied about who I was and what I thought, studied others, and mimicked them. It taught me something important: I don't know what it takes to be happy, but I know what it takes to be miserable—being anything other than who you are. It's a simple formula for guaranteed misery. So now, I'm accepting being me, at least unto myself. Sometimes I try to reach out, only to recoil from the fire. I dream of something that calms the storm, an answer to an unknown question.

After fighting in two wars, the hardest war I have ever fought is the one that rages daily in my mind. We have kept it mostly conventional, although I will admit I have resorted to nukes when greatly outnumbered and overpowered. There is, and most likely will always be, radioactive fallout that contaminates some areas of the battlefield. I have lived with significant physical pain for over ten years and ignore it daily. But the mental pain is real and sometimes unbearable. And what is it, really? Mainly just thoughts like these. Would I change myself if I could? Would I give up these thoughts? Would I trade being unique for being average? No. But one can daydream, can't they? For the first time, I am starting to understand why I do the things I do. That clarity and awareness are power. And the more I learn, the more I feel like I'm gaining the ability to control and understand my habits and choices. I'm realizing that it's up to me to educate myself about my body, mind, and psychology. If I don't like a pattern of behavior in my life, it's up to me to change it. And if the diagnosis that everyone keeps assigning to me doesn't feel accurate, it's up to me to keep searching, learning, and discovering until I find something that does.

This isn't the first time I've taken a hard look at the man in the mirror and told myself that I need to step up and take responsibility, but it is the first time I feel like I might actually have a chance at real change. In the past, I always felt suffocated under the weight of radical responsibility because I felt completely ill-equipped and incapable of change, unsure of why I was making those choices in the first place. No matter how hard I tried or how long I managed to keep my shit together, it never stuck. I always found myself fighting the same battles and falling back into the same patterns. But that's all changing now. I'm starting to see a much bigger picture...

JOURNAL ENTRY #15

I've started to realize that I have a deep-seated belief that I don't deserve anything good—not just success, but anything positive at all. There's a part of me that feels I don't deserve success in any form. I was subconsciously programmed to believe that I'm unworthy of nice things, love, or any form of happiness. Take relationships, for example. I'm currently alone. Sarah is gone. At first, all of this was just a big move to try and win her back. I went to rehab and came to Warriors Heart to save our relationship. But that's all changing. The thick walls of arrogance and bravado have come crumbling down. I'm not doing this for Sarah anymore; I'm doing it for me. I still get angry when I think of her in the truck, kissing him, or Vanessa choosing another man over me. I used to think I was blameless and had no part in the toxicity that surrounded me. Now, I see I was wrong. Whenever things start heading in a positive direction with a woman, I tend to sabotage it. I'm starting to think that's because I fundamentally believe I don't deserve it. It's easier to blame the other person or external circumstances than to look in the mirror. It's much harder to look inward and accept my own faults.

I'm starting to take full responsibility for my relationships and how they have failed in the past. Understanding why I behave this way, where it comes from, and how I can change it is a whole different can of worms. But hey, I've got time to open them while I'm here, so I might as well open the lid.

JOURNAL ENTRY #18

Forgiving myself is one of the hardest things I've ever had to do. I find it much easier to forgive others than to forgive myself. When it comes to relationships and love, I feel like I've made the same mistakes a thousand times. I still judge myself harshly for this and haven't fully forgiven myself. But that's a different issue. I'm working on forgiving myself for those mistakes and for everything else I've done.

Specifically, over the past three days, I've been reflecting and realizing that things didn't turn out as I had hoped. That's okay; it happens, and I can't change it. What I can do is stop judging myself, let go of that judgment, and focus on learning from the experience and moving forward. I won't keep punishing myself for something I no longer control. I have to concentrate on the way forward, not the way back.

JOURNAL ENTRY #21

It's becoming clear that a major cornerstone of rehab treatment is accepting a higher power in your life. I'm not really sure how to feel about that. In fact, I'm conflicted.

I clearly remember the day I decided there was no God. Mom and Dad sent me to a Christian camp which gave me more of a taste of hell than heaven. The camp counselors preached grace and forgiveness but acted with harsh, unfair judgment. Everywhere I turned was another example of hypocrisy in action. I hated every minute of it. I had so much night anxiety in fear that I would piss my pants that I actually shit myself instead. There, in that cramped outdoor bathroom, I felt alone and fucking angry. If this God they claimed was real was so loving and kind, why was I stuck alone in a bathroom cleaning up my own shit? If this God was truly loving, why would He create a special lake of fire just to torture anyone who had even a hint of doubt? And why were the people supposed to be His right-hand men at this camp such jackasses?

From that day on, I always said, "If there is a hell, I'll go there in protest." I wanted to see some shred of evidence that proves His existence. If that makes the so-called "all-loving and all-seeing God" mad enough to throw me into hell, then, as I said, I'll go there in protest. That day when Scott stood over my blown-out, raw-hamburger-meat of an arm, working against the clock to save my life, I acted tough, like I'd passed some test by NOT believing in God. But honestly, I wanted to feel something. I wanted to believe there was something bigger than me out there, that I wasn't alone, that I was connected to something. Maybe I didn't feel it then, or at that awful camp as a kid, but I do feel something now. It's not necessarily religion, at least not right now, but there's a deep awareness that there's something bigger than me, some source of higher power.

I realize now that there's a part of every single human designed to be spiritual. It's undeniable. We're not just physical and emotional beings; there's a spiritual part of us too. I've denied it for so long. Maybe I was afraid of what I couldn't understand or control, or maybe I couldn't reconcile how bad things can happen when there's a God out there. Now I'm coming to terms with not having all the answers but recognizing that there is something here. And I have a feeling that if there is an all-knowing, all-loving God out there, who's outside of time and space, He's big enough and patient enough to let me take my journey, deal with my doubts, and keep asking questions without throwing me into some fiery lake. And if, for some reason, I'm wrong about that and He does, as I said before, I'll go there in protest. As I said before, I'm a man who stands up for his convictions.

◆▶

I've always hated therapists, counselors, psychiatrists, and the like ever since I sat in a dreary room with my family for therapy when I was nine. But as I sit on a couch, staring at this kind woman with dark brown hair and wise eyes, I think I might have been wrong. The woman in front of me is more than just a therapist; she's a guide, navigating me through the wilderness of my mind. She offers me a road map so I don't feel lost, and shows me things I never even knew existed. Despite the challenges, she still smiles warmly at the end of our sessions, casting a nurturing glow over me as I leave. God knows I'm not an easy patient. Maybe therapists, counselors, and psychiatrists weren't all full of bullshit; maybe I just hadn't met the right one yet, or maybe I just wasn't ready.

It's been three weeks since I arrived at Warriors Heart–The Ranch, which sprawls across 534 acres of picturesque Texas landscape. Surprisingly larger than I anticipated, it resembles more of a compound than a typical ranch. Boasting a private lake, pastures, winding hiking trails, a swimming pool, a state-of-the-art fitness center, a ropes course, and courts for volleyball and basketball, the Ranch is teeming with military veterans as well as a handful of law enforcement officers and first responders. It's strange to be in a place with so many people from similar backgrounds.

It didn't take long for me to settle into the rhythm and way of life at the Ranch. Each day here follows pretty much the same routine: I wake up at 07:00, make my bed as required, and do an accountability check-in with the rest of the group. Then comes breakfast, class time, another break, another class, and lunch. After lunch, there are electives to choose from: a wood shop and metal shop where staff guide us in creating artwork that represents our healing process; a K-9 department where we learn about K-9 obedience training and bond with canine warriors; jiujitsu; art; and yoga. When the sun sets, everyone gathers around a campfire, and that's when the storytelling begins.

"The healing is not done in the classroom; it's done around the campfire," one of the instructors tells me with a knowing smile on day two. His statement proves true for most of the individuals here. It's around the campfire that war stories begin to surface. While I choose not to participate or share my own stories—it's never been my style—I find solace in sitting in the corner, reflecting, writing in my journal, and quietly observing the powerful moments unfolding around me. I spend the time gathering and piecing together clues.

This experience marks the first time in my life that I am dedicating each day to focusing intensely on myself, nurturing my body back to a state of cleanliness and health—a much-needed reprieve from the pain and discomfort it has endured. Most significantly, my mind feels clear and unburdened, allowing me to see things with newfound clarity and perspective. This isn't just about winning back Sarah anymore. I sense a profound transformation taking place within me. There's something powerful about the silence here—it's not just the absence of city noise and technology. The static noise in my mind has quieted down, and I am on the verge of a breakthrough. I can just feel it.

"Today, we're going to start working on a new project," Kelly says, rising from her chair. There's a knowing smile on her face as she moves across the room and grabs something. Suddenly, a piece of blank butcher paper eight feet long unfurls on the ground.

"So, we are going to start by drawing a line down the middle of this paper," she says, looking up to meet my eyes. I'm already intrigued. "On one side, write down every significant event in your life, starting from your very first memory. This will be your life line—a timeline of every major event that has ever taken place in your life. On the other side, list any negative things you've ever said or believed about yourself—your negative core beliefs. This can be anything from 'I'm a bad person' to 'I'm stupid.' Then, I want you to try and trace back when and why you began believing these things about yourself. This process will take you weeks, so don't rush it. Once it's finished, we'll gather a group of warriors together. You will stand up, show them your life line, and share your entire life story from start to finish. As you bring your story into the light—all those memories, negative core beliefs, and trapped emotions—you might be surprised to see how they connect in your life. You will begin to notice patterns that you hadn't seen before."

I walk out of Kelly's office with a giant piece of butcher paper and a mission. But the first letters I write on the paper look so small and insignificant that I doubt I'll ever come close to filling the entire sheet.

As I stare at the blank paper, my entire life begins to play out like a movie before my eyes. I watch with deliberate and methodical precision, scrutinizing every detail as if conducting a forensic analysis.

I see myself gazing at my dad's passive face, bathed in the blue glow of the television, mouth hanging open as he sleeps off the bottle of whisky he drank after making my mom cry.

...I'm not worthy of being loved and cared for.

I see Gauge and Desoto peering around the corner of the backyard tree, pistols blazing.

...*I am alone.*

I see a fist flying toward me as the neighborhood bully takes a swing.

...*I am vulnerable and unsafe.*

I see myself signing the papers to join the military. I see myself in the wilderness, hoping I'd make it through selection. I see gunfights and blood. I see my arm hanging like a rotting carcass beside me. I see Vanessa's smile. I see myself in that beige office, playing video games, with pink scars painted across my arm.

...*I'm pathetic.*

I see my hands shaking as I learn that Vanessa slept with another man.

...*I can't trust anyone.*

I see myself lying on the couch, drool pouring down my chin after taking the first round of medication recommended by the VA psychiatrist. I see myself standing like a gargoyle in a MAC cosmetic store.

...*I'm a loser.*

I see myself running to a burning building alongside the firefighters. I see myself yelling with a pack of GoRuck athletes as they plunge into the ice-cold waters of the Potomac River. I see myself snorting a white line of cocaine with a prostitute between my legs.

...*I am a bad person, and if people knew the real me, they would leave.*

I see myself on the set of *Suicide Squad*, watching the Joker fly in on a helicopter. I see myself back at Womack Medical Center seeking drugs because I can't go more than a few days without them.

...*I am not in control.*

I see the *SEAL Team* cast and crew hard at work. I see the world turning upside down as I fly above the handlebars of my motorcycle and roll onto the pavement. I see Sarah kissing him.

...*I don't deserve love.*

And now I see it. All these stories have one common denominator: me. For a long time, I felt as though life was happening to me, as if I were just a bystander watching the twists and turns of my life. "Why me?" I asked when Vanessa didn't stay and Sarah didn't either. *"What did I do to deserve this?"*

Just doing the best I can; I don't really have a choice. I hear my excuses as I pop a handful of painkillers into my mouth. *I'm a man who likes sex; what's the matter with that?* I hear myself rationalizing as I spend my hard-earned money on sex and drugs. *This isn't me. This isn't me. This isn't me.* I hear myself repeat the phrase a thousand times.

A thousand scenarios, a thousand choices, and a thousand moments flash before my eyes. And now I see exactly why me. I got exactly what I deserved. It's all me. The truth is that I was so emotionally fractured and unavailable that I wasn't capable of loving another person well.

Why? Because I didn't love myself.

The truth is that I wasn't really doing the best I could, and I really did have a choice. And I'm not just a man who likes sex; I'm a sex addict who has objectified women and used them for my own pleasure. It's all me. The gavel drops. I am solely accountable. For every choice I've made. For everything I've done. And it's time to stand up and take full responsibility for my life, my choices, and my actions.

For so long, I've been deeply aware of the friction I feel in every area of my life—the grinding, gnawing resistance that seems to accompany everything I do. I've been aware of the war inside my mind, the battle of duality between the Warrior and the Destroyer. I've felt the exhaustion of it, felt the fog this internal war has caused. I've wanted to change. But until now, I just couldn't see the big picture. I couldn't correlate a cause with an effect. I wanted to change but couldn't see how. I still don't see the entire picture yet, but I do see the puzzle pieces in front of me. Every day I'm here at Warriors Heart, another puzzle piece lands on my table.

As warrior after warrior stands up with that massive piece of butcher paper and shares his story, I'm beginning to see that my life is not a haphazard collection of experiences and stories. I'm starting to notice that the same themes, challenges, and patterns exist in almost every warrior I talk to. I feel like a detective now, slowly piecing together the clues. And honestly, things are getting kind of *weird*. There are glaring, uncanny, and strange similarities between all of us. This isn't just about personality. It's not just because we went through the same training program or because each of us had a traumatic event in our lives. This is different. There is an undeniable pattern here, and I need to figure out what the template is because I know there's a key to solving this mystery. Every day, I take notes in my journal, like a detective, chasing every shred of evidence I can find.

I've spent hours listening to the stories of some of the bravest, strongest, most resilient warriors the world has ever known, who feel worthless and alone, battling addiction, and struggling to piece together their shattered lives and families to understand why it all fell apart in the first place. Everywhere I turn, another story emerges, yet the symptoms remain consistent.

My butcher paper is almost full. I'm writing in the margins now, noting memories and clues, every important piece of evidence from my life. As I stand in front of this massive piece of butcher paper, a single question plays on a loop, and I will not rest until I find the answer: *If these are the symptoms, what is the disease?*

CHAPTER 29
ANATOMY OF A WARRIOR

ENDING THAT LAST CHAPTER WITH a powerful line like "If these are the symptoms, what is the disease?" practically demands a compelling breakthrough scene to follow. I would stand there looking at my life gutted and splayed across that massive sheet of butcher paper, searching for clues. The camera would zoom in on my face, eyebrows drawn in deep contemplation, until I shout, "I got it! I know the cure!" like one of those TV medical dramas where the doctors are all really attractive and cure rare, life-threatening diseases one minute and have sex in the supply closet the next. Honestly, I kind of hate those types of shows, but with a last line like that, it definitely popped into my mind.

The reality is that it took me years to track down the patterns, assemble the clues, educate myself, and grasp the true nature of the disease. Revelation, healing, recovery, and growth are gradual, messy, and imperfect processes. But on that particular day, as I stared at my life scrawled out on that butcher paper, something important did happen. I came to the realization that nearly every messy, toxic, painful situation in my life was a result of the same recurring issues. Once I identified the symptoms, I searched for the disease. When I found the disease, I searched for the cure. When I found the cure, my life completely changed. Suddenly, I began to experience growth, healing, and metamorphosis in a way that was powerful and transformative. For the first time, the space between my ears was a peaceful place to be. I no longer felt powerless in addiction's tight grip. I discovered new depths of giving and receiving love that I never imagined. My entire view of myself changed. Habits that I thought were unbreakable suddenly began to dissolve. Was I cured overnight? No, but the enigma that once shrouded that faceless enemy finally dissipated. In its place was a peaceful sense of clarity and a clear strategy for winning the battle. After years of repeatedly finding myself trapped in the same cycle, I had almost given up hope that change was attainable.

In the preceding pages, I've laid myself out on the examination table and shined a big, bright, unflattering fluorescent light on myself, and you've seen all the gross pockets of infection, weird ingrown abscesses, fractured this, and misshapen that of my life. It wasn't easy, but now we've reached the stage where we can link the symptoms to the clues and bring it all together. Don't worry, the story isn't over. There are a couple more big twists still to come. But first, let's put the puzzle pieces together so the whole picture becomes clear. If you'll remember, in the Introduction, I emphasized the importance of listening very carefully to every story, as each one—whether strange, funny, disturbing, bizarre, or heartbreaking—has a significant purpose. And you're about to see why. But before we begin to connect the dots, I want to establish a framework for our conversation.

When most people talk about warriors' struggles, I'm surprised by how much emphasis is placed on problems, symptoms, and challenges without first establishing the innate characteristics and environmental influences that shape warriors. Think of it this way: If you wanted to find a cure for a disease, wouldn't it make sense to start by acquiring a basic knowledge of human anatomy? If you don't know what a healthy body looks like, you might mistake something abnormal as normal. You could mistake a giant oozing abscess or oversized cyst as a standard part of the body, not realizing that it was actually never meant to be there in the first place. So let's start with a very simple question: How do you define what it means to be a warrior?

Many people think that being a warrior means being a fighter or a soldier. Some define it as a job required in times of danger and war. Others equate it with violent actions or aggression. I believe that a warrior is an identity or archetype—created by a combination of natural-born characteristics and environmental shaping. I like to use the analogy of iron being forged in fire—both the natural material and the environment are important in shaping the final product. While every person has a distinct set of inherent traits, talents, and propensities, it has become evident over time that certain archetypes exist universally and are essential for the well-being of any society. These recurring patterns, stereotypes, molds, models, or archetypes are timeless and recognizable. Throughout history, people have tried to establish a societal blueprint or framework based on these observations. The Swiss psychiatrist Carl Jung, for example, conceptualized twelve distinct archetypes: the Innocent, Everyman, Hero, Outlaw, Explorer, Creator, Ruler, Magician, Lover, Caregiver, Jester, and Sage. Others, such as Carol Pearson and Margaret Mark, have categorized these archetypes based on fundamental driving forces, grouping them into Ego types, Soul types, and Self types. In contrast, the Indian caste system, including Brahmins (priests, teachers), Kshatriyas (rulers, warriors), Vaishyas (landowners, merchants), Sudras (servants), and the untouchables, known as Dalits, serves as a highly controversial historical example.

Whether you agree with the specifics of each labeled type or not, the idea of archetypes is like a universal language. They are the original blueprints—the universal symbols that encapsulate ideas everyone can relate to, no matter when or where you find yourself on this big blue marble we call Earth. Archetypes are deep-seated characters and themes that keep popping up, no matter what cultural or social boundaries you might cross—from the epic tales carved into ancient tablets to the complex characters that live and breathe in your favorite Xbox games.

But there's one archetype that has stood the test of time, recurring repeatedly at nearly every point in history: the Warrior Class.

The Warrior archetype captures the essence of courage, mastery in battle, and honor—warriors are the heroes, the fighters, the protectors. From the sword-wielding legends of yore to the pixelated heroes saving virtual worlds, warriors are part of the collective narrative of human history—one of struggle, overcoming obstacles, and striving for something greater. The Warrior archetype also shows up in the animal kingdom. Think about a wolf pack, a popular example in military circles. Each wolf has an important role: the alpha leads, the betas support and keep order, and the omegas help reduce tensions. When pups are born, the whole pack gets involved in their care, pitching in to protect and raise them. This shows that the warrior is not just a protector but also a nurturer in the community—emphasizing that the Warrior archetype is founded on responsibility and unity as much as strength and protection.

Warriors are often drawn to roles and environments that enable them to serve the common good, defend the vulnerable and innocent, and fulfill a higher calling. You'll often find the Warrior Class within the ranks of the military, veterans, first responders, firefighters, law enforcement, medical staff, and many other professions—serving in every demanding and critical arena in today's world. But I want to be very clear on this: You can be a warrior and never pick up a gun in your entire life. You can be a warrior without ever encountering violence. The true mark of a warrior is found in the commitment to help and protect others, the pursuit of justice, and living with courage and integrity. This identity is defined not by the presence of conflict, but by the values and strength of character that are intrinsic to who you are. Being a warrior is an identity. It is who nature made you to be.

There are many characteristics of the Warrior Class. Warriors are born with a strong sense of duty to serve those around them. Warriors have an innate connection to a higher purpose and a clear mission. Warriors possess natural mental fortitude and a propensity for brave and bold action in the face of resistance. Warriors are protectors, keeping the young and more vulnerable members of the tribe safe. Warriors offer security for the assets and resources of the tribe, ensuring they are not stolen or lost. Warriors do not back down or surrender in the face of threats or danger; they stand up, push back, and hold the boundary to keep others safe. Warriors are willing to sacrifice themselves if necessary for the greater good, falling on their swords, giving their lives, and putting themselves in harm's way to protect others. Warriors have the ability to remain calm in the midst of chaos.

I want you to reread the last characteristic because it is one of the most important clues to what we are about to uncover. *Warriors have the ability to remain calm in the midst of chaos.* This is one of the most defining characteristics that sets warriors apart. When danger looms, emergencies arise, or threats are near, warriors possess the capability to think clearly and respond strategically, while others react in panic.

In high-pressure situations like combat, soldiers maintain focus, assess quickly, strategize, and engage with precision. Law enforcement officers advance toward active shooters, coordinate efforts, isolate threats, and resolve crises safely. First responders triage victims in emergencies, stabilize conditions, and provide immediate care. Firefighters analyze fire behavior, create fire lines, and evacuate people safely while staying composed.

"I don't know how you do it."

"That must be so stressful."

"I bet you're so glad to be home safe after such a dangerous ordeal."

Warriors often hear things like this from those who look on from the outside and imagine themselves reacting to a similar situation. While these kinds of statements are said with good intentions, they stem from a common misconception: the assumption that warriors perceive and react to high-stress environments in the same way as the average person. But talk to any warrior about their experience in high-stress environments, and you may be surprised by their response.

A typical physical response to danger or threat is a racing heartbeat, feeling faint, sweating, nausea, chest pain, shortness of breath, trembling, and confusion. This is usually accompanied by extreme mental fog and the desire to run away, hide, or impulsively react. Not for warriors.

We don't feel panicked and confused; we turn on in high-stress environments. The moment there is danger, threat, or emergency, we become acutely aware of our surroundings and feel an absolute sense of calm. High-stress environments activate our superpower: hypervigilance. When this is engaged, we are able to make tactical decisions rapidly, think clearly, and take strategic action. Every system of our body works together in perfect synchronization, we experience total clarity of mind, and we do what we are designed to do. We have an overwhelming sense that we were made for whatever challenge we are facing.

How is this possible? Our bodies and minds have learned to normalize high-stress environments and a state of hypervigilance, allowing us to thrive within that context. This superpower uniquely equips us to handle threats, danger, and chaos. I say this with confidence, not only from my own experience but from the hundreds, if not thousands, of warriors I've interacted with over the course of my life.

But, like all superpowers, this comes with a cost. Warriors live in a strange, inverted world: Most people feel happy, safe, and calm when it's time to stop working, unwind, and sleep. Not warriors. We feel most calm when our superpower, hypervigilance, is engaged and we have a clear target and mission to accomplish. We often experience anxiety when it's time to stop working, unwind, and sleep, because we constantly feel that the other shoe will drop and we'd better be on high alert and ready for action when it does.

This inverted reality really hit me when I found myself sprinting toward that burning building near Sunset Boulevard. That environment activated my superpower. I felt alive. I experienced more activation and mental clarity than I had in years. I felt like I was doing what I was born to do. And fuck, I'd missed it!

Countless soldiers have described feeling a "rush" or "high" in the midst of combat. First responders also report similar experiences when they operate in high-stress environments. Most people assume that soldiers must feel tremendous relief when they return to safe, suburban American life. People assume that first responders must be happy to get back home and relax after a busy shift. But we know differently. The environment that makes most people feel panicked and anxious makes us feel calm and clear-headed, whereas the environment that makes most people feel calm triggers panic and anxiety in us. We thrive in high-stress environments that provide a clear mission and objective, allowing us to utilize our skills to serve and protect others.

As I dug into the characteristics of the Warrior Class, it became clear that one of the greatest defining factors is the warrior's unique ability to remain calm in chaos and take measured, strategic action in high-stress and high-stakes environments. It doesn't matter how physically strong you are or how knowledgeable you are about proper protocol in high-stress situations—if you freak out when you're in one, you will not be able to make any meaningful contribution.

Is there a genetic component to this ability? Possibly. Some studies show that heart-rate variability could be an indicator of an individual's innate ability to handle stress and maintain homeostasis. In other words, how much your heart rate differs over a period of time could be a good metric to measure your resilience and ability to handle stressors such as traumatic incidents. These studies are fascinating, but we still don't have a clear answer on how much this factor helps someone stay calm in chaos. This suggests that the calmness-in-chaos characteristic that distinguishes warriors is mainly developed and cultivated through environmental conditioning. So, I had to ask the obvious question: What are the environments that shape warriors, and how does that conditioning happen? What is the forge that transforms raw iron into a mighty sword?

The most effective way to create an adaptation in the mind and body is through practice and repeated exposure to a condition until it becomes normalized. Think about the concept behind battle drills. A battle drill involves collective action executed without the need for a deliberate decision-making process. These drills are essential for carrying out complex combat operations without loss of life due to tactical or accidental hazards. They serve as the "fundamentals" that are constantly practiced until they become second nature. Battle drills provide the flexibility to respond to changing scenarios and ensure that everyone knows what to do; they are designed to keep soldiers safe and effective in combat. The ability to remain calm in chaos comes from being conditioned to normalize chaos. The more exposure you have to high-stress, chaotic environments, the better equipped you become to adapt and thrive within them.

Throughout history, when a child displayed strong natural warrior characteristics, parents, teachers, and other authority figures would encourage, cultivate, and refine those attributes. Fast forward to today, and we see a similar approach but with different talents. Kids who are naturally artistic, brainy, or inventive are encouraged through artist clubs, speech and debate camps, entrepreneur think tanks, and little innovators clubs.

In the past, warriors were considered essential, natural, and esteemed members of society. When the inherent warrior traits emerged in a young adult, they were nurtured. Back then, nurturing young warriors was all about building up their physical and mental toughness. Different cultures and societies had their own methods, but the goal was the same: to nurture them into strong, capable warriors—valued and highly respected contributors to their tribe. As they grew up and proved themselves, they earned high status and respect for their contributions. The process of cultivating a warrior involved fostering traits such as high resilience, physical endurance, pain tolerance, and the ability to thrive in high-stress environments. Young warriors were frequently exposed to controlled adversity and physical and mental challenges to enhance their capabilities. Masculine warriors were guided by strong male role models who passed down the ways of warriors and prepared them for adulthood, both physically and mentally. The Warrior Class held a revered, appreciated, and nurtured position within society.

But while that might have been true in times past, it's not anymore.

In today's world, when a kid shows warrior-like traits, those qualities are often suppressed, shamed, and diverted. There are limited physical activities provided to foster the development of young warriors, and this issue is even more pronounced for masculine warriors. With around 75 percent of teachers being female and schools focusing on nurturing nice, domesticated, polite little boys, the landscape for nurturing masculine traits is virtually nonexistent. Modern dads spend a lot of time "in the office" and prefer to relax in front of the television when they get home. Statistics show that most family activities are now planned by mothers.

In this environment, young, naturally masculine warriors feel out of place. And on top of that, there's the trend of medicating hyperactivity, fewer physical sports, and a general negative view of masculinity. All of this has created a climate where pretty much any type of masculine behavior is viewed in a bad light, not just the harmful stuff. Healthy male role models are scarce, making it difficult for these traits to be properly cultivated and celebrated in masculine warriors. Because warriors are not recognized as a natural archetype, the nurturing of young warriors is almost nonexistent in modern Western society.

The reason for this is simple: society no longer views warriors as a fundamentally necessary part of society. The presence of artist clubs, speech and debate camps, entrepreneur think tanks, and little innovators clubs reflects the value and emphasis society places on artists, debaters, entrepreneurs, and innovators. Society believes these archetypes are crucial for our continued survival and prosperity. The failure to acknowledge and nurture natural warrior characteristics today is a clear indication that society no longer recognizes warriors as an inherent archetype within its framework. It wasn't always this way. Once upon a time, children had opportunities to be adventurous, solve problems independently, and develop strength and resilience. There were numerous outlets for youth, such as the Boy Scouts, Girl Scouts, and sports leagues. While some of these still exist today, statistics show a massive decline in participation in recent years. Today, we have made the environment so sterile and safe that children no longer have the chance to make mistakes or face adversity, which is the only way we can learn, adapt, and improve.

In today's America, many people are shielded from real dangers like fires, violence, theft, and physical harm. They might read about them on social media or see videos, but they rarely face these realities firsthand. A lot of people live in a cozy bubble where they feel safe and might even think threats are a thing of the past. But if you hang out in a calm, protected environment for too long, you might forget there are wolves lurking just beyond the fence. While society continues to benefit from the defense, service, and protection that warriors offer—as these elements remain essential—young, natural-born warriors are not nurtured, recognized, or celebrated within our current societal framework.

But despite the fact that modern culture no longer recognizes and nurtures young warriors, our society is still producing warriors who are uniquely capable of remaining calm in chaos and thriving in such environments. This is where things get interesting.

For a long time, I believed that my military training shaped my ability to excel in high-stress environments. I viewed my struggle with LTSD as a consequence of my profession. I thought that the rewiring of my nervous system to remain calm in chaos was a result of intense military training, preparation for warfare, and repeated battle drills. I just figured that I'd practiced the "fundamentals" so extensively that they had become my default response—without the need for conscious decision-making. I assumed this conditioning began on day one of basic training when I joined the military. Turns out I was wrong. I'd been nurtured, shaped, and conditioned long before that.

The environment that groomed my body to see a state of hypervigilance as normal, and forged my unique ability to remain calm in chaos, wasn't the military; it was a traumatic childhood.

I came to this realization at Warriors Heart after spending weeks and hundreds of hours listening to stories from warriors across the country. Despite the wide range of personalities, ethnicities, education levels, characters, and professional backgrounds, there was one experience we all shared: a traumatic childhood. In a society that fails to cultivate young warriors, the predominant nurturing environment for many modern warriors today is childhood trauma, particularly abuse or neglect.

To be honest, it took me a while to acknowledge that my childhood had been traumatic, and I know that's true for a lot of warriors. We tend to downplay our tough experiences, rationalizing with "It's not that bad; others have it worse, so I can't complain." I always knew my childhood wasn't perfect, but I didn't fully realize how deeply it had affected me. I was the loner kid who got bullied and had imaginary friends, the sensitive one trying to fix my parents' marriage, the polite kid who got turned down by girls, and the independent type who thought I didn't need much from my parents. But that illustrates the whole point: Chaos and high stress were so deeply ingrained in my life that I was oblivious to the trauma that shaped me.

Throughout most of my life, I downplayed my childhood experiences as a coping mechanism. I minimized the pain, neglect, and trauma from my early years and normalized it, because that's my superpower. And it kept me calm in the midst of the chaos. In fact, I so normalized the pain, neglect, and trauma that I didn't even understand that my childhood was abnormal until I was at Warriors Heart and began untangling the negative core beliefs that had been impacting me.

My counselor Kelly, God bless her, pushed me to follow the breadcrumbs and unravel the core beliefs and negative self-talk until I uncovered their origins. Each time I pulled at the thread, I'd think, "Eureka! That's it! This is where it all began!" only to find that the thread continued further. I'd pull it again and again until I finally pinpointed the real starting point, which unfailingly led back to my childhood.

Is it possible that the men and women uniquely conditioned to serve, protect, defend, and safeguard modern society are those who have been shaped and forged through trauma? In a society that barely acknowledges threats and dangers from the outside, and suppresses instead of nurturing natural-born warriors, does it not stand to reason that those conditioned to thrive in high-stress environments are the ones who were forced to do so as children? New studies are now emerging on this subject as experts begin to piece together this major component of the puzzle, but we have yet to really address the implications of what this means.

The Warrior Class continues to play a vital and essential role in our society. When threats loom at our doorstep, we courageously rise to defend your freedom and safety. In moments of crisis, we enter blood-spattered rooms to shield you from harm. In the face of danger, we charge into fires to rescue you. When a loved one's life hangs in the balance, we hold the fragile threads of their humanity together, giving you the chance to see them once more. We are prepared to face the unimaginable because, for many of us, the unimaginable has already become our reality.

Unfortunately, most people don't stop to ask why we excel at enduring pain, pushing past discomfort, confronting evil, and staying calm amidst chaos. Today's finest warriors didn't grow up surrounded by a tribe of strong-minded, positive role models who nurtured and cultivated their abilities. With few exceptions, we didn't have sparring partners, mentors, or running companions to guide us. Most modern warriors were shaped by trauma. We were the misfits and outcasts in the classroom, the ones who were abused or neglected at home and bullied outside. The very superpower that enables us to endure pain, persevere, and remain calm in chaos was forged through trauma.

"Trauma" is a term that's thrown around quite often these days, and it can mean very different things to different people. For a long time, I was very resistant to the idea of using it to describe my own life experiences. I knew I'd had my share of hard knocks—just like anyone else—but calling it trauma? That felt like an overstatement. It wasn't until I fully grasped what trauma really means that I understood how deeply it had shaped me.

Ask a hundred people to share and compare "traumatic" experiences and you'll get a hundred very different answers. What registers as trauma for one person may not for another. Exactly which events or environments classify as traumatic is subjective. But what's not subjective is how your nervous system and subconscious react to them. When your brain perceives something as extremely frightening or life-threatening, it triggers your autonomic nervous system to switch into survival mode, altering your body's sense of safety.

Think of your nervous system like a traffic light. The colors represent the states of your nervous system: green represents homeostasis or calm, red signifies the fight-or-flight response, and yellow is somewhere in between.

Our bodies are designed to bounce back from a single frightening experience or dangerous situation. Children, in particular, are very adaptable and resilient, even in the face of adversity. A child may feel fear or discomfort for a while but will return to a normal baseline state when they feel safe. They may travel to the "red zone" or "yellow zone" a few times throughout their childhood but will return to "green" when the situation is resolved or the environment changes. But if a child lives in a constant state of never feeling safe, that's when a fundamental adaptation, or "rewiring," occurs.

If you endured repeated trauma or a consistent lack of safety as a child, you will eventually begin to accept that your environment isn't going to change. In response, your brain and body will start to normalize those conditions as a coping mechanism.

The brain adapts to protect your vulnerabilities as a child, leading to a perception of danger and chaos as a *normal state of being*. This altered reality becomes your baseline. A trauma-forged brain is wired very differently than one that has not developed within a traumatic environment. This isn't a conscious choice; it's a survival strategy, the body's way of adapting to constant turmoil. When this happens, your default mode as a child is to expect danger, unpredictability, and a lack of safety in everyday life, effectively normalizing danger or chaos. But for warriors, it goes a little deeper than just normalizing chaos. While many people might learn to live with chaos, warriors rise up and take decisive action in response to it. A victim says, "The world is a fucked-up, unsafe place full of danger and pain and there's nothing I can do about it. Might as well lay down and accept it or wait for someone to come along and save me."

A warrior says, "The world is a fucked-up, unsafe place full of danger and pain, but I'm going to stand up, face it, and learn to thrive within the chaos so that I can defend myself and others from the storm."

It's crucial to understand that the adverse childhood experiences that reshape the nervous system aren't always the gritty, violent scenarios you might picture. This kind of rewiring doesn't just happen to kids who survive brutal beatings or endure the harshest extremes, like going without food or living on the streets. Trauma comes in all shapes and sizes, and it's not always wrapped in violence.

For some, it might be the constant upheaval of constantly changing residences as a kid, never feeling settled, and always being forced to start over just when they began to find their footing. That nagging instability may have made the world feel uncertain and unsafe. For others, it's growing up in a home where parents had zero emotional regulation, where the adults in charge couldn't manage their own feelings and placed the weight of their emotions squarely on the child's shoulders. When you're a kid in that environment, constantly walking on eggshells, bracing for the next emotional storm, or feeling responsible for a parent's happiness—or worse, their misery—it leaves a mark. That silent, creeping trauma can burrow deep into the nervous system, altering the way you react to the world around you.

Whether it's the big, obvious wounds or the small, consistent cuts that come from daily instability and emotional chaos, the impact on the nervous system can be just as profound. Just because you don't think your own experiences are traumatic doesn't mean your body agrees.

I realized early on that life is cruel and doesn't give a shit about your feelings. I realized early on that no one was coming to save or support me—only I could defend myself. Eventually, I stopped waiting for my environment to change. I learned to expect danger and pain around every corner. And the only way I felt safe was to be on alert, activated, and hypervigilant.

I craved the activation of high-stress or chaotic environments because it turned on my superpower, hypervigilance. Warriors who were conditioned by a traumatic childhood don't struggle to stay calm and make deliberate decisions in the midst of high-stakes environments because they've been doing battle drills for them all their lives.

If you were shaped by trauma and made the choice to rise up in the face of pain, abandonment, and abuse, that makes you a warrior. The decision to dedicate your life to serving, protecting, and fighting for others—because you know all too well what it's like to face the unimaginable alone—carries immense value. In many ways, your trauma is a gift. It shaped you, it made you who you are, and it forged rare abilities and capacities in you that define the warrior you are today. The world needs those abilities—our superpowers. Society relies on us to step up, to defend, to lead.

But it's important to recognize this is a two-sided coin: Trauma may have conditioned us to be incredible warriors, but it comes at a significant cost. *Because the same superpower that makes us superheroes in other people's lives turns us into supervillains in our own.*

CHAPTER 30
THE FRACTURED WARRIOR

LOOKING BACK AT THE JOURNEY that shaped me into a warrior, it's clear that my "superpowers"—enduring pain, compartmentalizing emotions in times of high stress, and staying calm in chaos—weren't just handed to me. *They were forged in chaos.* They were forged in the fires of adversity and trauma. That's true for most warriors. For a long time, I brushed my experiences aside, convinced they were no big deal. I thought that talking about "childhood trauma" was a sign of weakness and I was a goddamned superhero, not some loser on a therapist's couch, right? Eventually, I realized that ignoring the two-sided nature of the environment and experiences that shaped me wasn't a strength, it was stupidity and arrogance. As I started to dig deeper into how my brain and body were shaped by trauma, I began to realize that the implications of being shaped by childhood trauma were extensive.

For many years, I felt the toll of the war that raged inside of me, and I became aware of the fact that there seemed to be a fracture in my identity. On one side was the natural-born Warrior. On the other was the Destroyer—a master of sabotaging my life, destroying any shred of peace and happiness, and the ultimate creator and whisperer of lies I believed about myself. For a long time, I was aware of the conflict, thinking the Destroyer was a product of my military training and combat experiences. But as I traced it back, I realized it started much earlier than that.

I began to ask myself, "When did I start forming the Destroyer? Why did I create it?" These questions led me all the way back to my childhood. And as I pulled the thread and understood more about the brain and body, I began to realize that when trauma takes place during a child's formative and malleable years, it can "cement" negative core beliefs into their very identity. This creates a fracture that can eventually lead to an internal war—a battle between who you truly are and who trauma forced you to become.

Kids have a way of seeing the world that's completely self-centered—and not in a bad way; it's just how their brains are wired at that age. They're still figuring out the difference between what they do and what happens around them. A child might think that if they arrange their stuffed animals just right before bed, it'll keep their family safe. Or if they overhear their parents talking about money problems, they'll start saving pennies in a piggy bank, thinking that'll somehow fix everything. They might even believe their mood controls the weather—if they're sad, it rains, and if they're happy, a rainbow appears. If a sibling gets sick, they might worry it's because they secretly wished their sibling would leave them alone. And when their parents split up, they might think it's because they weren't lovable enough or did something to make a parent angry.

As they grow up, kids usually learn that the world doesn't revolve around them (hopefully) and that not everything is their fault. But when you grow up in chaos or trauma, that self-centered thinking can get stuck. Kids who feel like they're responsible for everything around them might start to believe they're the reason for all the chaos and negativity. They think they're the problem, that they don't deserve a safe, loving environment. And that sense of unworthiness sticks around.

And yeah, that was me.

I spent years of my life trying to earn my parents' love, trying to change myself so that I wouldn't be neglected and bullied. But nothing worked. Over and over and over, no matter what I did, no matter how hard I tried, I was always overlooked, beaten down, and alone. I felt constantly vulnerable and unsafe. This formed questions inside of me that I would ask for years to come: *Am I a bad person? Do I deserve bad things? Is there something fundamentally wrong with me? Am I not worthy of love and safety?*

I wanted to be myself—that highly sensitive, natural-born warrior, protector, and defender with a big heart. But everything around me reinforced that being myself would only result in pain, shame, and harm. I tested it out time and time again and always got the same results. The boys bullied me, the girls rejected me, and my parents saw nothing about me that was valuable enough to deserve proper care or love. In every situation, I was the common denominator. *Cause and effect.* All the data seemed to point to one logical conclusion: The real me had to go. That's when my identity split in two, fractured right down the middle. I pushed my authentic, sensitive self into the background. He wasn't gone, but he was tucked far, far away from the cruel world filled with pain and suffering.

In his place, I created a fantastic, impenetrable, macho masterpiece of a character—a perfect, invincible alter ego designed for a dark, catastrophic, dangerous, pain-filled world such as the one I found myself in. The Destroyer was born. The Destroyer was just fine being alone; he was confident, ruthless, and aggressive, and he sure didn't need anyone's approval. Rejection from women? He'd shrug it off because he'd already beat them to the punch by objectifying first—keeping them at arm's length so they never got close enough to see the real me. I turned them into conquests in a game where I would never feel disappointed or hurt. The Destroyer didn't feel neglected because he could take care of himself. The Destroyer never had to defend himself in the storm of chaos because he was on the offensive; he was the storm's creator. The Destroyer didn't feel sad, disappointed, or scared because he switched off emotions like a light and didn't feel a damn thing.

The Destroyer is born out of a need to cope with the overwhelming, powerless feeling that comes when life's brutal realities hit you hard. As a kid, you start out with hope, trusting in the goodness of the world. You believe that if you love fully, if you hope for the best, good things will come your way. But then life comes along with a big fucking hammer and smashes those ideals to pieces. You get hurt. People let you down. You learn, painfully, that life is unfair, and no matter how hard you try, you can't change your environment. That's when the Destroyer steps in.

His job is to take control of the chaos before it controls you. He makes sure you're never caught off guard again. Sabotage a good relationship before you get attached? That's the Destroyer at work, protecting you from the pain of a broken heart. Convince yourself you're worthless and don't deserve good things? That's his way of shielding you from disappointment when things inevitably go wrong. The Destroyer isn't just a defense mechanism; it's a survival strategy, ensuring that you never have to feel the full weight of life's betrayals again.

But over time, the lines between who you are and who trauma made you become so blurred that it's hard to know who you really are. And you start to think that you might actually be that self-sabotaging, lying asshole, the Destroyer.

Living with a fractured identity means never really knowing who you are. It blurs the line between your true self and the roles you play in response to the world around you. Every event, every mistake, every act of service or sacrifice becomes a measure of your worth, a constant evaluation of whether you deserve love or respect.

This internal battle between who you truly are and the persona forged by trauma inevitably leads to collateral damage—the erosion of your self-worth, esteem, and capacity to love.

That was absolutely true for me. My life was a constant war between my fractured identity. On one side, the Destroyer convinced me that I was fundamentally broken, undeserving of love and acceptance. On the other, the Warrior inside me fought to recognize my intrinsic value and right to be loved. This conflict became a relentless search for proof, an endless quest to determine which side was right. Every achievement and every challenge became a piece of evidence, either supporting or refuting my worth.

When I earned money, drove a nice car, had a beautiful partner, or made meaningful contributions to my team, I'd think, *Maybe I'm not so bad after all. Look who wants to be with me; look at the car I'm driving; look at the houses I own; look at the positive impact I'm having on others. That's got to mean I'm worth something, that I'm a good person.*

But when I made a mistake, found myself alone, fell into addiction, or failed to perform in a way that validated my worthiness of love, my inner critic was brutal: *Look at yourself, you worthless piece of shit. You don't deserve anything good. You're not a good person; you're not a hero; you're not worthy of love or happiness. You got exactly what you deserve."*

But the fractured identity was just the beginning. Trauma doesn't just leave its mark on your sense of identity; it rewires your brain, setting you up to normalize—and even become addicted to—chaos. This is where LTSD (lack of traumatic stress disorder), or chaos addiction, comes into play, a survival mechanism crafted by the Destroyer to maintain control over the chaos.

Being raised in a traumatic environment fundamentally alters a child's nervous system. As they endure repeated trauma or a consistent lack of safety, the child will begin to accept that their environment will not change. In response, their brain and body start to normalize these conditions as a coping mechanism. The brain adapts to protect the child's vulnerabilities, leading to a perception of danger and chaos as a normal state of being. This altered reality becomes their baseline. A trauma-forged brain is wired very differently than one that has not been developed within a traumatic environment. This isn't a conscious choice; it's a survival strategy—the body's way of adapting to constant turmoil. When this happens, the child's default mode is to expect danger, unpredictability, and a lack of safety in their everyday life—effectively normalizing danger or chaos. And we're not just talking feelings and emotions here; we're talking about physical, demonstrable adaptations that arise from environmental conditioning.

Because I never truly felt safe during those formative years, my baseline state became one of hypervigilance—constantly on high alert for danger, catastrophe, and chaos. As I grew older, I found that calm, non-chaotic environments felt unsettling, almost alien. I was always bracing for the next disaster, convinced that something bad was just around the corner. Even when the immediate threat had passed, my body remained in a state of hypervigilance, unable to fully relax.

Inside my home as a child, I navigated a minefield of emotional volatility, with an alcoholic father and a landscape riddled with unpredictable outbursts. Outside, I faced bullies who saw my sensitive nature as a weakness to exploit. My brain and body became so accustomed to living in the yellow zone that the idea of a green zone—a place of safety and peace—was something I couldn't even conceive of. To me, there were no safe environments, only varying degrees of threat. This constant state of alertness became my default mode, my way of feeling some semblance of control in an unpredictable world. It didn't matter if the immediate threat had passed, my body refused to relax. The reality was simple: I believed there were no safe environments, and that meant I was better off maintaining a state of hypervigilance.

But what happens when your body gets stuck in a hyperalert state, always on guard, even during moments of peace? First off, our bodies aren't built to live in that kind of constant overdrive. The green zone is where we heal, process emotions, sleep, restore, regenerate, and tap into creativity. It's also where our brain lets us form social and emotional connections with others. But when your body shifts into hypervigilant mode, out of sheer necessity, all of that gets shut down. And when you've been conditioned to thrive in chaos, just flipping the switch off isn't that simple.

Most warriors live in a perpetual yellow zone, not quite panicking, but never entirely at peace either. It's a constant state of purgatory: not safe enough to relax but also not threatened enough to trigger a full fight-or-flight response. It's an eternal standby mode, braced for a danger that never fully materializes yet never dissipates. At least the red zone offers a clear directive: fight the threat or flee from it. The yellow zone leaves us in limbo. Our nervous system can't relax and we can't run. It's the anticipation, the fear of the impending punch, that's often more tormenting than the punch itself.

When your body's been trained to switch on in high-stress environments (your superpower), and then you suddenly find yourself somewhere that doesn't trigger that response, it's like going into withdrawal. LTSD is a concept I developed to describe the disorientation and withdrawal symptoms that hit when someone who is wired to normalize stress and chaos lands in a low-stress environment. You might feel anxious, out of place, like a fish out of water. Depressive feelings, vulnerability, unease, and a sense of detachment can creep in.

For some warriors, LTSD feels like a deep emptiness. You may feel disconnected, struggling to find motivation, excitement, or even happiness in your day-to-day life. Even with a loving family, a good job, and supportive friends, you might still be haunted by a black hole that seems to swallow up any positive emotion. This disorientation and withdrawal often stem from brain chemistry and structure that's adapted to make high-stress environments feel normal. And even if you don't turn to extreme behaviors for a quick fix, dealing with this inner turmoil can be one hell of a challenge.

Other warriors go searching for anything that can reactivate their superpower. When that familiar state of alertness suddenly switches off, it can trigger an impulsive craving for situations, environments, or substances that bring back that intensity. Chaos addiction, or LTSD, can show up in all sorts of ways—from gaming and doom-scrolling to excessive shopping or seeking out risky behaviors like gambling, soliciting sex, reckless driving, extreme sports, heavy drinking, smoking, and drug use. LTSD can set off a domino effect of destruction.

But the fracture in identity and the rewiring of the body to normalize chaos aren't the only costs of being trauma-forged. The harsh reality is that this kind of conditioning can also leave you physically vulnerable to addiction.

The worst-kept secret in the warrior community is that addiction is running rampant, primarily manifesting as alcohol and drug abuse, as well as sex and porn addiction. You've read about mine. For years, I couldn't understand why I was unable to break the cycle of sex and porn addiction, as well as excessive drug use, no matter how hard I tried. Every time, I felt as if someone or some*thing* had invaded my body, used me like a puppet, and then left me feeling utterly broken, morally degenerate, and worthless. My battle with addiction was a tremendous source of shame and guilt because I saw it as evidence that I was a morally flawed, bad person. I will be the first to take full responsibility and say that many of my choices were objectively, irrefutably against my moral code. There is no excuse for the choices I made that hurt myself and those I cared about.

For years, I believed I was just struggling with a lack of willpower and a fundamental moral defect in my character. I couldn't understand why I couldn't seem to break the destructive patterns of addiction in my life. But then I came across a book called *TINSA: A Neurological Approach to the Treatment of Sex Addiction* by Dr. Michael Barta. TINSA (Trauma Induced Sexual Addiction) is the innovative treatment model pioneered by Dr. Barta, and the following passage from his book changed my fucking life:

> The primary origin of sexual addiction lies in a damaged autonomic nervous system (ANS) due to developmental traumas. Early wounding events, such as a lack of attunement and emotional neglect, can predispose a person to addiction by incurring damage to a person's neurological systems. A lack of parental attunement and other adverse developmental events can cause damage to the brain and autonomic nervous system, stunting emotional and psychological growth. This can provoke an individual to seek outside substances or feel-good behaviors in an attempt to regulate this damaged system. When a person is raised in an emotionally vacant home, he or she is then being set up to seek alternative ways of producing dopamine, the main neurotransmitter associated with pleasure in the brain.
>
> Adverse childhood and environmental experiences can cause detrimental effects on the brain's dopamine receptors, leading to and being the catalyst for substance abuse. The reward system in our brain is what processes dopamine, the body's pleasure-producing neurochem-

ical. This system is comprised of dopamine receptors, and in a healthy, functioning brain, these receptors are able to receive and process dopamine at a normal rate, keeping us well-balanced. If, however, the amount of dopamine receptors that a person has is limited, then that person will process dopamine at a limited rate. In cases like these, what this means is that ordinary but pleasurable dopamine-producing activities don't feel as good as they should. *All of this can set a person up to seek more dopamine just to feel normal.* Whether through pleasure-producing substances or behaviors, there are countless ways to find outside sources of dopamine, many of which can be highly addictive, as they can cause the person to become hooked on the dopamine provided. This is the very definition of addiction.

But the brain is very adaptable. Although the brain can't regulate the amount of dopamine coming in (because it cannot control a person's behavior or make a person stop doing a behavior) what the brain *can* do is regulate how much dopamine gets through. It does so through a process called down-regulation in which, if the brain receives more dopamine than it can handle, it begins to take away or disable its dopamine receptors. It is important to note here that generally speaking, the higher the risk of sexual behavior, the more dopamine is produced. This is where progression and escalation kick in. Progression is where we need more of the same thing in order to get the same effect, and escalation is when we start to change or escalate into more risky behaviors or higher dopamine-producing behaviors in order to get the same effect. This leads to what is known as regulation. *Instead of doing something as a means of feeling good, now we experience a dependency or need to do it just so we can feel normal.* It's no longer about the high, but instead, it becomes solely about overcoming withdrawals just to get back to our baseline. We need a dopamine fix to self-regulate, which initiates the pathological pursuit of rewards and relief through the use of substances and behaviors. When dopamine receptors drop after too much stimulation, the brain doesn't respond as much, and we feel less reward from pleasure. That drives us to search even harder for feelings of satisfaction."

It's not an accident that addiction runs rampant among warriors. First of all, we've already established that many of our modern warriors come from backgrounds scarred by childhood trauma, which often inflicts lasting damage on both the brain and the autonomic nervous system. This disruption can significantly hinder emotional and psychological maturity, creating a state of chronic dysregulation that provokes many warriors to seek outside substances or behaviors in an attempt to regulate this damaged system.

But addiction among warriors isn't just about childhood conditioning; it's also tied to their training and experiences. Intense experiences can actually rewire the brain's reward system, making combat veterans more prone to addiction as they seek out substances or behaviors that give them the same adrenaline rush they felt in combat. This alteration in brain chemistry helps explain why so many warriors find themselves unable to escape the grip of addiction. The potent rush of biochemicals that comes from surviving life-threatening situations can create a strong dependence. The body and mind get used to the flood of adrenaline and endorphins from high-stress experiences, driving them to constantly seek out ways to replicate that feeling, often resorting to destructive behaviors.

The science behind this is irrefutable. Addiction's toll is catastrophic and far-reaching, with impacts that span the physical, mental, and emotional landscape of life. Addiction can hijack the brain's reward systems, leading to mental health disorders like depression and anxiety. This alteration of brain chemistry makes recovery and the return to a non-addicted state a challenging journey that can take years.

Throughout my life, as I struggled with addiction, I felt intense guilt and shame. It ate away at my self-esteem and made me question who I was. The impact on my romantic relationships was also significant, as it damaged trust, eroded connections, and caused me to feel isolated. The stigma surrounding addiction made reaching out for help even harder. It tore my relationships apart, disrupted my social life, and damaged my body. Unfortunately, this is true for a lot of warriors.

It took me a long time to face the reality that childhood trauma played a huge role in shaping who I am today. I know that's not an easy thing for most warriors to admit. But recognizing the impact of trauma doesn't make you weak—it makes you smart. Our families, communities, nation, and the world all benefit from the protection, security, and service we provide—service that often comes from the unique training and conditioning rooted in our traumatic pasts. We can ignore it, pretend it doesn't exist, or blame one event for the collateral damage in our lives. Or we can get real about the fact that the same adaptations that make us goddamned superheroes also come with a price. To give you an example of exactly how this shows up in real life, I'm going to lay my life out on the examination table once again and shine a big ol' surgical light on it.

TYLER, A NATURAL-BORN WARRIOR...

I am a Warrior. I was born with a strong sense of duty to serve those around me. I have an innate connection to a higher purpose and a clear mission. I possess natural mental fortitude and a propensity for brave and bold action in the face of resistance. I am a protector by nature, devoted to keeping the young and vulnerable safe. I instinctively have the desire to provide security for those around me. I do not back down in the face of danger; I stand up and hold the boundary to keep others safe. I am willing to sacrifice myself for the greater good, putting myself in harm's way if necessary to protect others. That is the real me.

TYLER, A WARRIOR SHAPED BY TRAUMA...

I was raised by an emotionally absent alcoholic father and a fragile mother. From a young age, I was severely neglected, left to fend for myself, lacking a sense of safety within my own home. The constant harm, physical violence, and verbal abuse inflicted by bullies in my community only compounded this. At school, I was an outsider, disconnected from social groups and unable to fit into society's mold. The world outside my home felt just as unsafe as it did inside. Gradually, my mind and body adapted to this environment, accepting chaos and danger as the norm. But all the evidence pointed to one inevitable decision: If I was going to survive, I had to conceal my true self.

The trauma was an attack on my authenticity. My identity split in two, fractured to the core. Similar to the creation of Tyler Durden in *Fight Club*, I buried my authentic self, distancing it from the cruel world in order to shield it from further hurt and pain, and I created an alter ego designed for a dark, catastrophic, dangerous, pain-filled world: the Destroyer. The Destroyer was confident, ruthless, and aggressive. He didn't need anyone's approval. Emotions were a foreign concept; he simply shut them off and felt nothing. In the chaos, he took charge, making it his own. Now, I was a Warrior and a Destroyer.

TYLER...THE WARRIOR, THE DESTROYER, AND THE GODDAMNED SUPERHERO

Then I joined the military. And I'll tell you what, growing up in a traumatic environment made me one hell of a soldier. I was calm in the midst of chaos because my brain and body were already adapted to it. Pain hardly affected me because I'd endured far worse before. I was a master of compartmentalizing my emotions and disassociating when necessary. After a lonely childhood and starving for a sense of belonging, I found a family and brotherhood that accepted me. Without any internal sense of self-esteem, I had an opportunity to prove my worth based on my willingness to sacrifice myself for the team. I was hungry for validation and external proof that I had value, and it made me willing to do just about anything necessary to earn my stripes.

The military was also the perfect home for my overconfident alter ego, the Destroyer. I fully embodied the persona I had crafted for myself: a gun-wielding, fearless, unstoppable knuckle dragger and force to be reckoned with. The military environment constantly engaged my superpower and gave me a sense that I was controlling the chaos. Don't get me wrong, the natural-born Warrior in me also thrived there. I discovered a greater purpose and a definitive mission. I found myself in circumstances where I could boldly and courageously confront danger, safeguard the young and vulnerable, sacrifice for the greater good, and bravely defend against evil to ensure the safety of others. And for a while, everything seemed okay. The chaotic environment felt familiar. The Warrior and the Destroyer thrived there. Until it all came crashing down.

TYLER...A BATTLEGROUND FOR THE WAR WITHIN

The military served as a splint that held together my fractured identity. When it was gone, I fell apart, and suddenly I was dealing with the brokenness that had taken place long ago. While I was busy fighting an external war on foreign soil, I felt okay. But the moment I stopped, the Warrior and the Destroyer turned inward and began to battle against each other, and I suddenly found myself fighting battles on multiple fronts. This fracture in identity created an internal battle of epic proportions: a war between the Warrior and the Destroyer. And damn, they were both so strong. Which leads us to our next subject: the *War Within*.

CHAPTER 31

THE WAR WITHIN

WHAT EXACTLY IS THE WAR Within? People often talk about the "internal battle" that warriors face but rarely ask where it comes from or why it exists. For years, I felt the fog, exhaustion, and pain of internal conflict. I described it as an unseen battle, an undiagnosed disease, a black hole—it was a War Within me that I couldn't quite name.

To quote Carl von Clausewitz, a classic military theorist, "War occurs when states seek goals that clash with the goals of other states and choose to pursue them through violent means. The decision to use force must be mutual." He goes on to say, "Each tries through physical force to compel the other to do his will; his immediate aim is to throw his opponent in order to make him incapable of further resistance."

Digging deeper to understand the source of the conflict inside myself created this War Within. I started with the simplest definition of what war is. I figured that if war is the clash of two opposing forces, then it stands to reason that a War Within would be no different—there would be two forces inside me battling for control. That led me to ask the natural next question: What two opposing forces are at war within me? Why is there friction, conflict, and struggle?

These questions led me to understand that the War Within was a battle between the Warrior and the Destroyer—two identities locked in a struggle for dominance. On one side was the Warrior, representing my true self, my natural-born purpose to serve, protect, and live authentically. On the other side was the Destroyer, the persona shaped by trauma, hell-bent on controlling chaos, sabotaging every good thing in life, and creating destruction wherever it went.

Forged in Chaos

The Destroyer didn't just appear out of nowhere—it was forged in response to trauma, a defense mechanism designed to protect me from life's brutality. The Destroyer's intent was clear: to control and sabotage. It was born from a deep need to feel safe in a world that felt anything but. The Destroyer's job was to take control of the chaos before it could control me. He made sure I was never caught off guard, disappointed, or hurt again. He sabotaged anything good before I had a chance to get my hopes up or trust in something good. Yet in its attempt to protect me, the Destroyer was also tearing me apart, dismantling every opportunity for growth, happiness, and connection.

The War Within was a battle to see whether the Warrior or the Destroyer would gain control of my life. For a long time, this war raged beneath the surface, buried in the shadows of my subconscious. It was a shadow war—a term from military strategy that describes a conflict where a greater force hovers over a smaller dispute, steering it without getting its hands dirty. In this hazy zone between war and peace, battles are fought in the dark, often without any clear idea of who the enemy is or what the stakes really are. That was me—just an observer in my own shadow war, watching the conflict from a distance, trying to keep the collateral damage in check. I didn't fully understand who was at war or why—I just knew there was this deep internal conflict that wouldn't let up.

But as time went on, I began to recognize the shadow war for what it was, and I knew that I could no longer stand idly by. The time had come to plant my flag in the soil, declare the battle lines, and understand the strategy of my enemy so I could finally gain victory in my life. Trying to keep the conflict hidden was draining my energy and resources, sucking the life out of me, and leaving a path of destruction in its wake. Eventually, I'd had enough. I knew it was time to drag this war out of the shadows. I declared all-out war, planted my flag, and took a hard look at my enemy: the Destroyer. My first move was to understand exactly who I was up against and where the real conflict lay. Only by deciphering the strategy, tactics, and intent of the Destroyer could I start to reclaim control of my life and let the Warrior rise. So I laid it all out—every trait, every tactic of the Destroyer—and prepared myself for the battle ahead. I started by making a list of characteristics that defined my enemy: the Destroyer Mentality.

Terminal Uniqueness: The Destroyer Mentality convinces you that no one could possibly understand who you are or what you're going through. It's the voice in your head telling you that your struggles are insurmountable, that you're beyond repair, and that no one else can ever truly relate. This isolating belief leaves you trapped in self-imposed solitude, drowning in a sense of hopelessness.

External Validation Quest: The Destroyer Mentality is like a relentless drill sergeant, driving you on an endless mission to find worth outside yourself. It makes you crave approval and constantly seek validation from others because it's convinced you that don't have any value on your own. This was my constant battle when I left the military. Without the structure and validation that came from sacrifice and service, I felt utterly worthless. I latched onto anything that could prove my value—Vanessa was my last anchor. When I lost her, I spiraled downward, chasing validation in every corner, whether through sexual conquests, wealth, or social status, desperate to fill the void left by the absence of self-love.

Escapism/Fantasy: The Destroyer Mentality thrives on avoidance, leading you to every possible escape route to dodge the reality of who you are and the emotions you've locked away. Whether it's drowning in substances, getting lost in unhealthy coping mechanisms, or diving headfirst into risky behaviors, it's all about running from the pain you're too scared to face.

Adopting a Facade and Chameleon Behavior: The Destroyer Mentality hides behind masks, creating personas to protect you from rejection and vulnerability. Whether you're the Bloodthirsty Villain, the Overconfident Playboy, or the Polite "Nice Guy" who lets everyone walk all over him, it's all a facade. These are just survival tactics that have you shifting like a chameleon to whatever shade you think will keep you safe or earn approval.

Approval Seeking: The Destroyer Mentality sometimes manifests as passive compliance, a desperate need to gain approval by becoming a yes-man. It shows up in that subtle, sneaky way of never standing up for yourself, never voicing an opinion, and always trying to make everyone else happy to earn their approval. For many guys (myself included), this shows up in relationships, where we constantly seek approval from the women in our lives, mistakenly believing that by catering to their every whim, we're showing love. But it's not love—it's a tactic, a way to meet your own need for approval under the guise of caring for someone else. The sad truth is most women can sense the difference. I remember Vanessa saying to me, "Just be a man," or "I wish you would just lead," and it drove me fucking nuts because I was doing EVERYTHING she wanted. It turns out that all I was doing was seeking approval, not truly loving or leading.

Emotional Avoidance: The Destroyer Mentality locks away your emotions in a vault, keeping you from dealing with the messy stuff that makes you human. It compartmentalizes, dissociates, and buries feelings deep, leaving you emotionally stunted and disconnected. My own unprocessed emotions piled up like a toxic landfill, poisoning my relationships and wreaking havoc on my physical and mental health.

Self-Destructive Coping Mechanisms: The Destroyer Mentality doesn't just protect, it destroys. It brings with it a host of self-destructive behaviors, coping mechanisms that tear you down instead of building you up. These habits don't just hurt you, they ripple out, causing collateral damage to everyone in your orbit.

Perfectionism and Self-Criticism: The Destroyer Mentality sets you up as your own worst enemy, pushing you toward impossible standards and tearing you apart for every tiny flaw. It's an all-or-nothing mindset—one slip, and it feels like the whole damn world is crashing down.

Control Disorder: The Destroyer Mentality is, at its core, a control disorder. It's a desperate need to manage the chaos inside, which shows up as a need to control everything outside. Whether it's your relationships, your work, or your own self-destruction, the Destroyer Mentality grabs the reins and refuses to let go because letting go would mean facing the unknown.

Impulsive Behavior: The chaos that defines the Destroyer Mentality fuels impulsive decisions, making you act without thinking to chase the immediate thrill or relief, no matter the cost. These impulsive actions often lead to a downward spiral of destruction, feeding the cycle the Destroyer thrives on.

Difficulty in Forming and Maintaining Relationships: The Destroyer Mentality sabotages your ability to connect with others. It fills your head with feelings of worthlessness and a fear of vulnerability, making trust nearly impossible. It's the reason relationships crumble, why intimacy feels out of reach. Even when the Warrior in you steps up, trying to create real love and connection, the Destroyer is right there, ready to tear it all apart, create chaos, and foster codependency. Authenticity and wholeness are prerequisites for true intimacy, but the Destroyer Mentality keeps you from ever knowing who you really are, making genuine connection feel like a distant dream.

Isolation and Withdrawal: The Destroyer Mentality is a master of pushing you into the shadows, making you isolate yourself from the world as a twisted form of emotional self-defense. It's like building walls so high that nothing—and no one—can get in, leaving you alone with your thoughts, your pain, and your regrets. This withdrawal leads to compartmentalizing your emotions, tucking them away in dark corners where they fester and grow. The isolation often springs from a deep, unsettling realization that you're not living as your true self, compounded by that feeling of terminal uniqueness, the belief that no one can possibly understand what you're going through, so why even bother trying to connect?

Addiction to Chaos: The Destroyer Mentality and chaos addiction feed off each other like a twisted symbiotic relationship. Born from a desperate need to maintain control in a chaotic world, the Destroyer Mentality can lead to the rewiring of the brain—not just to normalize chaos but to actually thrive in it. The ability to stay calm in the midst of chaos isn't inherently bad; in fact, it's one of the greatest assets a warrior can possess. LTSD often occurs in warriors who've undergone intense training, causing their brain and body to crave stress. These adaptations aren't inherently negative, they're survival tools. But when the Destroyer takes hold of that adaptation, it twists it, turning that calm into a driving need to create chaos as a way to control it. This is where chaos addiction, or LTSD, comes into play. The Destroyer exploits that need for control and the comfort found in chaos, pushing you to seek out chaotic situations—whether through drugs, dangerous risk-taking, toxic relationships, or more subtle forms like endless scrolling or emotional withdrawal.

After medically retiring from active duty, I experienced intense LTSD. The military had provided a steady drip of dopamine, high stress, and activation that made my nervous system feel right at home. When that disappeared, my whole body freaked the fuck out. I felt anxious, depressed, and constant fear that the other shoe was about to drop. At first, my LTSD manifested as a profound sense of emptiness. I felt detached and struggled to find motivation, connection, excitement, and happiness. While I had a beautiful, loving girlfriend, a nice house, and was seemingly "living the dream" in Vegas, I found myself isolated in that beige office, feeling depressed and questioning why that black hole inside me seemed to swallow up every shred of happiness or motivation I once had. I hated myself for becoming that guy. My self-esteem went down the toilet, and I felt like a loser.

The Warrior hated the "depressed guy in the office." The Warrior rose up, taking steps toward a better career, starting to exercise, and embracing a good dose of healthy discipline. The Destroyer, on the other hand, sought out just about every form of chaos imaginable—especially after feeling betrayed and rejected in my relationship, which only reinforced my belief that I was worthless and that my authentic self was better off hidden behind the mask of the Destroyer. Excessive drinking and drugs were my top chaos devices of choice, but sex addiction was my primary tool. This book is filled to the brim with examples of what LTSD looks like in real life.

My brain and body had grown so accustomed to high stress that I actually felt more at ease in that intense state. Take a look at my experiences: While jetting around the world leading back-to-back GoRuck events without a break, I turned to central nervous system stimulants and risky sexual encounters to help me "relax" in my off time. The buzz of risk and excitement I got from seeking out those encounters, combined with the high of the drugs, replicated the high activation and adrenaline rush I had known in combat. This pattern continued during my time on the *Suicide Squad* set and filming *SEAL Team*. As long as I pushed myself to the brink of exhaustion through work and exercise, I was okay. When it was time to stop working, instead of winding down like most people, I craved chaos and constant excitement because that was my brain and body's normal baseline.

The collateral damage from my battle with LTSD was extensive. As I look back, I see the substantial amount of time, money, and energy I poured into my self-destructive behaviors. I recognize how my body endured the exhaustion from being repeatedly pushed into that state. The impact wasn't confined to me; it also took a toll on those closest to me. My addiction to chaos played a significant role in the deterioration of my relationships with both Vanessa and Sarah. As time went on, the situation only intensified.

This quote from *TINSA* says it well.

> As our dopamine receptors keep declining and weakening, we need more and more dopamine to get the same effect. All of this can set us up to be constantly seeking higher-risk sexual activities. For example, by seeking out more extreme sexual stimuli, longer porn sessions, or more frequent porn viewing—thus further numbing

the brain. This is why, especially into adulthood, sex addicts will often seek high-risk sexual activity, such as paying for sex or having extramarital affairs, because if sex is mixed with either fear, pain, or shame, it increases the rush, secreting higher levels of dopamine and creating greater amounts of pleasure. There is nothing fun about living life as a sex addict. Shame, guilt, extreme self-loathing, and depression are just a few of the internal conflicts that most addicts wrestle with daily. Addicts regularly report dealing the loss of employment, deterioration of marriage or relationships, and loss of social reputation.

My use of drugs, pornography, and sex were glaring wrecking balls that caused significant damage to authentic love and connection in my romantic relationships, especially as it continued to escalate. The longer my addictive behaviors remained unchecked, the more I found myself developing an appetite for talking about and fantasizing about risky sexual behaviors that were not only unhealthy but were things I didn't really want to do. But I needed the escalation and novelty to experience the same hit of dopamine.

But the issue ran deeper than that. I also struggled to be present and at ease without constantly being in motion. I was, quite literally, a workaholic, always moving from one task to the next, convincing myself that I was doing it all for *her*—to be a good provider, to show acts of service that would make her feel loved and cared for. While that was partly true, the constant craving for motion, chaos, challenge, and a heightened sense of activation (often achieved through extensive work hours) to feel "okay" left me internally restless and unable to establish deep emotional connections. These factors, among others, initiated toxic patterns in our relationships, leading me to actually become addicted to the explosiveness of that toxicity, causing it to amplify. It was a destructive cycle that never ended. Looking back, I can now see it clearly, but at the time, everything seemed perfectly normal.

The Destroyer Mentality and LTSD/chaos addiction feed off each other synergistically. In my life, the more chaos I generated, the more guilt I felt, reinforcing the belief that I was truly worthless. This heightened my feelings of low self-worth and self-blame, with each instance further cementing my negative self-image. I found myself trapped in a destructive cycle of creating chaos, taking responsibility for it, and then berating myself for my actions. This destructive loop was vividly exemplified by addiction. When the external representation of the alter ego I had constructed began to crumble as I transitioned into the civilian world, I wasn't the muscular, battle-hardened knuckle dragger who wouldn't take shit from anyone. For many years, I was a skinny guy with a gimpy arm and few marketable skills in the civilian world. The Destroyer Mentality sought out any means to incite chaos and unleash its power. The internal battle between my authentic self and the distorted persona shaped by trauma unfolded as a path of destruction, causing harm not only to myself but also to those closest to me. Additionally, all that emotion I had suppressed for years began to surface, but in unhealthy ways. I spent a lifetime shutting off my emotions by adopting the Destroyer Mentality. Only I didn't really shut them off. Just because you choose not to feel emotion or properly process it doesn't mean it goes away. The emotion is simply stored until your brain and body feel safe enough to process it.

Most warriors aren't just fighting one battle, they're fighting two. The first is against external threats: foreign enemies, crime, disasters, fires, and whatever else life throws at us. But the second battle is the one that rages within, a struggle between our true warrior nature and the mental and physical adaptations born from trauma and the intense conditioning of our professions.

Once I understood that my deep sense of inner conflict, that constant tension and friction, was a battle between the Warrior and the Destroyer, I knew I had to dig deeper. I started looking at every single area of my life to figure out where these battles were being fought, and what I discovered was eye-opening. These battles weren't confined to one area of my life, they were raging across multiple areas, each with its own unique challenges. I started by dividing each area into separate "terrains" where the battle was being fought. While some terrains overlapped, I was able to address each separately.

The Physical Terrain: Here, the clash between the Warrior and the Destroyer was like a daily fight. The Warrior wanted me to push my limits, to build strength, to care for my body and treat it well. But the Destroyer? He was hell-bent on tearing all of that down. My battles with sex addiction and heavy drug and alcohol use were classic examples. The Destroyer mentality drove me to abuse my body, pushing me toward behaviors that wrecked my health and left me feeling like shit. I was trapped in a vicious cycle of using substances to numb the pain, only to wake up feeling even more broken. The Warrior was there, fighting to keep me strong, but the Destroyer made sure I stayed locked in self-destructive patterns that tore me apart from the inside out.

The Mental Terrain: The battlefield of the mind was where the Destroyer loved to play dirty. The Warrior was all about clarity, focus, and a mindset grounded in truth. But the Destroyer thrived on confusion, self-doubt, lies, and negative core beliefs. He was that voice in my head whispering that I wasn't good enough, that I didn't deserve happiness or success, that I was nothing but a worthless piece of shit. He kept me trapped in this twisted loop of self-sabotage, using every dirty trick in the book to make sure I stayed down. Every time I tried to push forward, the Destroyer was right there, whispering doubts, fanning the flames of fear, and convincing me that failure was my destiny. The lies he fed me became the core beliefs that haunted me for years—beliefs that I wasn't worth fighting for, that I wasn't capable of anything better.

The Emotional Terrain: Emotions? The Destroyer saw them as the enemy. The Warrior wanted me to feel, to connect, and to love with everything I had. But the Destroyer knew emotions were dangerous—they made you vulnerable. So he taught me to avoid them, to bury them deep, to shut down and shut out. My inability to regulate emotions created chaos in my relationships. One minute I was completely shut down, and the next I felt like I wanted to explode. The Destroyer made sure I never got too close and rarely let anyone see the real me, because that would mean opening up to the possibility of pain, rejection, or disappointment. The Warrior was fighting to keep my heart open, but the Destroyer kept me locked in this cycle of suppression and eruption, wreaking havoc on everyone around me and leaving me more isolated than ever.

The Spiritual Terrain: The Warrior wanted purpose, meaning, and a connection to something greater than myself. The Destroyer feared that more than anything. Because if I found purpose, if I found something to believe in, something that gave me hope, it could shift the balance of power. The Destroyer filled my head with doubt, cynicism, and despair, making me question everything. I had a deep resistance to even the notion of a higher power because the Destroyer knew that a Warrior with a purpose was a force to be reckoned with. So he kept me lost, disconnected, hopeless—a Warrior without a mission.

The Social/Relational Terrain: This is where the Destroyer really did some damage. Relationships are where the Warrior wanted to shine—building connections, forging bonds of loyalty and trust, and loving fiercely. But the Destroyer? He was terrified of that shit. I was so scared of being hurt, of being vulnerable, that I would sabotage my relationships, objectify women, or just shut down emotionally. This was the Destroyer's way of keeping me safe from getting hurt, but it was incredibly damaging both to me and those I tried to connect with. The Destroyer kept my true self the shadows, never allowing me to see who I really was, because that would mean risking rejection, and he wasn't about to let that happen.

The Professional Terrain: Money is more than just currency; it's power, it's freedom, and it's a tool to build the life you want. The Warrior saw money as a means to create stability, secure the future, and fuel my mission. The Destroyer saw money as a status symbol and a ticking time bomb. With every big move I made—whether it was working on the set of *Suicide Squad* or *SEAL Team*, or starting my own security business—the battle inside me was brutal. The Destroyer filled my head with doubts, telling me I wasn't cut out for it, that I'd fail, that I didn't have what it took. But the Warrior pushed back, reminding me of my purpose, telling me I was made for more. It was an all-out war, and every time I took a leap, I had to fight like hell to keep the Destroyer from pulling me back into the shadows.

In every terrain, the Warrior's mission was clear: to act with purpose, with passion, to fulfill the calling inside me. The Destroyer's mission was just as clear: to control, to sabotage, to destroy every effort the Warrior made to grow, to advance, to expand. The Destroyer was terrified of anything good—any shred of hope, any positive belief, any trust—because he knew that if I let those things in, if I let the Warrior win, his reign of chaos would come to an end. So he fought with everything he had to keep me small, to crush any possibility of growth, to make sure every inch the Warrior gained was met with brutal resistance.

Understanding the terrain was like shining a spotlight on the battlefield, exposing exactly where the Destroyer had dug in and was launching his attacks. Knowing where the fights were happening allowed me to map out the battlefield, anticipate the Destroyer's next move, and counter it with the strength, resilience, and truth that only the Warrior could bring.

By now, you're starting to see how this all comes together. We're getting to the heart of the War Within—the clash between the Warrior and the Destroyer, between who you were born to be and who trauma forced you to become. We've laid out the terrain where these battles are being fought and the battlefield is clear.

In the next chapter, I'll break down how I formed a war plan by creating very specific strategies, techniques, and tactics to win the battles that raged across every terrain of my life. But first, there's something else we need to talk about: obstacles. There are obstacles—real, tangible, and challenging—that complicate the battles for hundreds of warriors I've worked with. These aren't just minor setbacks; they're unique challenges that can add layers of struggle and make the fight even more brutal.

So before we get into the tactics and strategies for victory, it's crucial to bring these obstacles into the light. Because understanding them is key to navigating the battlefield and, ultimately, winning the war.

OBSTACLE: TRAUMATIC BRAIN INJURY (TBI)

TBI is like a hidden land mine that can destroy you from the inside out if you're not careful, and we're just now beginning to understand how pervasive it is in the warrior community. While many assume that TBI is only caused by blunt-force trauma, the surprising truth is that blast-wave exposure can also lead to it. Warriors often experience TBI without a direct impact to the head. The symptoms are often difficult to pinpoint—low mood, sleep disturbances, irritability, and a brain that just won't focus. Special Operations personnel, due to their extensive work with explosives and heavy weaponry, are particularly at risk. The stats are staggering—over 85 percent may suffer from TBI as a result of their training, a rate far higher than in conventional forces. But the damage doesn't stop there. Veterans with TBI often face additional hurdles like disruptions in levels of hormones, such as cortisol and testosterone, which can mimic depression and wreak havoc on sleep and cognition. It's like fighting a war on two fronts: the War Within and the war waged by TBI on your body and mind. The lines blur, making it nearly impossible to know where one battle ends and another begins.

The hormonal chaos, mood swings, and mental fog that come with TBI create a whole new level of complexity in the War Within. It's damn near impossible to differentiate between the battles caused by the clash between the Warrior and the Destroyer, and those that are the physical fallout from TBI. But one thing's for sure: The Destroyer will pounce on this obstacle, using it as ammunition to undercut the Warrior at every turn. If TBI is part of your fight, your battle strategy has to include bringing in proper support. This isn't a battle to fight solo. You need to pull out the big guns, rally the right allies, and be strategic in navigating this terrain, so you don't end up overwhelmed.

OBSTACLE: LOSS OF MISSION AND PURPOSE

When I transitioned into civilian life after my injury, I found myself completely unmoored, drifting without the structure, discipline, and sense of purpose that had once been my lifeline. The Warrior in me was desperate for a mission—a cause to fight for, a purpose to protect. I had spent years honing my mind and body to rescue the weak, stand up to the world's bullies, and face down the darkest threats. But suddenly, I was starting from square one—no mission, no purpose, and a hollow sense of worth. The Destroyer thrived in that emptiness, whispering that my only value was tied to how much I could sacrifice and serve. Without a mission to anchor me, I felt like a shell of the man I used to be.

I spent years lost in that vast emptiness, without a compass, fighting off the despair that comes when you feel like you've lost your reason for being. This loss of direction didn't just hurt, it handed the Destroyer even more power, making it even harder for the Warrior to stand his ground. The Destroyer fed me lies, telling me I was worthless, that I had nothing left to offer, that the world was too far gone, and that without a mission or purpose, life itself was meaningless. That void made it even more difficult to push back against the Destroyer as he reveled in the chaos left behind by my lost sense of purpose.

OBSTACLE: UNRESOLVED GRIEF

Unresolved grief is a heavy burden that many warriors carry. Whether it's the loss of a brother in arms or the fallout from a brutal battle, grief sticks with you, even when you think you've outrun it. It's not something you can just power through. For us warriors, grief is often entangled with trauma and the harsh realities of a dangerous and unforgiving world. But when you're living in a state of constant hypervigilance, there's no space for grief—you shove it down, lock it away, and keep moving, because that's what you've been trained to do.

But here's the hard truth: Grief doesn't vanish just because you've buried it. It lingers in the darkest corners of your mind, waiting for the right moment to resurface. Unresolved grief doesn't follow any rules. It can show up long after the event that caused it, even when life seems to be going well. And it's not just about losing someone you loved. You could be grieving the loss of your career, your identity, a sense of brotherhood you once experienced, or even your physical capabilities.

The Destroyer thrives on that unresolved grief, using it as a weapon to deepen the chaos within. He's a master at creating confusion, making it nearly impossible to tell if you're dealing with grief, depression, or just another one of the Destroyer's twisted games. The Destroyer will twist that loss into something even darker, whispering lies that this world is irredeemably fucked up, that vengeance, anger, and bitterness are worth clinging to, and that you shouldn't let yourself love or get close to anyone because they'll inevitably be ripped away.

Unresolved grief muddies the waters of the War Within. It creates an emotional fog that makes it tough to see the battle lines clearly. The Destroyer loves that fog, using grief to sap the Warrior's strength, keeping him off balance and magnifying the pain and chaos. Recognizing and confronting that grief is essential because if left unchecked, the Destroyer will use it to twist your view of the world, making you see love and connection as risks not worth taking, and leaving you isolated in your pain.

OBSTACLE: SICKNESS, DISEASE, OR INJURY

Sickness, disease, or injury can create tremendous obstacles that turn the conflict within your physical terrain into an uphill battle. When your body is compromised, every fight on this front becomes an incredible challenge. For warriors, it's easy to overlook the toll illness or injury takes because we've been conditioned to push through the pain, to ignore the signals our bodies are sending us because, in the heat of action, there's no time for weakness. But the reality is that you can't separate your mental health from your physical health. They're connected, and when one goes down, the other usually follows.

When sickness, disease, or injury hits, it makes the War Within far more lethal. The Destroyer doesn't just sit back and wait—he seizes the opportunity, capitalizing on your infirmity to demotivate you from fulfilling your mission and purpose. He uses your physical struggles to amplify feelings of worthlessness, to drive home the idea that you're not the Warrior you once were. The Destroyer knows that a weakened body can lead to a weakened mind, making it harder to differentiate between the physical symptoms and the mental battles you're facing. And when you're already worn down, it's easy to believe those lies.

This obstacle doesn't just add a layer of physical pain and fatigue to the battles you're already fighting; it also creates a complex web of symptoms that is hard to untangle. Hormonal imbalances like low testosterone or thyroid issues can mimic depression, sapping your energy, clouding your mind, and making you feel like you're trudging through quicksand. Adrenal fatigue can leave you feeling like you're running on empty, making it nearly impossible to summon the strength to fight back. Gut health problems can lead to brain fog, anxiety, and mood swings that make it hard to think clearly or stay focused. Burn-pit exposure can cause neurological damage, leading to a host of cognitive and emotional issues that can feel like you're losing the battle before it even begins.

The Destroyer will use these confusing, overlapping symptoms to create a fog of war, making it hard to differentiate between physical and mental or emotional issues. This makes the War Within even more brutal, leaving you feeling lost and overwhelmed. The Destroyer will whisper that you're too broken to keep fighting, that you'll never be at full strength again, and that you might as well give up now.

But this is where the Warrior needs to dig deep. Recognizing that you can't win the War Within without taking care of your physical health is crucial. You can't fight effectively if your body is breaking down. The Destroyer wants you to ignore the physical side of the battle, to push through the pain until you collapse. But the Warrior knows better. Taking care of your physical health isn't a sign of weakness; it's a strategic move to ensure you're fighting at full strength. Ignoring your health is like going into battle with one hand tied behind your back—it's only a matter of time before the Destroyer gains the upper hand.

OBSTACLE: MORAL INJURY

Moral injury is a wound to the soul that leaves a deep scar that doesn't just fade away with time. It happens when your moral compass—those deeply held beliefs and values that guide your actions—is shattered by something you've done, witnessed, or been forced to participate in. For military and law enforcement personnel, this often comes from being required to act in ways that clash with everything you believe in. Whether it's something you did yourself or something you were part of, the result is the same: a profound sense of guilt, shame, and moral confusion that gnaws at you from the inside out.

But here's where the Destroyer sees an opening. He'll take that moral injury and twist the knife, using it as proof that you're a bad person, that you're beyond redemption. The Destroyer will seize on the guilt and shame, whispering lies that you're irredeemable, that the things you've done are unforgivable, and that there's no coming back from the darkness you've seen or been a part of. He'll use that moral injury as ammunition to undermine every positive step you try to take, feeding the belief that you're not worthy of healing, not deserving of peace.

Healing from moral injury isn't about forgetting or erasing the past; it's about finding a way to integrate those experiences into your life without letting them destroy you. But if you're unaware of the obstacle and not astute to the strategic way the Destroyer will exploit this, it can be absolutely detrimental. The burden of moral injury can be overwhelming, adding another layer of complexity to the War Within, as the lines between right and wrong blur, and the weight of your actions—or inactions—feels like an anchor dragging you down. The Destroyer thrives in this confusion, using it to erode your sense of self-worth and keep you trapped in a cycle of self-blame and despair.

OBSTACLE: A FRAGMENTED MEDICAL SYSTEM THAT DOESN'T ADDRESS PSYCHOPHYSIOLOGY

This chapter is called "The War Within," and the focus has been on you, as an individual—your story, the environments that shaped you, the fractures in your identity, the rewiring of your nervous system, and everything fueling the battle raging inside you. But here's the thing: I can't, in good conscience, just talk about the war inside you without addressing the battlefield you're up against—your external environment.

Let me be clear: What I'm about to say is not coming from an "everyone's corrupt and the government's watching you through your microwave" type of person. But if you're battling any mental or physical challenges right now, I've got news for you: Our conventional Western medical system is fucking you over. And yeah, I know that's a heavy thing to say, so let me clarify. I'm NOT talking about the incredible people, the doctors, nurses, mental health specialists, and all those who've devoted their lives to helping and healing others. I am not anti-Western medicine. I'm not against conventional medicine. It didn't just save my arm—it saved my life. I am living proof of what modern science and medicine can do when it's at its best—precision, innovation, and the power to rewrite fate. But the *system*? That's a different story. The system is failing you, and it's got to change.

Here's the story I see time and time again: You realize you've got health problems and need support. You're in the trenches, mentally and physically beat to hell, and after slogging it out for who knows how long, you finally reach that moment where you're ready to ask for help. And let's not downplay that—just getting there is huge. As warriors, we've been taught to grit our teeth, keep giving till there's nothing left, and shove our own pain into a dark corner somewhere. So, when you finally say, "Alright, I need some backup here," you're putting it all on the line. That's a massive step.

And what happens next? Well, usually, you get handed a PTSD diagnosis (more on this shortly) like it's a lifetime membership to the Trauma Lifestyle Club. Congrats! You're in! Your "treatment" options?

You've got two flavors on the menu: talk therapy and/or meds. Like trauma recovery is an ice cream shop with exactly two flavors. Chocolate or vanilla. Or maybe the chocolate-vanilla swirl if you're feeling adventurous. But does it work? Are we seeing a drop in suicide rates? No. In fact, they're rising. Are we actually tackling the root causes of these issues? Nope. They're just getting buried under a pile of medication, numbed and masked instead of healed.

Why? Well, first of all, the conventional medical approach hasn't caught up with the science. Thanks to breakthroughs in research, we now know that trauma isn't some mystical, emotional dark cloud hanging over you. It's not a personality flaw or some abstract disorder. Trauma is a physical injury, as real as a broken leg or a gunshot wound. Your body isn't betraying you—it's doing exactly what it was designed to do: survive. Trauma is a biological response hardwired into our DNA, but when that response doesn't shut off, it rewires your brain and body, trapping you in survival mode. This overactive survival response floods your system with stress hormones, triggering symptoms like anxiety, insomnia, paranoia, hypervigilance, and even suicidal or homicidal thoughts. We now know that trauma *physically* changes your brain. Thanks to breakthroughs in science and technology, we can now see it on brain scans. The neural pathways themselves are altered—regions of the brain that process memory, fear, and stress responses actually shrink or swell in response to trauma. Your brain is literally rewired by trauma. And for most warriors, that rewiring becomes addictive (aka LTSD).

But here's the thing that most people don't talk about: Did you know that when you've been rewired by trauma, *every system in your body* is affected? Science is finally showing us the truth: trauma doesn't just haunt your mind; it invades your entire body. Your nervous system stays on high alert, constantly pumping out stress hormones like cortisol and adrenaline, which wreak havoc on your heart, blood pressure, and immune system. This constant flood of stress hormones leaves your body in a state of *chronic* stress, causing widespread inflammation. And that's a gateway to a whole host of health issues: digestive problems, gut imbalances, fatigue, headaches, joint pain, skin disorders, cardiovascular disease, and even cognitive decline. It disrupts sleep patterns, making true rest seem impossible. It messes with hormone production, leading to everything from thyroid issues to adrenal fatigue and even weak bones over time. It messes with gut health, which impacts digestion and even your mood—because, yes, there's a direct link between the gut and the brain. Trauma's effects ripple through your entire being, attacking your ability to think clearly, sleep deeply, heal properly, and even feel safe in your own skin.

Trauma rewires you in ways that keep you stuck in survival mode. For many of us, that ripple effect has been happening since we were children. And until we start treating trauma as a full-body experience, it won't be just your mind that pays the price—it'll be your entire well-being.

Trauma isn't just something you "get over." It's like a virus that embeds itself in your core, rewriting the way you think, feel, and function. And yes, while there are brutal effects that come with it, there's no denying that trauma also forges some of the toughest warriors. It's not all bad—it builds resilience, grit, and an ability to withstand the worst. But you have to be aware of the flip side: Those same traits that make you a fierce warrior can sometimes make you blind to the toll they're taking on your body and mind.

For too long, we've ignored this reality, treating trauma as just a mental "disorder." But science is showing us something much bigger: Trauma is a whole-body experience, and healing it requires a whole-body approach.

Case in point: if your leg were broken, would anyone tell you to just walk it off? Of course not. You'd get a cast, some crutches, and time to heal. But with trauma, the message is often, "Suck it up. Deal with it. Here's some meds to take the edge off."

That's not healing—that's survival on life support.

For years, we've treated the effects of trauma as purely psychological, overlooking the domino effect it has on the entire body. Trauma impacts both the mind and the body (after all, the mind *is* in the body), yet Western medicine treats them as separate entities. This disconnect leaves far too many people caught in an endless loop of unresolved trauma and lingering physical symptoms.

And not only have we missed this fundamental mind-body connection, but our Western medical approach to treatment is hopelessly fragmented. Got hormone issues? They'll send you to an endocrinologist. Feeling depressed? Off to the psychiatrist. Stomach problems? Time to see the gastroenterologist. And here's the kicker: None of these specialists communicate with each other. Your nervous system, gut, hormones, and mental health are treated as if they belong to separate people. Your therapist doesn't look at your cortisol levels, and your endocrinologist isn't interested in your childhood trauma. Everyone's working in their own little silo, tossing solutions at symptoms but never addressing the root cause. This siloed approach keeps people managing symptoms rather than actually healing.

And let me be clear: I don't blame the incredible people, the real warriors, who wake up every day and work within this broken system. They give everything to serve and heal, but they're forced to function as cogs in a machine that's not designed for true healing. They're working within a structure that doesn't give them the time or the tools to actually fix what's wrong. Everyone's doing the best they can, but the system they're stuck in? It's fundamentally flawed.

It's a system that treats pieces, not people.

We need a whole new approach—one that attacks the root cause, not just the symptoms. We're sitting on a gold mine of data showing how trauma physically rewires the brain, wreaks havoc on the nervous system, derails hormones, wrecks the immune system, and sends shockwaves through everything else, including your genetics. We're understanding the mind-body connection in a way we never have before. This isn't just "emerging science"—this is game-changing evidence that could flip the whole system on its head.

Forged in Chaos

So why haven't we seen massive changes in how we diagnose and treat trauma? Right now, I'll give the benefit of the doubt and say it's due to outdated thinking, ignorance, and an obsession with efficiency. But let's be real—that benefit of the doubt has a hard expiration date. I'll give it a sliver of time to catch up, but if we don't see *massive* changes now, if we don't see treatments that address trauma's full-body impact, then let's call it what it is: a system built to keep you sick, to profit off your pain, and to block real solutions from ever seeing the light of day. Is this about profit? Damn right it is. But it's more than just greed. The real problem is a system that refuses to grasp the true nature of trauma, a system that's allergic to treating the whole body as one interconnected being. The system wasn't built to see *you*. This isn't healing; it's symptom control for profit. And you know what? I'm going to say it. It's bullshit. And it doesn't fucking work. And you, your family, and your future are the ones paying the price.

The cold, hard truth is that you getting healthy probably doesn't fit their business model. Because if trauma can actually be treated and healed, that's one less lifelong "customer" for the system. Real healing? Healthy people? That's just not profitable, is it? Because here's the bottom line: We know better now. We have the brain scans, the research, the data. If we don't see massive changes in how we approach trauma in the next few years, it's not ignorance—it's intentional. So mark my words: With the scientific firepower we have now, there's zero excuse for the lack of change. If nothing happens, understand this—*your pain, your trauma, your life has become a product, a revenue stream for companies cashing in on your suffering.*

Don't let your life—your health, your family, your well-being—be sacrificed on the altar of greed and outdated thinking. It's about damn time we said *enough*.

I know I've probably made a few of you uncomfortable just now, but I also know there are a lot of you who are fired up and ready to lead the charge with me. Let's face it: Most of us know deep down that the conventional approach needs a massive overhaul. As a result, we're seeing a surge in alternative therapies, especially within warrior care.

There's no shortage of options out there—psychedelics, cold plunges, ketamine therapy, 4:00 a.m. workouts, somatic breathwork, hyperbaric chambers, you name it. And behind each one? A person as passionate as a preacher with their gospel. If psychedelics are their cure, they're the modern-day shaman. If it's ice baths, strict macros, and waking up before the sun rises, they're a monk of discipline. If it's the gospel, they're Jesus. "Just try this supplement, it'll change your life." "Do this therapy, it'll change your life." Sound familiar?

The problem is that there's so much conflicting information on all sides—some proving effectiveness, some debunking it—that we end up buried in a mess of "it works" and "it'll kill you." One blog swears by a supplement; Reddit has someone claiming it almost killed them. One expert says it'll change your life; another says it's a scam. Your buddy tells you it's a miracle cure; your other buddy calls it snake oil. You end up spending years and thousands of dollars sifting through this whirlwind of conflicting advice.

Some of these therapies? Sure, they're straight-up bologna with zero scientific backing. But many others are backed by credible research, real data, and proven cases that show they are effective treatments, protocols, or support systems. And behind each one you'll find someone convinced it's the silver bullet. And that's where the real problem lies: *No therapy is a one-size-fits-all solution.* What works wonders for one person might do absolutely nothing for the next. The thing is, a lot of these therapies *do* work—*for the right person and when combined with the right approach.* But without any central diagnostic system or a cohesive treatment plan that layers and sequences these therapies, we're all just green-guessing our way to health.

Just like with the conventional medical approach, everything's fragmented. Your psychedelics group isn't working on your gut health, hormone balance, or nervous system reset. Your fitness crowd isn't addressing your thyroid or mental health. You're out there trying one therapy after another, but nothing's connected, nothing's layered, and nothing's centralized.

What we need are clear diagnostics and a centralized approach—a way to layer and combine therapies into a personalized treatment that actually targets and supports every part of who you are. The entire conventional approach to treating the human body needs a revolution—the current system is fragmented, profit-driven, and designed for efficiency over true healing. And the alternative approach? It's got potential, but it's scattered, drowning in conflicting advice, and missing the centralized system we need to verify, diagnose, and combine therapies that would actually get the job done.

This is a massive obstacle, but let me be clear: I'm not here to sit on the sidelines and wait for the cavalry to show up. In the next chapter, I'll lay out exactly what I plan to do about it.

OBSTACLE: PTSD

At this point, you might have noticed that I haven't brought up post-traumatic stress disorder even once in this conversation, which probably seems a bit odd. After all, PTSD has become the catch-all diagnosis for just about every symptom, struggle, and battle that warriors face today. And while it's true that many warriors do suffer from PTSD, I believe it's an incomplete—and in some cases, even an inaccurate—diagnosis for the expansive challenges we're up against. I'm convinced that this overreliance on such a broad label is one of the biggest roadblocks to creating real, effective solutions for warrior recovery and care. You can't develop an effective cure if you're treating the wrong disease. To put it another way, you can't craft a winning battle strategy if you don't fully understand the nature of the war. This tendency to lean on PTSD as a comprehensive explanation for every warrior-related struggle is actually a massive obstacle in itself, blurring the true nature of the War Within. I know that's a pretty big statement to make, so before I ruffle any feathers, let me explain exactly what I mean. We're going to dig a little deep into this obstacle because it's crucial to examine and fully understand it in order to create an effective strategy for dealing with it. First, let's start with a simple question: What exactly is PTSD?

Post-traumatic stress disorder is defined as a mental and behavioral disorder that develops from experiencing a traumatic event, such as sexual assault, warfare, traffic collision, child abuse, domestic violence, or other threats to a person's life or sense of well-being. Symptoms may include disturbing thoughts, feelings, or dreams related to the event; mental or physical distress triggered by trauma-related cues; avoiding thoughts or conversations about the traumatic event; and steering clear of places, activities, or people that remind you of the traumatic experience. Symptoms of PTSD are said to start within three months of the traumatic event. To receive a PTSD diagnosis, a person must have symptoms for longer than one month after the event, and these symptoms must be severe enough to interfere with aspects of daily life, such as relationships or work.

PTSD was known to previous generations as "shell shock." The term itself first appeared in the medical journal *The Lancet* in February 1915, some six months after the Great War began. Captain Charles Myers of the Royal Army Medical Corps documented soldiers who experienced a range of severe symptoms—including anxiety, nightmares, tremors, and impaired sight and hearing—after being exposed to exploding shells on the battlefield. PTSD gained public awareness when the American Psychiatric Association included it in its diagnostic manual of mental disorders in the 1980s.

The logic behind the diagnosis is straightforward. Consider this scenario: Jennifer is a normal, healthy, functioning adult. She was brutally raped in a gas station bathroom. Following the traumatic event, Jennifer no longer feels like herself. She experiences flashbacks and nightmares related to the incident. Jennifer feels anxious each time she drives near the location where the event occurred and has panic attacks at gas stations. She wrongly blames herself and feels sad, anxious, and depressed more often now than she used to. In terms of the nervous system, Jennifer typically resides in the green zone (homeostasis). However, when the traumatic event occurred, her body shifted into the red zone (fight, flight, or freeze). Now, even though the event has passed, she frequently finds herself transitioning into a yellow or even red state when memories of the event arise.

I have experienced PTSD. However, it wasn't tied to a single military experience but rather to my motorcycle accident. Following the crash, I felt anxious whenever memories of the car coming toward me and being thrown over the handlebars resurfaced. After the accident, I didn't buy another motorcycle and avoided riding for years until I was forced to do so for a large riding event. After that weeklong group ride, my symptoms lessened, and now I only occasionally experience effects from the incident. This is PTSD. Given these circumstances, it's understandable that some soldiers may encounter similar symptoms following events like a significant explosion or close combat. That, too, is PTSD.

These days, however, PTSD has become a broad diagnosis for every warrior-related struggle. It's a big fat label that gets slapped on just about every symptom a warrior might have. From addiction to mental health, physical health to suicide, nearly every challenge warriors encounter is attributed to one or more isolated traumatic events. Relationship problems? PTSD. Addiction? PTSD. Trouble sleeping? PTSD. Low self-esteem? PTSD. Loss of purpose and mission? PTSD. Depression? PTSD. PTSD has become a broad brush by which all warriors are painted, but there are some major problems with this as a comprehensive theory.

PTSD ISN'T WARRIOR-SPECIFIC

PTSD is a diagnosis given to warriors as well as everyday people who have endured severe trauma, but their experiences, for the most part, are incomparable. Ask any warrior, and they'll tell you their experiences in combat, crime response, or fire intervention are nothing like surviving an earthquake, car wreck, or assault. Individuals who've endured sexual assault, natural disasters, traffic accidents, child abuse, or domestic violence are survivors and victims in the truest sense of the words. They are everyday people who were suddenly forced into a traumatic situation. They were unprepared, overpowered, and surprised by the event.

Being a warrior or experiencing active combat could not be more different. The conflict, friction, resistance, high stress, and danger we face as warriors are not random or unexpected. We are trained to handle danger and chaos; that's what our minds and bodies are conditioned for, and it's what we signed up to do. Our brains and bodies are naturally wired, conditioned, and well-prepared to function effectively in high-stress environments. In fact, these environments feel completely normal to us. And this leads to the next point…

PTSD ASSUMES EVERYONE HAS THE SAME BASELINE

The basis of PTSD assumes that everyone starts from the same "green" baseline and perceives stressful situations the same way.

To demonstrate this, let's remove Jennifer from the previous scenario and substitute Dave as the example. Dave, an average infantry officer, is accustomed to maintaining a state of homeostasis, also known as the green zone. Dave is hit by an IED during combat. This situation is so shocking to his system that his brain and body flip into the red zone. Following this traumatic event, Dave no longer feels like himself. He experiences flashbacks and nightmares related to the incident. Dave feels anxious each time he's near the location where the event occurred and has panic attacks in similar situations. He wrongly blames himself and feels sadness, anxiety, and depression more frequently than before. In terms of the nervous system, Dave typically resides in the green zone (homeostasis), but the traumatic event causes his body to shift into the red zone (fight, flight, or freeze). Now, even though the event has passed, he often finds himself transitioning into a yellow or red state when memories or flashbacks of the event arise. Okay, no shockers here.

This is the PTSD stereotype.

But let me give you another scenario: Dave, an average infantry officer, is conditioned for high-stress situations and lives in a state of hypervigilance, also known as the yellow zone. During combat, Dave thrives and operates effectively in intense circumstances. He experiences complete mental clarity, takes bold strategic action, remains calm in chaos, and feels like he's doing what he was born to do. However, upon returning to civilian life, Dave finds himself on a couch, watching talk shows and eating takeout. He struggles with feelings of depression, emptiness, anxiety, and exhaustion due to his inability to switch off his hypervigilance. Nothing really excites Dave, and he doesn't want to admit to anyone just how boring and unfulfilling his life feels because, on the outside, he's living the dream. Dave finds himself compulsively looking at porn even though he's happily married and attracted to his wife. He feels incredibly guilty about this and tries to make up for it by working hard and trying to be a good provider. Despite these difficulties, Dave loves looking at old pictures from his military days, swapping combat stories with his buddies, and listening to military podcasts. He longs for the mental clarity, strategic action, and execution his brain and body were capable of during combat and misses the sense of purpose and camaraderie that came with it. Dave finds it challenging to discover motivation, passion, and purpose in the civilian world. After experiencing the adrenaline and fulfillment of active service, everyday suburban life seems monotonous and devoid of meaning.

The reality is that many of us warriors have grown up in challenging environments and live in a constant state of hypervigilance—our baseline is more like yellow than green. This means that events most civilians would consider high-stress or traumatic don't affect us in the same way because we operate from a different baseline. Of course, there are situations that could cause significant distress, even to the most seasoned warriors, such as witnessing the gory death of a close friend or teammate. But if we compare the number of such documented incidents to the number of veterans and first responders dealing with what they call "PTSD," the numbers don't add up. I would venture to say that LTSD is a far more pervasive struggle than isolated event-related PTSD.

THE AVOIDANCE FACTOR

One of the fundamental criteria for a PTSD diagnosis is feelings and actions that revolve around the avoidance of memories or reminders of the traumatic event. The diagnosis states that people with PTSD will struggle with frequent and unwanted thoughts about a traumatic incident, including vivid flashbacks, distressing dreams, and extreme emotional or physical responses to reminders of the trauma, alongside a tendency to actively avoid situations or people related to the event to escape these memories. If you take a look at the DSM-5 criteria for diagnosing PTSD, "Avoidance" is a specific category, and an individual must exhibit one or more avoidance feelings or behaviors.

In the scenario above, Jennifer meets the criteria. My reaction after the motorcycle accident also meets the criteria. A Vietnam vet who flips his shit when a plate of rice is set down in front of him because it reminds him of being tortured in POW camps meets the criteria. A veteran who feels anxious when he hears fireworks on the Fourth of July because he was hit by an IED meets the criteria. It's logical for medical and mental health professionals to initially think that all warfighters and first responders share similar responses to high-stress and combat situations due to the intense nature of these experiences.

We warriors know differently. If PTSD were the only disease running rampant among our warriors, then we'd have hundreds of thousands of warriors avoiding every reminder of their trauma on the battlefield. Warriors wouldn't talk about their combat experiences on podcasts; they'd have panic attacks. Warriors would be the first to heed trigger warnings on social media posts so they could avoid flashbacks. Warriors would struggle to watch movies that depict combat or avoid them altogether. We all know this is far from reality.

The truth is that most of us miss the action. We don't avoid reminders of it; we run to them. We don't shy away from discussing combat, guns, or operations. We don't actively avoid situations or individuals connected to the events or environments to evade these memories; we seek them out. We write books about the action, spend hours discussing it on podcasts, and create movies based on our experiences. Interestingly, the warriors who do exhibit avoidance symptoms almost always do so because of a moral injury incurred during an experience, not the experience itself.

If PTSD were the issue, warriors would be triggered all the time. Our society, families, and media would have adapted to be sensitive to the many soldiers struggling with PTSD. But where's the avoidance?

Most of us don't shy away from reminders of high-stress or dangerous situations; in fact, we often seek them out.

THE NON-COMBATANT PTSD PHENOMENON

Interestingly, symptoms typically associated with PTSD are present in both combat and noncombat soldiers. That's pretty odd when you consider that PTSD is supposed to be related to a specific event. According to the DSM, you're required to wait at least a month after the event to receive a diagnosis of PTSD. However, data indicates that many noncombat warriors are experiencing mental health challenges, addiction issues, relationship struggles, and more without having experienced a specific traumatic event. Doesn't this raise questions about the validity of the current diagnostic criteria?

PTSD is one condition that affects warriors due to their exposure to traumatic events, but it's just one piece of a much bigger puzzle. It fails to capture the full complexity of the challenges that warriors are actually facing. What's more, PTSD's narrow focus on specific events often pressures warriors to pinpoint a single traumatic incident from their past to explain their current struggles. This can be incredibly frustrating because the reality is that many warriors felt calm and composed during events that civilians or mental health professionals might classify as traumatic. This obsession with tying everything back to one moment can lead us down the wrong path, overlooking the underlying causes behind pervasive issues like addiction, struggles with self-love and self-esteem, and the attraction to high-stress situations rather than avoidance.

There's no denying that some of the push for PTSD as a catch-all diagnosis might be tied to a larger profit-driven agenda. But it's also important to recognize that PTSD has become the go-to diagnosis largely because the civilian mental health community lacks direct experience or intimate knowledge of the unique challenges faced by warriors in combat and military environments. When civilians compare combat experiences to a car wreck, it's not out of a lack of empathy or willingness to understand, but because they're drawing from their own frame of reference. They're doing their best to comprehend the intensity and impact of such events, but without firsthand experience, they can't fully grasp the depth of what warriors go through.

The sad reality is that more than a dozen warriors take their own lives every single day. Awareness is higher than ever, but if we don't get honest with ourselves about the real problem we're facing, we'll keep missing the mark. PTSD is an obstacle that warriors must learn to navigate, but it's not the entire war. We will never win the battle if we don't get clear on the real nature of the conflict we're dealing with.

As I close this chapter, there's one more thing I need to address, and it's crucial. This chapter is titled "The War Within" because the battle that raged inside me was undoubtedly the hardest fight I've ever faced. Unfortunately, the damage from this war didn't affect just me; I wish it had. The truth is my internal struggle caused real harm to others, especially to women I encountered throughout my journey. I may have never physically harmed a woman, but that shouldn't be the metric by which any man measures himself to feel proud.

One of my greatest regrets is that many good and decent women encountered the Destroyer within me—an asshole alter ego who objectified and mistreated them—rather than the real me. Hurt people hurt people, and I certainly did. And I can't sit here and discuss the War Within without acknowledging the collateral damage that extended far beyond myself.

To every woman who met the Destroyer instead of the Warrior, I apologize. If I connected with you during the years when the Destroyer was in charge, I have no doubt that you were hurt in the process. The way I treated you was a reflection of me, not you. You are not a mirror, a trophy, or a game in the Destroyer's quest for validation. A true warrior's strength will make you feel safe, valued, and protected. You deserved more, and you deserved better. I cannot rewind the past or undo the damage caused, but I am doing everything I can to remove other Destroyers from power.

CHAPTER 32

WAR PLAN

WE'VE SPENT A LOT OF time discussing the War Within, dragging that unseen battle out of the shadows so we can finally get a clear view of what's really going on. But diagnosing the disease and understanding the conflict aren't enough. We're not here just to identify the problem; we're here to conquer it. Now it's time to ask the big question: *How do we win the War Within?*

The truth is that winning the War Within looks a little different for every person, but I will share with you what worked for me and what I have seen effective in the lives of the warriors I've worked with.

IDENTIFY THE ENEMY

First and foremost, before you can develop any kind of war strategy, *you must identify the enemy.*

As these pages bear witness, I spent years trapped in an unseen battle—a shadow war that tore through every terrain of my life: physical, mental, emotional, social, and financial. The toll was immense, hitting me in every fiber of my being. I was exhausted, lost in the fog, confused about who the enemy even was, and completely clueless about how to gain the upper hand. I threw everything I had at it, but nothing seemed to stick. Just when I thought I was making progress, I'd find myself right back where I started, stuck in the same damn cycle. The problem wasn't that I lacked the will to fight—it was that I didn't even know who I was fighting. And deep down, I feared I was fighting myself. I was terrified that the Destroyer *was my true identity*—an identity I had to hide and disguise so no one around me would see the monster I thought I was.

And you know what? The Destroyer thrives on that lie and the fear it creates. He fed off of my belief that my biggest failures, my fuck-ups, and my self-sabotage were proof of who I really was. That's how he kept me trapped. The Destroyer's greatest power was in the lies he made me believe about myself. And belief is everything. Every action, every choice we make is rooted in what each of us truly believes about ourselves and the world around us—not what we want to believe, but what we *actually* believe.

A lot of people think they have a weak mind, weak willpower, or weak motivation. But I would argue *that your mind is weak because your lies are strong*. And the truth is that you will only progress as far as your lies allow. Mental strength doesn't come from sheer will—it comes from truth. Until you accept the bare-bones truth about yourself, you will continue to have a weak mind and weak motivation. It takes real strength to face the truth, to strip away the comfortable lies and stand in the harsh light of reality. We live in a world that embraces comfortable lies because it cannot handle the truth. But make no mistake, it's better to live in truth.

Why? *Because all progress must be based on truth.* If your foundation is built on lies, everything you build on top of it will eventually crumble. The Destroyer knows this and uses it to keep you spinning in circles, fighting the wrong battles, stuck in the same cycles. But once I realized that who I am at my core is good and valuable, that the Warrior within me is my *true self*, I was able to separate myself from the Destroyer's actions. That's when everything changed. The lies lost their grip, and I could finally start fighting the real enemy with the strength that comes from knowing the truth. The biggest breakthrough in my life came when I finally understood the origin of the Destroyer within me and realized that my true identity, at my core, is the Warrior, not the Destroyer. I began to understand the fact that while I was *responsible* for every thought, action, and choice the Destroyer made—because I gave him power and let him take hold in my life—they *weren't a reflection of who I really am*. When you learn to differentiate between who you are at your core—the Natural Born Warrior—and the persona that trauma forced you to become—the Destroyer—everything changes. This realization is liberating because it separates your core identity from the choices you make and the events around you. Even if you screw up, it doesn't mean you're fundamentally a bad person.

When I finally separated myself from the Destroyer, I began to trace him back to his roots—to the moment I brought him into existence. I realized that the Destroyer wasn't born out of malice or evil intentions; it was born out of sheer survival instinct. I created him to protect me, to help me navigate a world that felt hostile and unforgiving. This realization robbed the Destroyer of one of his greatest sources of ammunition because the Destroyer thrives on hatred, conflict, friction, and lies—on convincing you that you need to keep running from yourself. But when you start to integrate and accept all the parts of who you are—both the real you and the version that trauma forced you to become—without shame, you begin to starve the Destroyer of the fuel that keeps him alive.

When I learned to accept, and even appreciate, how the Destroyer stepped up to defend me, to keep me alive, everything began to shift. When you trace the Destroyer back to his origins, you'll see that you created him to survive some truly tough shit—and there's no shame in that. If you've endured trauma, the Destroyer's inception was your way of staying alive. The compartmentalization, the drive to survive, the instinct to obliterate anything that poses a threat—these are all natural responses. The fracture happened because I found myself in environments where my true self was abused, neglected, overlooked, rejected, and in danger. This constant state of vulnerability and self-doubt forced me to bury my real self under layers of defense mechanisms to avoid further pain and rejection. The trauma I endured during those years twisted my perception, making me believe that I was somehow responsible for the chaos around me, locking those negative self-beliefs deep inside.

The truth is you can't erase trauma. Trying to do so will only lead to frustration. When money is printed, the ink is applied to the fabric with such force that it becomes embedded in it. This makes it impossible to remove the ink from the paper; they become one, creating something of value. Printing only on the surface would produce a counterfeit; it's the deep infusion of ink into the fabric that creates the value. Similarly, a warrior who has not integrated their inner Destroyer will constantly live with the fear of being discovered as a counterfeit. Experiencing trauma is similar. You can't separate from it, and you can't pretend it's not there. But that's where the value lies—in the deep infusion of those experiences, in the way they shape who you are, giving you depth, strength, and resilience.

You can't change the environments that shaped you or the adaptations trauma forced on you. Instead, you've got to accept the entirety of who you are—both nature and nurture. Integrate these aspects to become the authentic, unique warrior you were meant to be. Your experiences, like the inseparable ink and fabric, make you who you are and give you your strength.

When you strip away the shame and mystery surrounding the Destroyer and understand why he was created in the first place—when you recognize that you did what you had to do to survive—you immediately weaken the Destroyer's hold on your life. But you can't stop there.

It's not enough to shrug and say, "Oh, that's not who I am, so I don't need to feel bad about the Destroyer's path of destruction."

Fuck no.

Once the battle lines are drawn, it's time to declare all-out war on the Destroyer in your life.

You allowed the Destroyer to take control, and now it's time to strip him of his rank and authority. It's on you to take lethal, forceful, and decisive action to make damn sure the Destroyer no longer holds power over your life.

Once you've separated the Warrior from the Destroyer, you have to plant your flag and declare, "I know who I am, and I will fight for myself." When you do that, you drag the shadow war out into the light. You finally give yourself the chance to form a clear strategy because you now know where the real battle lies: between the Warrior and the Destroyer.

During the weeks I spent at Warriors Heart, something shifted inside of me. I finally stopped fighting a subconscious shadow war and began to consciously understand what was happening in my life and why. I realized that I wasn't broken, powerless, or ill-equipped to handle the battle. I was a goddamned superhero—one of the world's best-trained soldiers. I had spent years studying military strategy and doctrine, honing my brain to solve problems in the highest-stakes situations across the globe. My divergent thinking was *exactly* what I needed to put to use in my life. I possessed an entire skill set that could be used to analyze my life, understand the intent and strategy of the enemy, see where he was gaining momentum and traction, recognize the unique challenges of each terrain, identify the obstacles that made the battle more complex, and then map out a clear strategy to win.

Developing a war plan for life and strategic op orders for each battle is something I've poured tremendous time and resources into—not just for myself but for others as well. Crafting this plan is an intricate process, one that demands deep understanding and precision. It's a conversation that goes far beyond these pages—a mission that extends into the broader community and movement that I am honored to lead, where the Warrior Class comes together to create intelligent strategies and win the war in every area of their lives. There is a depth, breadth, and complexity to the process I've developed to help all types of warriors and leaders accurately assess their lives and develop intelligent strategies for winning the War Within—it's quite literally an entire other book. While we don't have the time and space to take a deep dive into it here, I want to leave you with a few key takeaways that can start guiding you in the right direction.

YOU GOTTA GET IN THE GREEN ZONE

One of the first things you can do to weaken the Destroyer is to get in the green zone. (No, not that Green Zone. Just had to throw in a little Iraq joke here…good times, good times.) In all seriousness, the link between warriors and the nervous system cannot be underestimated. As a warrior, your mind and body have been rewired to normalize high stress. Your nervous system has grown accustomed to being in that yellow or red zone. This is exhausting for the mind and body, and it's a context in which the Destroyer thrives. The green zone is where your body can function properly, sleep deeply, and heal itself. It's where your body signals your mind that the danger has passed, allowing you to process emotions, feelings, and memories. When you are in a state of hypervigilance, the brain will compartmentalize and suppress emotions. This means that pockets of emotion may be stored for months or even years before they can be fully processed. The green zone is also where your nervous system is relaxed enough to socially connect with others. It's science. Fortunately, this means that science also has solutions for helping warriors with LTSD and other nervous system–related challenges. There are countless ways to work with your body as you struggle with withdrawal symptoms, addiction, and a nervous system that isn't accustomed to living life in the green zone.

But gaining an awareness of your nervous system and training your brain to signal a sense of safety, or live in the green zone, is not as straightforward as just trying to relax. It's not helpful for me to say, "You don't need to be hypervigilant! The world isn't that bad. Everything is safe." That would probably just irritate the hell out of you more. I know because that's exactly how I feel every time someone says it to me. Your experiences as a warrior have shown you the dark side of the world that most people will never see. And unfortunately, that is reality. Even if we live in a society that chooses to experience the world in a censored bubble of selective reality, that doesn't change the fact that international threats, crime, tragedy, and disaster exist. I know you have walked the streets where the worst of humanity enacts its evil. You've faced the burning buildings. You know firsthand that the world can be a hard, cruel place, and that vigilance is often what ensures survival. You have taken a stand on that wall and witnessed the dangers lurking beyond it.

So I'm not going to tell you that the world is all safe and hunky-dory, or ask you to change your worldview and relax. What I will tell you is that you have to learn when to engage and when to disengage your superpower. If you don't understand how your body works and how to work with it, it's going to continue to cause damage and lead to destruction in your life. There are many scientifically proven solutions and treatment options available for LTSD. I have partnered with a handful of leading medical and mental health professionals to develop a comprehensive recovery method for warriors, which is explained in further detail on other platforms. Getting your body into the green zone is one of the most powerful and significant steps you can make toward winning the War Within.

ARM YOURSELF WITH INTELLIGENCE AND TRAINING

There's a big motivational culture and movement among warriors right now. The leaders on the front lines are always screaming to "Keep going!" " Never quit!" and "Push through no matter what!" It's true that this mindset is crucial when you're balls-deep in adversity.

You need that relentless, no-quit attitude to survive the heat of battle. But here's the thing: Before you even think about charging into action, you've got to have an intelligent strategy. Charging forward without a plan? That's not bravery—that's stupidity. In war, it's not just the guy who refuses to quit that gains the upper hand; it's the one who first crafts a smart, well-thought-out plan, executes it with ruthless precision, and adapts to the ever-changing battlefield. Perseverance without direction is just spinning your wheels even deeper in the mud, which will get you nowhere fast.

Part of developing that strategy is arming and training yourself. You can have all the grit and determination in the world, but if you're not properly equipped and educated, you're setting yourself up to fail. Real power lies in knowing what you're up against, understanding the tools at your disposal, and using them with deadly accuracy.

I can tell you from my own experience, learning how the brain and body work is an absolute game changer. When you understand the science behind your mental and physical struggles, the stigma and shame start to dissolve. Suddenly, you're not just some broken mess; you're someone with a real, understandable challenge that can be faced head-on. That sense of clarity gives you hope, hope that things don't always have to be as brutal as they've been, that you can actually change, heal, and find peace. Education arms you with the tools to see your struggles clearly and tackle them with confidence, knowing that recovery isn't just possible—it's within reach.

Case in point: At this point in this book, you're already familiar with my battles with addiction. For years, I couldn't figure out why I kept falling back into the same destructive habits I'd sworn to break. Willpower alone didn't seem to cut it. But here's the kicker: The day I picked up *TINSA: A Neurological Approach to the Treatment of Sex Addiction* and started to understand that my struggle with addiction had a physical component, everything changed. Knowing that the problem wasn't rooted in some dark moral failing but in a very real, explainable adaptation in my brain gave me the clarity I needed to seek help. Within a week, I felt a massive shift. Within a month, the battle with porn and sex addiction that had plagued me my entire life just dissipated. Once I understood the physical aspect of addiction and how it was tied to the brain's rewiring from childhood trauma, all the shame and guilt I'd been carrying for years began to lift. Without that cloud hanging over me, I could finally start supporting my brain and nervous system properly. And suddenly, the power that addiction had over me started to disappear.

Now that I understand my mind and body and have the right tools and support, I'm no longer losing the battle. That's the power of education. So before you charge ahead, make damn sure you gather the intel you need and educate yourself. Understand the enemy, know your own mind and body inside and out, and then take action. Because when you combine that warrior spirit with an intelligent, well-crafted strategy, you're not just fighting—you're winning. And that's what it's all about.

DEVELOPING YOUR WAR PLAN: A SIMPLE BLUEPRINT

So, how do you develop an intelligent strategy? Again, this is a much deeper conversation that we'll continue on other platforms beyond this book, but for now, let me leave you with a simple, straightforward blueprint to help you develop a war plan. This isn't just some theoretical idea—it's a practical strategy you can start implementing right now.

1. *Identify the Enemy and Source of Conflict*

You've got to know where the conflict is and who the enemy is. You can't fight what you can't see, and you sure as hell can't win if you don't know who you're up against. Once you drag that subconscious, hidden war into the light and differentiate the authentic Warrior in you from the Destroyer, you'll be able to develop a clear strategy to win.

2. *Assess the Terrain in Your Life*

Take a hard look at the terrain where these battles are taking place:

- Physical Terrain
- Mental Terrain
- Emotional Terrain
- Spiritual Terrain
- Social/Relational Terrain
- Financial Terrain

3. *Identity Obstacles*

Take inventory and identify the unique obstacles that might be in your battlefield: TBI, PTSD, moral injury, or maybe something else. These are the things that can complicate the fight, but they don't have to derail you if you're prepared.

4. *Formulate an Intelligent Strategy, Execute to Win*

Once you've locked onto the enemy, mapped out the terrain, and identified the obstacles in your way, it's time to craft a strategy that'll lead you to victory. This isn't about charging ahead blindly—it's about gathering intel, analyzing every angle, and understanding the Destroyer's game plan. There is no one-size-fits-all solution. This comes down to knowing yourself, understanding your battlefield, and developing a game plan that leverages your strengths and counters the Destroyer's every move. Over the years, I've developed a set of criteria that's been a game changer for me and for the warriors I've helped. It's called the Lethality Scale, and it's a hierarchy of criteria that predicts who will gain the upper hand in any type of conflict. These are listed in order of importance, and each level builds on the one before it. If you're weak at the top, it doesn't matter how strong you are at the bottom—you're setting yourself up to lose. You can use this to assess the battle between the Warrior and the Destroyer in every terrain of your life and understand which set of actions needs to be taken to weaken the Destroyer and strengthen the Warrior.

LETHALITY SCALE

1. Mindset

Mindset isn't just important, it's the foundation of all effective action. If your mindset is at 1 percent and your enemy's is at 99 percent, you're done before you even start. Even with the best strategy or the most advanced gear, a weak mindset will cause it all to crumble. But if your mindset is rock-solid, you can overcome almost any obstacle. Your mindset is the engine that drives your actions, shapes your perceptions, and builds your resilience. Every move you make on the battlefield, every decision, every strategy, stems from the quality of your mindset. This is the first thing you need to strengthen.

2. Strategy

Once your mindset is locked in, the next step is strategy. This is your battle plan, the blueprint for how you're going to win. It's not enough to just grit your teeth and push forward; you need a strategy that's intelligent, well thought-out, and tailored to the unique battles you're facing. And once that strategy is in place, don't deviate. Stick to it with relentless focus. Your strategy channels your mindset into effective action. Without it, even the strongest mindset can become aimless and ineffective.

3. Tactics

Tactics are the boots on the ground, the maneuvers that bring your strategy to life. They're the day-to-day actions that keep you on track and push you closer to victory. Tactics are flexible; they need to adapt as the battle unfolds. The key is to stay one step ahead, constantly adjusting based on what the enemy throws at you. But remember, tactics are only as effective as the mindset and strategy they're built upon. They're the muscle, but without the brain and heart behind them, they won't get you far.

4. Techniques

Techniques are your skills, the methods you use to execute your tactics. These are the things you refine and perfect over time, making you more efficient and effective on the battlefield. Techniques are important, but they're not the be-all and end-all. They need to evolve and adapt, just like tactics.

5. Gear

Finally, there's gear, the physical tools and resources at your disposal. Gear can give you an edge, but it's actually the least important element in the Lethality Scale. You could have the best gear in the world, but if your mindset is weak, your strategy is flawed, and your tactics and techniques are off, that gear won't save you. However, with the right mindset, strategy, tactics, and techniques, even the most basic gear can become a deadly asset in your hands.

STRENGTHENING THE WARRIOR VS. EMPOWERING THE DESTROYER

To demonstrate how to apply the Lethality Scale to guide you in crafting and executing a winning strategy, I'll give you an example. Think of your life like a video game where you've got two characters, the Warrior and the Destroyer. Every choice you make, every action you take, either levels up the Warrior or powers up the Destroyer. Just like in a game, you're constantly collecting power-ups, leveling up, and acquiring new skills to make your character more lethal. The same goes for your life. Every time you invest in your mindset, sharpen your strategy, and upgrade your gear, you're making the Warrior in you stronger.

But when you're drowning in stress, self-doubt, and unresolved trauma, the Destroyer thrives. His mindset is fueled by lies, self-deception, and fear. He whispers that you're not good enough, that you'll never measure up. The more you buy into these lies, the stronger he gets. The Destroyer's strategy? Keep you trapped in a cycle of self-sabotage, convincing you that you're powerless to change. His tactics? Wear you down, isolate you, and push you toward his gear—porn, alcohol, or pills. These are his weapons, numbing you and keeping you disconnected. His techniques evolve with your vulnerabilities, always adapting to keep you off balance, ensuring you never find the strength to fight back. Every time you feed the Destroyer with these destructive choices, he grows more lethal, sinking you deeper into the cycle, making you feel more isolated and further from who you really are. The flip side is just as true.

Your life is a game where you choose every single day whether to power up the Warrior or the Destroyer. As you progress, you collect items that boost your resilience, sharpen your strategy, and equip you with better tools (the Warrior), or you gather items that make you more vulnerable to negativity, fear, and self-sabotage (the Destroyer). The choice of which character you power up is yours. Just like in the game, you've got to make daily decisions about which side of you gets stronger. Are you feeding the Warrior or the Destroyer? Each choice, each action, each thought either strengthens your ability to fight or gives more power to the enemy.

The battle is constant, and the outcome depends entirely on which side you choose to empower.

As we bring this book to a close, I want to leave you with something that I've emphasized throughout these pages: *This isn't the end; it's just the beginning.* Let me say it again—this book doesn't signify the end; instead, it marks the beginning of a new conversation, strategy, approach, and action plan for the Warrior Class. We're standing on the brink of a paradigm shift in how we understand the minds and bodies of warriors, pushing constraints that have confined us for far too long.

For years, warrior care has been shackled by a narrow understanding, with PTSD as a catch-all explanation and a diagnosable disorder for warriors. Treatment has been limited to talk therapy and medication. And while talk therapy—and in some cases, medication—has its place, it's only one piece of the puzzle. Conventional methods have ignored critical elements like the nervous system (LTSD), hormonal imbalances, addiction, and the deep connection between warriors and the environments that have shaped them, especially childhood trauma.

But here's the good news: The field of science has already made leaps that can revolutionize warrior care. We now have access to proven data and real solutions that can transform the landscape of warrior treatment, recovery, and support. I know this shift will face resistance, especially from those who stand to lose profits from the disruption of traditional practices—but that won't stop us. When the attacks come, pay attention to where the resistance is coming from and what they stand to lose. Those who benefit from your continued treatment will be the first to push back. But by uniting and taking ownership of the mission to save our fellow warriors, we can achieve victory together.

We're not in this alone. Alongside us is a dedicated group of professionals—doctors, researchers, healers, counselors, and therapists—who are all rallying to revolutionize warrior care. This collective effort requires a foundation of education, training, strategic planning, and actionable steps. Every warrior deserves a comprehensive understanding of their own mind and body: how they function, how to nurture them, and how to collaborate with them instead of working against them.

YOU HAVE TO TREAT YOUR ENTIRE BODY SIMULTANEOUSLY

Winning the War Within demands addressing every system in your body and treating the mind and body simultaneously. I've been blunt about calling out the conventional medical system—and even parts of the alternative treatment world—because the stakes are too high to pull punches. We know that traditional Western medicine treats mental and physical health like they exist in different worlds. That split isn't just outdated—it's dangerous. Mental and physical health are inseparable; they influence each other in ways most people don't even realize.

To truly win the War Within, you need a strategy that hits both the mind and body together, because, let's face it, you can't have one without the other. Trying to process emotions, heal, and grow while dealing with a chemically depressed, hormonally imbalanced, constantly on-edge body is like trying to run a marathon on a broken leg. Even if you make it a few miles, it's going to be slow, grueling, and painful. And on the flip side, focusing solely on physical healing without addressing trauma, buried emotions, and the Destroyer Mentality is like fixing up a car without touching the engine. It might look good on the outside, but it's not going anywhere.

Effective warrior care demands a full-body, integrated approach, one that tackles mental and physical health as a single, interconnected system. It's not about quick fixes or covering up symptoms. It's about digging deep, confronting every layer, and building true health from the inside out. But our medical system wasn't designed for that kind of real, comprehensive healing; it was built for efficiency, not transformation. But as I said from the start, I'm not here just to talk about problems. I'm here to bring solutions. I've poured time, grit, and everything I had into building the healthcare company I wish had existed when I was at my worst. And I definitely didn't pull it off alone. Don't get me wrong, I'm good, but nobody tackles a mission this big solo. I partnered with powerhouse experts—people with the credentials, experience, and sheer fire to flip the status quo.

Together, we're creating a movement. This isn't just another wellness company; it's a fully integrated health revolution. This vision is powered by a team that's here to rewrite the rules. We didn't set out to build a brand. We set out to build the healthcare system people *deserve*—backed by science, using diagnostics to cut out the guesswork, and rooted in actually listening to each person's story. We're not just "analyzing data";

we're digging deep into the full story of *you*: your history, your trauma, your lifestyle, all of it. We're pairing this with advanced biomarker analysis, DNA insights, genetic profiles—the works—to build a treatment plan that is customized and comprehensive. Everything from nervous system resets to hormone therapy to functional medicine. This isn't some cookie-cutter plan. This is a full-body, full-life transformation. This whole thing was built on one purpose: to take hard data and create a full health story for every single person—past, present, and future—and then provide the tools, treatments, and therapies they need in an *accessible way*—through telehealth, clinical partnerships, and in-home care so nobody has to suffer in silence or isolation.

This isn't about slapping a Band-Aid on symptoms or selling people the latest health fad. It's about giving people a clear path forward, built on science and backed by solid principles. We've rounded up the best of the best: top-tier providers, specialists, therapies, and treatments, all in one place. We don't just treat the mind and body as connected systems; we treat *you* as a whole person. No more piecing together solutions from here, there, and everywhere. No more isolated symptom treatments. We go straight to the root cause and fix what's broken.

The driving passion in my head as I worked on creating this was simple: What do I wish I'd had when I was at my absolute bottom? What might have saved the lives of some of my friends who lost hope somewhere along the way? Like I said, this isn't a company; this is the *revolution*. I'm not going to dive into all the business details here; that's not what this book is about. But if what I've said resonates with you and you're ready to join me, let's fucking go. While I my heart's in helping to create a health revolution for the world, my first and foremost priority is caring for my fellow warriors. As in all other areas of life, warriors lead the way. If we can get our shit together, we can lead the charge and create a better, healthier place for our families, communities, and nation at large.

This mission is massive, and we're going to run headfirst into resistance from those who stand to lose the most when we start taking back control of our bodies, our trauma, and our lives. But sitting back and waiting? That's not how warriors win wars. The fight to save our warriors is raging right now, and if we're going to turn the tide, we need to stand united and be ready to raise hell. And when we do, we'll have an even bigger mission, because *the revolution for the health of our nation has just begun, and we need the entire Warrior Class locked, loaded, and ready to take it on.*

This is our fight, and I plan on winning.

In closing, I want to leave you with this: You alone have the power to decide who has authority in your life, and you're fully responsible for the choices you make. No traumatic event can strip you of your identity. You are a warrior. If you're fighting a War Within, know there is hope. If anything I've shared in this book resonates with you, I invite you to join a community of warriors who are choosing to stand up, take intelligent, strategic action, and reclaim their lives. If you're drowning in your own War Within, it's time to stop lying back and letting yourself get taken down in the fight. You are a goddamned warrior, built not just to fight but to win.

And I want to be very clear: Getting back in the game doesn't necessarily mean wearing a uniform or picking up a weapon. It means serving, protecting, and leading others. It means being a lighthouse of strength and calm in our chaotic world. It means nurturing the next generation of young warriors and setting an example of strength, resilience, integrity, and excellence. It means embodying the characteristics of a natural-born warrior: to lead, nurture, and protect others. But you can't do that if all your energy, time, and resources are being sucked down into your shadow war. So don't be selfish. Don't allow your unique skill set to be wasted while you doomscroll, play the victim, surrender to mediocrity, or walk around in an alcohol- or medication-induced haze. *Remember who you are.*

If you choose to sit on the sidelines, to keep fighting a losing internal shadow war instead of drawing your battle lines and declaring all-out war on the Destroyer in your life, then you, your family, your community, and the world will pay the price. We need you. Your family, your community, your nation, and this world need you now more than ever.

We need you to stand up, lead, nurture the next generation, and fight for those who cannot fight for themselves.

If you have disconnected from your sense of purpose and feel like you've lost your mission and compass, that's okay. I promise that as you heal, strengthen, and take time to create an intelligent strategy to win the War Within and reconnect with who you are at your core, your next mission will naturally reveal itself. And you will reclaim your purpose. How do I know that? Because you're a warrior. *And that's just who you are.*

CHAPTER 33

SEVEN MINUTES

THERE'S ONE LAST STORY I want to share, one from my selection and assessment process for joining the Unit. I know, I know, you thought I wasn't going to tell any training or selection stories, but I couldn't resist. And I saved this one for the very end for a reason.

For those who may not be familiar, the Unit selection takes place over three to four weeks at Camp Dawson, West Virginia. Those who succeed are put through the Operator Training Course, a six-month, constantly evolving education that covers marksmanship, demolitions and breaching, and executive protection. Qualifying for the Unit includes the completion of all-night land navigation courses, a mental evaluation by a review board, and a test of stamina known as the Long Walk—a forty-mile march with a forty-five-pound rucksack that must be completed within a time limit. Roughly nine out of ten candidates fail the selection process. The time standards and criteria are kept highly confidential. Even those of us who successfully completed the process and were selected remain unaware of the specific time standards and criteria for who is selected and who is not. The details I do know from experience, I cannot share, unfortunately. Everything I've disclosed here is googleable information; otherwise, my good buddies at the Department of Defense might not have let this book see the light of day. So, while I can't tell you anything about the mysterious selection process that you couldn't find online, I can tell you this story.

The moment I open my eyes on the last day of selection, I know this is the beginning of the end. The excitement that accompanied me during the first week has long since been released in droplets of sweat, giving way to a deep fatigue that spreads throughout every part of my body. I am strong, pack-mule strong, but they sure knew how to make us pack mules suffer.

We're not supposed to know how long the selection will last or which day will be the final one, but it doesn't take a genius to figure it out. I've been counting the days and observing the challenges, and I just know that today is the last day. Only one more day to find out whether or not I've been selected. Well, one more day and the Long Walk, that is.

The Long Walk isn't just about seeing if we can slog through a forty-mile ruck; it's also a test of land navigation skills. You start with a set of coordinates, and if you find your way there on time, you get a new set. If you nail that one, you get another, and it keeps going until you either make a mistake, give up, or reach the finish line. At each checkpoint, your rucksack is weighed, and if it's even a few ounces lighter than the forty-five pounds it should be, you're out. Trust me, if there's a sneaky strategy to alleviate even a little bit of the pure suck, they've already thought of it and made a rule to ensure that you can't get away with it. Without any idea of the time standard for completing the Long Walk, we all have the same strategy: get it done as fast as possible without burning out.

As the sun starts to set, a truck drops me off at the starting point for the Long Walk. I'm alone and the first to begin the challenge. Unless I screw up big time and fall behind, I shouldn't see anyone else for the rest of the day. The moment my boots touch the ground, I set off at a steady pace down a narrow trail. My mind is clear and focused, my feet steady. For three hours, I stick to the trail until it's obvious that heavy rain has washed it out. I veer onto a small mountainside path, still heading in the direction of the coordinates for the next checkpoint.

As the path begins to slope downhill, I'm suddenly engulfed in a dense web of branches and leaves. The darkness seems to close in around me as I push through the tangled brush, expecting to break into open terrain at any moment. But with each step, the web of branches only grows denser and the undergrowth thicker. It's not just in front of me; it's on every side. I know exactly what this is: *fucking mountain laurel*.

I've heard all the horror stories—men cursing the evergreen bushes that crushed their lifelong dream of becoming an operator. West Virginia's dense thickets of mountain laurel are like a graveyard, holding the shattered dreams of far too many soldiers to count.

You got nothing on me, you flowery, shrubby little bitch. Not me. Not today.

At first, I'm confident I'll get through this in no time. An hour later, I'm starting to doubt it. My pace has slowed to a crawl, and with every step, it feels like a thousand hands are reaching out to hold me back from the mission ahead. The dense foliage weighs heavily on me, and each small step forward feels like a victory over a seemingly impenetrable maze. Just when I think it can't get any worse, it does. I drop to the ground and begin inching forward on my belly, pulling my rucksack behind me, every movement painstakingly slow. My body aches with exhaustion, and each scrape against the thorny branches is a reminder of how far I still have to go. Progress is slow. *Agonizingly slow.*

This is it. You failed. You made it this far, and you just lost everything.

Every inch of my body is weighed down by deep exhaustion. This isn't the kind of tiredness that can be cured by a single night's sleep; it's the kind that builds up over days and weeks of my body struggling to obey the relentless demands of my mind to push harder and faster. My body isn't just protesting anymore; it's pleading with me. I can't do this anymore. All I can see around me are vines, dirt, and my rucksack, just inches from my face as I push it forward. When everything starts to blur, I realize there are tears in my eyes, liquid exhaustion spilling over that I can't seem to control.

Two hours later, I emerge from the mountain laurel and continue walking toward the checkpoint. I know it's over; I've lost far too much time to meet the time requirement. The moment I roll up to the checkpoint, I'll be pulled for time. I could quit now. Send up my flare and let them take me. But I'm not going to quit, not going to stop until they fucking say I have to. They're going to have to say it to my face. The knowledge of impending defeat makes my pace slow. My body is exhausted, and the knowledge that I am no longer in the game has seized the mind-over-body power that formerly ruled my performance. An hour later, I hear a rustling sound through the thick forest and see another selection candidate emerging through the trees. *Fuck*. Minutes later, two others emerge. We're all converging at the same checkpoint, but I had a head start. Just another confirmation that I'm way behind.

When I see the checkpoint in front of me, it feels like a death march. When I make it, I stand still, waiting for an audible confirmation of what I already know. But to my shock, another set of coordinates is given to me. I guess they'll pull me at the next one.

I push forward to the next checkpoint. When I arrive, I again wait to be pulled for time, but I'm handed a set of coordinates for the next checkpoint. I'm surprised and set off once more, this time through a thick forest. Two other candidates are walking in the same direction and fall in step beside me. Within half an hour, two more join us. We move quietly, the only sounds being our steady footsteps and the occasional rustle of leaves.

After what seems like a few hours, one of the candidates finally vocalizes what we're all wondering: "Did we pass the checkpoint already?" Another guy thinks it's still up ahead. They launch into a discussion, and I listen. We're not supposed to talk, but everyone seems to be getting desperate. I listen closely as one of the louder guys makes a compelling case for turning around and backtracking. After more time passes and there's still no checkpoint in sight, the group comes to the consensus that it must be behind us. But I don't think so.

I stare at my map, recount every step we've taken, and make my decision. I'm not going to turn around. I don't think the checkpoint we're looking for is behind us; I think it's deeper into the forest than we thought. Then the moment comes. The others turn around to search behind us, and I press forward alone.

It's got to be deeper than this. It's got to be deeper.

For several more hours, I continue to press on. Doubt gnaws at me, but I trust my instincts. When I finally spot the checkpoint up ahead, a surge of confidence washes over me. I trusted my gut, and it was the right call. I'm still in the game. As I clutch the next coordinates in my hand, I realize that victory is within reach.

With every step, I get faster and faster. Every time I drink water, I shove a rock into my rucksack. No chance in hell I'm going to come this far and lose everything because of a light pack. When my full bladder pushes against the waistband of my pants, I curse my stupid body and its stupid needs. If I lose this because I stopped to take a piss, I will never forgive myself. Suddenly, I have an idea. I turn around and begin to walk backwards. Simultaneously, I unzip my pants, point Little Tyler straight ahead, and let it go. *You're one smart motherfucker, aren't you?*

As a stream of urine sprays the ground, I continue my fast pace, congratulating myself for my ingenuity and resourcefulness. There's a reason they picked guys like me for this job. Then the back of my boots makes contact with something hard. I lose my balance and fall backward, and now I'm staring up at the sky as a urine streams across my face and body. I tripped over a log, dick in hand, and landed flat on my rucksack, spraying the skyline. Cue the laugh track. At least there was no one there to witness my humiliation.

I wipe my eyes, jump to my feet, and continue forward.

Faster...Harder...More...More...More... My body obeys.

Faster...Harder...More...More...More... My body pleads with me but still obeys.

Faster...Harder...More...More...More... This time, my body starts shutting down. I've whipped it into submission over and over again, but it has nothing left. That's when I realize I need to change my strategy. I need to take a minute and refresh my body, reset my mind. I take a seat on a fallen log and check my watch. *You've got seven minutes.*

My muscles cry in relief after countless hours of nonstop movement. I chomp on an MRE bar, drink from my canteen, and then put two rocks in my rucksack to make up for the water loss. It's time to finish strong.

Seven minutes later, I'm back on my feet and moving again, feeling like a new man. My mind is clear and focused, my body is nourished and strong, and my pace has nearly tripled. As the sun begins to set, the checkpoint comes into view.

I have no idea if I'll be selected or not, but I know that I'm proud of the way I finished. At the checkpoint, I'm handed another set of coordinates. Robotically, I plot the course for another ten-mile trek and show it to a sergeant major, who seems to have appeared out of nowhere. He nods, and I set off once more. But this time, I'm stopped by a firm hand on my shoulder. I whip around to find the sergeant major staring me down.

"Sergeant, you successfully completed selection."

My eyes meet his, and I nod.

"Okay, great," I answer and keep walking. I have another ten miles ahead of me and not a moment to lose.

The hand is on my shoulder again, harder and firmer this time.

"Sergeant, it's over. You're done. That's it."

There it was, the moment I'd worked for my whole life, and I was so exhausted from the journey that I couldn't even process that my dream had finally come true.

As I look back over my journey to get here, I see years of my life when I felt I had failed, fallen behind the pack, and gotten so lost in the wilderness of my own mind that I thought I would never emerge. There were years when all I could see were the tangled vines of mental confusion, crawling through the darkness of the unknown, not even sure what I was fighting. Years when it took all the strength I had just to inch forward, struggling to pull the weight of my past with me. But I stayed the course; I never gave up. When everyone around me said we had gone too far, told us to turn around and go back, I kept pushing onward, going deeper, believing that what we were looking for was still out there, beyond us, waiting to be found.

For years, I was the "crazy guy" pushing deeper to understand the true nature of this War Within that we, as warriors, are facing. I pissed off a lot of people. But I kept asking questions, piecing together clues, and plotting a new path forward. Even when countless people told me that we already had the answers, that what I was searching for was behind me, I didn't stop saying, "It's got to be deeper than this. It's got to be deeper."

As it turns out I wasn't crazy. I'm just beginning to uncover the answers I've been seeking. And I promise you this: I will never stop pressing forward. I will continue to push deeper into the unknown, as long as it takes.

But the metaphor of my own life isn't the only reason I told you this story. Let's be honest, I didn't need to tell you about taking a seven-minute break on the way to finishing selection. In fact, it's a little off-brand for the no-quit, breaks-are-for-losers, I'll-rest-when-I-die mentality that warriors thrive on. But here's why it is important for me to tell you this entire story. For years, I tried every type of self-destructive, self-abasing, self-sacrificing thing I knew to gain the upper hand on the War Within. The only catalysts for growth that I knew were pain and adversity, breaking and rebuilding. I thought I could muscle my way through growth and recovery. I thought I could don't-miss-a-workout my way through mental health. I thought I could force, push, and grit-my-teeth my way to healing, recovery, and finding the life and love I wanted.

But when I had exhausted every single method I knew without any lasting results, I realized that for once in my life, I should try something different, something I hadn't tried, something new. Since nothing else had worked, I figured I might as well try something besides *Faster…Harder…More…More…More.* I might as well try taking a step back, refreshing my body, resetting my mind, and getting the support I needed. For once in my life, I tried loving my mind and body instead of abusing them. For once in my life, I took time to heal my mind. And guess what? When I stood back up and started moving again, my mind was clear and focused; my body was nourished and strong; and yeah, my pace of fulfilling my purpose and reaching my mission was a hell of a lot quicker. Turns out that taking a minute to restore my body and get my head in the game was the best way to go faster and harder, to do more.

To the Warrior Class,

I don't need to tell you that you have a mission that you were put on this earth to complete. I don't need to tell you that your life has a purpose, because you already know that. You're a warrior; it's in your nature. I don't know what fire forged you into who you are today, nor do I know the environment that gave you the unique ability to withstand pain, endure adversity, and remain calm in the midst of chaos, but I bet that it wasn't easy. What I can tell you is that your family, community, nation, and world need you more than ever.

Maybe you are exhausted right now. Maybe you are struggling to gain the upper hand in a battle that is raging within your mind. Maybe you are broken and bleeding but still putting one foot in front of the other. Maybe you feel like a failure, like you're losing the fight, and want to quit. Maybe you think it's too late, maybe you've given up hope, maybe you feel like you're too far gone. But I'm here to tell you that there is hope. My story is filled with collateral damage, pain, and chaos, but looking back now, I can honestly say I'm grateful for every experience. Each one shaped me into the person I am today and forged in me the capacity to help others.

All your life, you've been told to ignore the pain, to silently suffer, to endure adversity, to go harder and faster, and to push yourself to do more, more, more. But maybe, just maybe, it's time to try something different. Maybe it's time to heed the signals your mind and body are sending instead of ignoring them. Maybe it's time to practice self-love rather than self-destruction. Maybe it's time to get support rather than pushing forward alone. Maybe it's time to take those seven minutes, reset your mind, nourish your body, and recover so that you can regain focus on your mission and purpose.

In closing, I want to say one more very important thing. Throughout your life, I'm sure many people have said, "Thank you for your service." I will not be one of them today. Ever since you became a protector, you've been appreciated for what you do. You've been valued for the fact that you are willing to bleed so others don't have to, face the darkness so they may live in the light, and give your last breath to protect, defend, and serve our nation. Today, I want to tell you that your value is more than your ability to endure pain and give your last breath so that others may live. Your value is more than your sacrifices and your service.

Today, I do not want to shine a light on your service or thank you for what you do. Instead, I want to thank you for *who you are*. When life knocked you down, pushed you into a corner, and caused you pain, you didn't stay there. You stood up and pushed back. You may have been forged in chaos, but you made yourself strong and devoted your life to being the defender you never had so that others would not face the pain you did alone. When your entire world felt unsafe and you had nowhere to run, you chose to remain calm in the chaos and devoted your life to making the world a safer place for others. So today, I will not say thank you for your service; I will say thank you for being who you are.

And in case it's been a while since you felt connected to the authentic, natural-born warrior inside of you, let me remind you:

You are born with a strong sense of duty to serve those around you.

You have an innate connection to a higher purpose and a clear mission.

You possess natural mental fortitude and a propensity for brave and bold action in the face of resistance.

You are a protector, keeping the young and vulnerable members of the tribe safe.

You offer security for the assets and resources of our community, so they are not stolen or lost.

You do not back down or surrender in the face of threats or danger; you stand up, push back, and hold the boundary to keep others safe. You are willing to sacrifice yourself if necessary for the greater good.

And you have the ability to remain calm in the midst of chaos…

…but that doesn't mean you have to stay in the chaos forever.

Even warriors need to lay down the sword once in a while.

It's okay to take seven minutes.

CHAPTER 34
IT'S NOT THE END

I AM SITTING IN A café with a glass of water in front of me. I've already scanned the entrance four times, waiting to glimpse Vanessa's shiny blonde hair. I take a sip of the water and focus on another part of the room, but my eyes can't help but dart back to the entrance every few seconds. After seven years apart, Vanessa is about to have dinner with me. It's all so strange it hardly feels real. Then I see her. Her eyes glide across the room and lock onto mine. She's older now, no longer the young, innocent girl who came to see me after I'd been released from the hospital, but she's just as beautiful. I stand to greet her, and she pauses for a moment as she looks me over from head to toe. I know I look different from the man she said goodbye to seven years ago. She wraps her arms around me gently and doesn't move. With her face buried in my chest, she cries softly, her fingers tightly grasping the back of my shirt, pulling me close. She doesn't let go for a while. When she does, she wipes away her tears, and a smile breaks out on her face.

"I'm so happy to see you." Her eyes are shining. "You have no idea."

As she sits down in front of me, I feel like I'm in a dream. For so long, I've hated her, blamed her for not choosing me and for all the pain I've endured. Now, she's here in front of me, but the hatred is nowhere to be found. As I stare into her eyes, I see my reflection once again. I see the past flash before my eyes, snapshots of the years we shared together. I see myself absorbing her energy and care like oxygen. I see her venturing into the darkness when I lost myself, trying to find the man she once knew. I see her holding together the bleeding fragments of my shattered identity for as long as she could. I see her crumbling under the weight of loving someone more than they loved themselves, and I understand now that it was more than any human could handle. I see us clinging to each other like life rafts as we tried to survive the chaos, as we became the chaos—our white-knuckled grip choking the life out of each other until every shred of innocent love was gone.

But that's not all I see. As I stare into her eyes, I also see the two kids we used to be, face-to-face on that street corner in downtown Dallas, hoping to see each other just one more time. I see us laughing across that white-clothed table at South Beach, Florida's best fine dining restaurant. I see us buying our first house in Vegas and making big dreams and plans for the future. And I remember. I remember us before the chaos, before that tender, innocent love became toxic. Suddenly, I want to say, "I'm sorry, I don't hate you anymore" and "Thank you." I want to say that I understand now. The words aren't easy to find, but our eyes hold the weight of history between us, and we both know its value, communicating a thousand things we will forever leave unsaid.

"So, is being a mom as good as you thought it would be?" I ask, and she smiles. She's still with *him*, has a beautiful home, and the two kids she always dreamed about. And I'm happy for her, truly happy.

"Even better," she smiles.

We begin to talk and fall into a rhythm like an old song. As the words flow between us, I feel something shifting, changing. Those green eyes are still the same ones that stared at me in Dallas, the same ones that lit up with joy when we decided to take a chance and move to Vegas, the ones that looked at me like I was the only man in the world in the Med Shed as my world crumbled. We were so young then, so naïve and unprepared for what lay ahead. We thought we were Bonnie and Fucking Clyde—coconspirators, allies, and partners. We were definitely just two broken kids trying to surf the chaos of life, arm in arm as we faced the trauma of a cruel world. And we did ride the waves together, at least for a while. When she stands to leave, I stand too. She looks at me before saying anything and then wraps her arms around me one last time. She doesn't let go for a while. When she does, she wipes away her tears and a smile breaks out on her face.

"I hope you find that love you're looking for, Tyler. You deserve it," she says. We both know I'll never stop looking until I find it. As I watch her disappear, it's not sadness I feel; it's closure. *It's not the end; it's just the beginning.*

CHAPTER 35
EVERYTHING WILL BE OKAY

I OPEN MY EYES TO see the love of my life sleeping beside me. Her chest rises and falls gently as she dreams, and I wrap my arms around her, careful not to wake her, and wait in the silence of the morning. In this peaceful environment, I feel calm. I feel happy. I feel like the luckiest man in the world.

My world was once filled with nothing but dirt, grime, bullets, blood, and rocks. Even then, I always knew that if there was a beauty in this world who would look at me and love me, everything would be okay. And now that feeling is here again, a deep sense that my heart has come home. I know for a fact that life isn't all suffering and brutality; it can't be. Not with a beautiful soul like my Cristiane still roaming the earth. I feel a sense of anticipation rising in me, but it's more than that; it's purpose. I always hoped I'd find my match. I always hoped I would experience one big, epic love story at least once in my life. And it turns out I was right. It seems the Man Upstairs must have really smiled when he wrote my Christiane into this crazy, twisted script of my life. Who better than a real-live Wonder Woman for this superhero to fall in love with? If I spent years painting a picture of my ideal woman, I couldn't have imagined her. Her magnificent grace, peaceful spirit, and devoted heart—I never even knew such love was possible.

There are days when the storms of chaos still rage around me, and nights when she holds me tight as I wait for them to pass. But I am not clinging to her like a life raft, because I am no longer drowning. My mind isn't the vicious place it used to be. There are days when the Warrior in me shines, and she celebrates the victories with me. On other days, a battle erupts as the Destroyer fights to gain the upper hand in this War Within. Once, the Destroyer reared his ugly head and looked at her—my beautiful, pure-hearted Cris—with pure destruction. He took out his sword and pulled it back, ready to sabotage it all.

"I'm not good enough for you; I don't think I deserve you," the Destroyer declared, ready for battle. But she leaned in closer, and fire flashed behind her eyes.

"You don't get to make that decision," she said, staring fiercely at the Destroyer. "You don't get to decide who deserves my love. Only I can do that."

The Destroyer was no match for my beautiful Brazilian Wonder Woman. With one statement, her Lasso of Truth knocked the Destroyer flat on his back. In his place stood the Warrior, shields down, basking in the light of unconditional love. She paused for a minute, her eyes sweeping across the Warrior—scarred, imperfect, and longing to love and be loved.

"I choose you," she said, closing the gap between us. We didn't speak as she held me. She'd already said it all, and I gave her my all in return.

And so, as I lie here, waiting in the silence of the morning, watching the rise and fall of her chest, I feel gratitude like I have never felt before. Today, I am not calm in chaos but in peace.

Maybe my life is not a perfect portrait of a role model to emulate or a champion to salute, but if I'm being honest with myself, I do want to be a hero. More than anything in the world, I want to be a hero for my wife and kids. I want to be a hero for my community and a world that needs me. So, I will never stop striving to be a man worthy of this woman who loves me so purely. I will never stop fighting with courage until I claim victory over this War Within. It will not be easy. I will win some battles and lose others. It may be brutal and definitely unpredictable, but then again, war always is. But I know that I will win.

How can I be so sure?

Because I'm a Warrior.

A Destroyer.

And a Goddamn Superhero.

ACKNOWLEDGMENTS

WRITING THIS BOOK HAS BEEN an incredible journey, made possible by the support, guidance, and inspiration of many people.

First and foremost, I want to thank **Lauren Ungeldi**, my co-author, for her dedication, hard work, and invaluable contribution to bringing this project to life. Your insight and collaboration made this process smoother and more meaningful.

To **Scott A. Huesing**, my agent and fellow warrior—thank you for caring about this story, believing in this book from the start, and guiding me through the process. Your expertise and support have been instrumental in making this a reality.

Thank you to **Benjamin Sledge**, who initially connected us all, and for his exceptional talent in designing the cover of *Forged in Chaos*. He is a fellow warrior, author, and talented artist.

Thanks to my editor, **Alex Novak**, for your encouragement and input along the way. Your perspective, vast experience, and advice have been invaluable.

I also want to extend my gratitude to **Warriors Heart** for the incredible work you do and for being the organization you are. Being at the facility for forty-two days was the spark that lit the fire for me writing this book—many of the ideas expressed came directly from my notebook written during my stay. I deeply respect and appreciate your dedication to helping those who serve.

Finally, a special thank you to **Shawn Ryan** for having me on his show and facilitating a conversation that helped me recognize the shared experiences and values connecting so many of us—that realization played a crucial role in shaping the message of this book.

Tyler Grey and Lauren Ungeldi

Thank you to everyone who contributed—through direct involvement, encouragement, or simply by inspiring me. This book wouldn't exist without you.

With gratitude,
Tyler Grey